A Voice of One's Own

A VOICE OF ONE'S OWN

Conversations with America's Writing Women

* * *

Mickey Pearlman
AND
Katherine Usher Henderson

HOUGHTON MIFFLIN COMPANY
Boston New York London

PHOTO CREDITS: M.A. Armstrong (Alice McDermott), Jerry Bauer (Kate Braverman, Louise Erdrich, Gail Godwin, Josephine Humphreys), Brian Berman (Joyce Carol Oates), Nancy Crampton (Laurie Colwin), Donna DeCesare (Gloria Naylor), Robert Foothorap (Amy Tan), Paul Fraughton (Francine Prose), Alvah Henderson (Janet Lewis), Marv Hoffman (Rosellen Brown), Doug Kirkland (Carolyn See), Carol Lazar (Shirley Ann Grau), Eric Lindbloom (Nancy Willard), Neil Schaeffer (Susan Fromberg Schaeffer), Jimm Roberts (Alison Lurie), Thomas Victor (Harriet Doerr, Diane Johnson, Anne Lamott, Carole Maso, Marge Piercy, Lynne Sharon Schwartz, Irini Spanidou, Mona Simpson), Ellen Warner (Elizabeth Winthrop).

This edition contains editorial revisions made by the authors
after the hardcover edition was published.

Library of Congress Cataloging-in-Publication Data
Pearlman, Mickey, date.
A voice of one's own : talks with America's writing women / Mickey Pearlman and Katherine Usher Henderson.
p.   cm.
Includes index.
ISBN 0-395-59972-5
1. Women authors, American — 20th century — Interviews.
2. Women and literature — United States — History — 20th century.
3. American literature — Women authors — History and criticism.
4. American literature — 20th century — History and criticism.
I. Henderson, Katherine U.   II. Title.
PS 151.P42   1992   91-36186
810.9′9287′09045 — dc20   CIP

Printed in the United States of America

Book design by Robert Overholtzer

BBS 10 9 8 7 6 5 4 3

Previously published in hardcover under the title
Inter/View: Talks with America's Writing Women.

For Mia Bess Pearlman, Mickey's best
and most demanding editor
and
for Joan Usher Nolan, Kathie's sister
and most generous friend

ACKNOWLEDGMENTS

WE WANT to thank those enthusiastic friends who read portions of the interviews and those with whom we stayed on our travels to the interviews: Brigitte and Bliss Carnochan, Katy Gottschalk and John Paul, Jack and Barbara McManus, Gayle Shomer, and Ann and Chris Stone.

Katherine Henderson would like to thank the 1988–89 Visiting and Affiliated Scholars of the Institute for Research on Women and Gender at Stanford University, especially Edith Gelles, for their excellent insights into this project.

"And all these questions, according to the Angel of the House, cannot be dealt with freely and openly by women: they must charm, they must conciliate, they must — to put it bluntly — tell lies if they are to succeed. Thus, whenever I felt the shadow of her wing or the radiance of her halo upon my page, I took up the inkpot and flung it at her. She died hard."

Virginia Woolf, "Professions for Women," 1929

CONTENTS

INTRODUCTION

MANY HOURS of careful listening have gone into the creation of *A Voice of One's Own*, a forum for twenty-eight people who have three labels in common: they are women, Americans, and writers. They represent, too, all of the borders that we have systematically attempted to cross — those of race, religion, ethnicity, sexual preference, marital status, age, "lifestyle," and geography. Given the generous profusion of women writing in America, it was, of course, impossible to include every writer in every place worth listening and talking to. But we did manage to interview writers who are white, black, Asian, and Native American, and women ranging in age from thirty-two (Mona Simpson) to ninety (Janet Lewis). We made a considerable effort to represent the country geographically because wonderful words by women are being written from coast to coast, north to south; a limited budget made this extremely difficult to do. Many writers, however, live in the Northeast in order to be close to the powerbrokers (publishers, agents, and editors) — among them, Lurie, Naylor, Godwin, Oates, Schaeffer, Piercy, Prose, Maso, Colwin, Winthrop, Spanidou, Willard, Simpson, Erdrich, and Schwartz. The West Coast is also rich in writers — Johnson, See, Fisher, Tan, Braverman, Doerr, Thomas, Lamott, and Lewis — many of whom talked about the disadvantages of living and writing far from the publishers in New York and Boston. The South and Southwest probably deserve their own collection, but their representatives here are Josephine Humphreys, from South Carolina; Gail Godwin, who lives now in Woodstock but is from North Carolina; Rosellen Brown, from Houston; and Shirley Ann Grau, who lives in New Orleans. We tried also to balance instantly recognizable authors such as Joyce Carol Oates, Gail Godwin, Gloria Naylor, and Alison Lurie (among others) with first novelists to whom much talent has been given and of whom much production is expected: Carole Maso, Amy Tan, Elizabeth Winthrop, Mona Simpson, Irini Spanidou. We expended *no* effort to include the currently "hot" writer, who is often the creation of an expensive and intensive publicity campaign waged by publishers absorbed by the financial bottom line.

Another motivation for doing *A Voice of One's Own* was our perception that most collections of interviews with working writers are skewed, lopsided, and often wrongheaded: "women writers" are usually tokens, one or two of whom are tucked into a collection with "men writers" (a label nobody uses), mostly, it seems, to avoid feminist wrath. The *Paris Review* interviews, for example (called *Writers at Work*), have been published in eight volumes and include 113 interviews, *of which only nineteen are with women*. Each volume includes at least one interview with a woman; no volume includes more than three women. The volume published in 1988 includes eleven men and two women, although in 1989 they issued a separate volume of previously published interviews called *Women Writers at Work*. Some of those writers are now dead. A careful examination of those texts reveals that the women were usually asked different, more stereotypically gender-defined questions, resulting in interviews that were markedly different in tone and seriousness and were often less evocative and useful. One of the reasons, as Gail Godwin suggested, is that women are more used to revealing themselves, making them "open to ridicule or attack." Many interviewers in these collections conflated the life of the woman writer with that of a female character. As Susan Fromberg Schaeffer remarked, "Nobody inquires about the relationship between a man's latest marriage or affair and what's going on in his books, but this is a regular, chronic reflex action when you read about a woman novelist. If [interviewers and reviewers] did this to men, they would be taken out behind a building and kicked in the mouth."

Several of these conversations took place on or near campuses, since even many financially successful writers continue to teach and to maintain their affiliations with colleges and universities: Lurie (Cornell), Oates (Princeton), Spanidou (Sarah Lawrence), Schaeffer (Brooklyn College), Johnson (University of California, Davis), Simpson (Columbia), Colwin (New York University), Braverman (California State-Los Angeles), Willard (Vassar), and See (UCLA). They are, with few exceptions, college graduates, several of whom have done graduate work in literature. Some, in fact, have Ph.D.s in American or English literature: Schaeffer (University of Chicago), Godwin (University of Iowa), Willard (University of Michigan), See and Johnson (UCLA). Many would feel represented by Josephine Humphreys's comment that "a lot of my narrative, my ideas . . . come [as much] from my reading as they do from my experience" because these twenty-eight women are a literate group. They refer often to fellow writers, such as Muriel Spark, Henry James, the Brontës, Faulkner, Joan Didion, Melville, Virginia Woolf, Tom Wolfe, Robertson Davies, Eudora Welty, Toni Morrison, Proust; to Latin American, Russian, and Eastern European writers; and, very often, to each other.

Among the twenty-eight are the determined urbanites such as Simpson (a runner), Colwin, Schwartz, who "now can write anywhere," and Spanidou, who "stop[s] listening" to the noise of the city when she concentrates, Naylor, who always "has to have a little piece of sky," Maso, who often works at a writer's colony in France, and Schaeffer, whose mother insists she was born saying, "Take me to the country." Others live far from the *Sturm und Drang* of the cities: Piercy (in Wellfleet, Massachusetts), Prose (in the woods near Kingston, New York), Oates (in the woods near Princeton), Lamott (in the woods near San Francisco), Godwin (in Woodstock, New York), M.F.K. Fisher (on a ranch in the Sonoma Valley of California), Doerr (in small-town Pasadena), Erdrich (in Cornish Flats, New Hampshire), and Lurie (in Ithaca, New York). Some of them write surrounded by skyscrapers and city life, and some want to see nothing but trees out the window. As Godwin says, "I've gotten so spoiled that I don't even want to see a telephone pole."

To quote Francine Prose, "It's not about the space you're in, it's about the space that's in your head. . . . It's not accidental, it's not biological, that women tend to write about the family, the garden, and [that] men, for whatever reason, feel free to write about seafaring and wargoing. That's about the life you live. Jane Austen was not going to write *Moby-Dick*." Alison Lurie talked about "the war between men and women for the control of space." Where women are concerned, "If you can't range freely, then the space you live in becomes more important to you." The "landscapes" of men and women, said Alice McDermott, "probably are different." Much more conversation took place in these interviews about the usually enclosed emotional, physical, psychological, and financial spaces of women, fictional or otherwise, and about what we might call the "right space." Louise Erdrich, for example, said she "was probably an easterner who mistakenly grew up in the midwest where I never felt very accepted or at home."

Both of the interviewers — one whose most recent book concerns English Renaissance feminism and one who is most involved with American fiction, women, and concepts of space — wanted to know how memory is linked to writing, to concepts of family, to the myths in which a family is invested, and to ideas like those of Oates, who said, "Much of my writing is energized by unresolved memories — something like ghosts in the psychological sense." All writers, without exception, depend on stored memories (and on invention), but it is in the selection from those memories and in the change that memory undergoes as it is transferred into fiction that the art of writing occurs. "That's where," as Rosellen Brown says, "the strange alchemy comes in: Why do you choose *what* you choose to make into your element?" Maso, for instance, says that "characters are both real and invented" and that novels "are sometimes *emotionally* autobiographical. . . . But," she has often asked critics, " 'do you think my life would be so structured and artful that I could just transfer it to the page and make it work?' " Prose adds that "any time you change anything, even a name, it changes everything." And Gloria Naylor explained that "you are taking the memory of your personal self, your historical self, and your familial self because your writing filters through all of these things." Anne Lamott probably spoke for all twenty-eight writers when she said she tries "to write about what we're *all* like on the inside, what it is to be human, what it is to be female."

The writers do use family memories differently when they write. Diane Johnson thinks that "memory is the realm of powerlessness," noting that old people in nursing homes often live in the past. (In her current fiction she has deliberately created women characters who have short memories, who live in the present.) Marge Piercy agrees that women are often "too captured by memory," although she adds, "None of our capacities are empowering or weakening in themselves; it depends on how we use them." At the other end of that spectrum are writers like M.F.K. Fisher, who prefers the form of the personal memoir to that of fiction; Lynne Sharon Schwartz, whose *Leaving Brooklyn* "used memory the most"; and Godwin, who found the writing of *A Southern Family,* a novel based on personal family tragedy, "an act of healing." Godwin believes that we all live to some degree in our memories: "What person in the world goes through life in a straight line?"

Most of the writers also talked about how they developed as artists, including the moment when they realized they were writers. Godwin, Lewis, Schwartz, Willard, and Fisher could not remember a time when they did not write. Amy Tan turned to writing fiction to cure herself of workaholism after she left therapy because her (male) therapist kept falling asleep. Harriet Doerr did not consider herself a serious, professional writer until she returned to college as a sixty-five-year-old widow and saw her talent reflected in the comments of her instructors. Alice McDermott had not planned to become a writer until her sophomore year in college, when her writing teacher called her into his office and said, "I've got bad news for you. You're a writer; you are never going to shake it." Lynne Sharon Schwartz, who realized at thirty-two that she "had to be a 'good girl' or a writer," made the right choice.

Although these women began their professional writing careers at different points in life (as a child, Nancy Willard was putting out a hometown newspaper in Oxford, Michigan, on a jelly press), they are equally and deeply committed to the process, and to the product, because that commitment is a matter of personal integrity. Probably as a result of that commitment, they lack as a group the material wealth of doctors, lawyers, and investment bankers. If a few are indeed wealthy, not one of them is a candidate for "Lifestyles of the Rich and Famous." There are no Rolls Royces in the garages, no staffs of servants in the houses. Most live modestly, even frugally. The only extravagance they *all* share is books; they read voraciously, and books (on tables, floors, beds, sofas, and in the bathrooms) are everywhere in their homes. Sometimes we had to clear a spot in which to sit, but since we are writers ourselves, this was a familiar experience. They may have individual extravagances — Godwin's indoor pool, Fisher's large plant-filled bathroom, Oates's glass house, Lurie's hideaway in Key West, Piercy's purebred cats (many, *many* have cats, possibly to assuage the loneliness of writing; Willard's has one eye "like Odin") — but none of these possessions resembles the familiar glitzy materialism associated with similarly successful people in other professions. They have created pockets of order and beauty in the places where they write, but they have done this with time and thought and taste rather than with money. Willard's 1950s blue bike ("no gears, no brakes"), Schwartz's bulletin board on which was pinned her police clearance for jury duty ("NO CRIMINAL RECORD"), and Prose's collection of papier mache masks are more typical of the treasured possessions we saw.

We did not ask those writers without children (Oates, Tan, Godwin, Simpson, Piercy, Naylor, Maso, Spanidou) if that choice was deliberate, but Humphreys told us that, as much as she loved children, she chose a third book over a third child. Many left career paths already traveled, especially full-time positions in teaching (Willard gave up tenure for time) or in publishing, for the economically insecure life of a writer. See said that when she was divorced with two children to support, "There were dark days when I thought, 'I have to get on welfare,' but I never thought, 'I have to go out and get a job' " other than writing. They do not have much leisure or the kind of social lives which are painstakingly chronicled in the *Los Angeles* or *New York Times* because most of them value solitude over invitations. But not one regretted her decision to write. In fact, it is fair to say that once you are a *writer*, you *are* a writer, and you simply have no choice. That was clear in all the interviews.

Most *do* have children. Some raised their children in nuclear families; others raised their children alone, with the help of friends (as Naylor is planning to do), or, in the case of M.F.K. Fisher, with the help of a sister. Most of the writers have two or three children; Johnson and Grau have four (now grown) and Erdrich and her husband Michael Dorris have six, three adopted, three biological. We know that including these facts skirts close to the sexist point of view that confuses a woman's personal life with her work (to which we would strenuously object), but we feel that the topic of a woman's children is relevant to her status as a professional writer. It is relevant because women who write usually do so (at least initially) with precarious financial backing coupled with the major responsibility for the emotional upkeep of family members and the literal upkeep of family "mansions." In many cases, writing comes fourth (or forth) after mates, children, and earning money to support the writing habit, at least until the habit becomes self-supporting. See said, "I try in my mind to put my books and my family exactly on a par," but achieving that balance in the real world is often illusory. Alice McDermott thinks there is still the sense that " 'It's very nice that you're writing your little stories, but you really shouldn't neglect your children. . . . I mean, what's more important?' "

That the majority of these writers have children is also a fact of historical significance, evidence that the nineteenth- and early twentieth-century idea that a woman must choose between career and motherhood is *almost* dead, although Francine Prose, for example, says, "Female students are still being told, 'You have to choose to be a writer or have a family,' but it's just bullshit; you don't." Think of the great women novelists of the twenties — or skim through any anthology of literature by women between

1890 and 1940 — and you will find that none of these women had children: Edith Wharton, Willa Cather, Katherine Anne Porter, Virginia Woolf, Ellen Glasgow, Gertrude Stein, Marianne Moore, Isak Dinesen. Only one of our writers, Janet Lewis, is of that generation, and as a mother of two children she is an exception, having resisted the social pressures on early twentieth-century women writers *not* to mother children. With the practical and emotional support of her husband, the critic Yvor Winters, she kept writing, typing her first novel as her baby daughter sat on her lap. She reminded us, "The funny thing about history and women is that there have been startling and tremendous women all along, regardless of what the culture thought."

Of course there are many differences between the social climates of earlier periods and what is happening now. The sheer numbers of women writing today and the high quality of poetry, drama, and fiction by those women are by-products of the second women's movement and the social, political, and psychological changes it has wrought. Those numbers are responsible for the endlessly debatable and finally unanswerable question about who dominates contemporary American writing. (See, Schwartz, and Johnson address the issue with perceptive comments.) But the fact that it can be debated at all testifies to the numbers of women writing first-rate fiction in America today. It is significant, therefore, that most collections of interviews (as well as many established book review sections) fail to acknowledge this. This book is our contribution to restoring the balance.

For a variety of reasons, we have chosen to write mini-essays with long quotations from the writers, rather than use the Q and A format. The mini-essay enabled us to describe the writer's geographical space and to insert background information at relevant points in the interview. The mini-essay also allowed us to bring together quotations on the same topic (we sometimes moved them, but never changed them) to achieve greater coherence and readability. Sometimes we summarized interview segments so we would have space for more interviews, but we tried hard to preserve both the essence of each writer's unique colloquial style and the essence of her statements. The mini-essay format placed the emphasis always on the writer and her answers because we feel that the emphasis is too often on the interviewer and her questions. The interviews are of different lengths, not because we value the writers differently but because of other variables: for example, some writers could give us more time than others; some interviews did not take place in quiet houses or private offices that permitted few interruptions. (See Pearlman's interviews with Maso and Humphreys in New York coffee shops, with Rosellen Brown in Boston, and her description of the telephone interview with Louise Erdrich.) We encouraged many of the writers to talk about the ideas of memory, space, and family in their fiction, but many talked instead about politics, children, dreams, book reviewing, their mothers, race relations, their alma maters, agents, publishers, editors, *and each other*. "Off the tape" conversations remained off the tape. We had no rigid format and no formal lists of questions. We allowed each interview to develop the configuration which every interview develops naturally. What also became clear as the collection progressed to its conclusion is that any literate and enthusiastic reader could have compiled a very different list of twenty-eight other writers, and that our choices depend partly on taste, on our own training at Columbia and the Graduate School of the City University of New York, on our already stated desire to be inclusive, and on a panoply of factors, including geography and availability.

We are grateful to have been allowed to enter the physical and emotional spaces of so many women who write. As Shirley Ann Grau said, there is a "wonderful thing about words and their overtones, and the meanings they drag along with them," both for the writer and for the reader. Good fiction energizes all of us, and the experience of reading these twenty-eight women is on the short list of things that are satisfying, inexpensive, readily-available, and durable. We thank them, most of all, for their time, but also for their patience, insight, honesty, and enthusiasm, and for giving us and their other readers an incalculably valuable part of themselves.

Alison Lurie

ALISON LURIE, who won the Pulitzer Prize for *Foreign Affairs* in 1984, lives in a dark-red clapboard house on one of the many tree-shaded streets of Ithaca, New York, home of Cornell University, where she is a professor of English. Somehow one expects America's most famous social satirist of the fictional intelligentsia, who has a house in Key West and a flat in London, to be surrounded by Chippendale chairs and Waterford glass. Instead, the Alison Lurie I met has giant pots of geraniums and healthy trailing plants in every window, a collection of baskets hanging on the garage wall, postcards from England under the glass-topped coffee table, and an open pantry well stocked with Campbell's soups. She works in a cozy upstairs bedroom that has a flowery, blue-cushioned window seat and two desks. Our conversation took place over salad and homemade lentil soup on the sunny deck behind her house, and I washed the dishes while Lurie changed from her denim skirt and red T-shirt into her "professor's clothes" for a conference on upstate writers at which she was speaking that afternoon. In other words, anyone looking for the artifice, pretension, and superficiality that Lurie regularly skewers in her novels won't find it at her house!

We discussed the reviews of *The Truth about Lorin Jones,* a novel that some feminists have found less than amusing. The bisexual heroine, Polly Alter, herself a failed painter who lives with the lesbian, man-hating Jeanne, has taken a year's leave from her museum job to research and write the biography of the deceased painter Lorin Jones. Polly spends most of the novel either overidentifying with or vilifying her subject, confusing the job of the biographer with that of the makeover artist. In the interim she also manages to sleep with Jones's husband and to spend considerable time reexperiencing her own anger at an abusive husband and an emotionally impotent father. Polly, and every one else in this novel, has a not-too-well-hidden investment in how the "truth" about Lorin Jones will be written. Whether she was indeed another female victim of the male establishment is the crux of the issue. And Polly's dilemma, according to Edmund White in his *New York Times* review, is whether she will "end up a lesbian feminist separatist or . . . remain unregenerate and heterosexual."

Lurie says that she expected the occasionally hostile review "because I think that [some readers] don't realize that there are different kinds of feminists." More importantly, "It's always risky to point out the flaws in any group that's beleaguered." For instance, "We mustn't say that the mayor of Washington may have cocaine connections, because he's Black. But I'm very disturbed by feminist separatism, though I understand it and think it's a natural reaction in some women. In an earlier draft of the book, there was a lot more about Polly's roommate, including her childhood: she was a battered and abused child, and her mother was a battered woman, and therefore she couldn't trust men. I thought she was well motivated to become what she became, and I think now that I shouldn't have left that out because this might be a natural reaction in some women, and maybe even the right one. If you are abused and can't get over it, and you are naturally attracted to women, why not? Some women have good reason to distrust men.

"I guess what I'm saying is that I'm upset by the *results* of separatism. I'm not sure that women are strong enough yet to profit by withdrawing from the male world. I think we're more apt to just be crowded into a corner. For example, in the academy, a women's studies department will set up a course in 'Women Writers,' and the result will be that only *women* will take this course. The men who teach modern or early twentieth-century fiction will say, 'Oh, now we don't have to include Virginia Woolf or Edith Wharton' and they'll cut these writers out of their courses, and male students will never hear of them. We'll be back to where we were fifty years ago. Separatism can be very divisive." Many of us, as Lurie well knows, remember that even in the sixties women read Woolf and men read Steinbeck. "I think a lot of people didn't realize that this is what I was saying. They just thought, 'She's against women, she doesn't like lesbians,' even though I put a very nice lesbian" in the novel. "People don't necessarily hear everything you say."

As for the character of Lorin Jones, Lurie says, "She comes out of a generation in which women were allowed or encouraged to be more anonymous than men. Therefore the people who remember her remember different people." A man "would have felt that he had to establish himself as a character quite early on. I know that when I was in college, men had to present a persona even if they were very young. They'd make it out of bits and pieces, their own male relatives, books they'd read, or professors they admired. Some of the women were also doing this, but others were deliberately keeping themselves anonymous. Someone once said to me, 'I'm not sure what I like until I know who I'm going to marry.' This wasn't true of all of us! Some of us were busy becoming characters just as fast as the men." In *Lorin Jones,* she said, "I wanted someone who seemed different to different people, and she had to be anonymous in this sense. But of course there is a relationship between what Lorin made of reality and what other people made of her." Polly "takes on the memories of this person she's never met, but I think this is also something that could happen to a man."

When I asked how she came to know so much about the art world, which many people have said is so corrupt it makes the publishing world look pure (see interview with Francine Prose), Lurie said, "I'm afraid this is true. One of my best friends works at the Whitney Museum, and she read the book before it went to the publisher and gave me some advice. The reason the art world is more corrupt is economic. If you write a book, its potential consumer is anyone who can afford to buy a paperback or go to the library. So the constituency you have to please is very large. If you are an artist, you are dependent on the whims of a few very rich people who are not always sure what they want. Some collectors are wonderful, interesting, educated people who happen to be rich, and some are ignorant and mean. This is true of readers of books too, but a publisher doesn't gain anything by 'making up' to an individual reader because there are too many of them. But a dealer gains a great deal by 'making up' to rich collectors, so the art world self-selects a certain type of person. What is selected is not the artists but the dealers. An art dealer has to be someone who can flatter and manipulate rich clients. There is also pressure on the artists themselves, who have to go to fancy dinner parties and be nice; an artist who won't do that is handicapped."

I mentioned that in *Lorin Jones* the emotional and physical spaces themselves seem to close in around the artist when she enters them, and I asked her if she had considered this. Lurie said she had not thought of the issue of space in the context of this novel but that "historically, women are more enclosed; this is true. And the space she is enclosed in is probably more important to a woman. In the past, a woman couldn't get out of her space, and this unfortunate situation is now being reproduced in places like New York City, where women are afraid to go out on the street or walk in the park. In many cities women are now being forced back into the enclosed spaces that they escaped from for a while. We forget that one hundred years ago a 'nice girl' didn't go out on the street alone, especially after dark. There are still places where there has never been a break. In most Moslem countries, a woman who walks on the street by herself is going to be subjected to abuse." Space then does become an issue, I suggested, and in

Lorin Jones spaces that were not intrinsically threatening do perhaps become threatening. Lurie replied that "Lorin Jones is very, very determined to have a room of her own and she does manage to have a room of her own throughout most of the book. She leaves her husband because he keeps trying to get into her room — not necessarily because he wants to sleep with her, but because he wants to get in there and look at her paintings, and invade her privacy, and tell her what she should be doing, and she has to leave him for that reason. And she ends up with her own space. The problem is that she also becomes very isolated because she is so desperate for her own space that other things have to go by the board.

"Another thing that happens in the novel which is very typical of the modern world, particularly of cities, is the war between people for the control of space, and particularly between women. If you are forced to live indoors, if you can't range freely, then the space you live in becomes more important to you. You can't get away from it the way a man can. So you get this war between Polly and Jeanne for the control of the apartment. There is a point where Polly asks Jeanne to get out of the way so [Polly] can talk to her son. And Jeanne says she doesn't want to go walk around the block because it's dangerous. A man would say, 'Sure, I'll go down to the corner and have a beer.' " It seems to me, as I said to Lurie, that the issue of space is always an underlying component in the experience of women, fictional or otherwise. Lurie agreed that "there is a tradition that women create nests for men and for children and that a woman is judged on the quality of her nest, whereas a man isn't. If a man lives alone and his apartment is messy, people might say, 'Well, he's preoccupied, he doesn't have time, he probably eats out most evenings.' They don't judge him by what his apartment looks like. But with a woman, if her house is ugly or messy, it's reflected back on her. The woman's house is more like her body. But there is a positive side to it. You can say, 'Look, this whole house can become my body. I can have a good time with it and make it agreeable and expressive.' For a lot of women their house is their art form, and they would feel unhappy and deprived if they were told, 'You don't have to worry about the house now. You can live in identical dwellings and no one will judge you by them; they're all going to be decorated by Howard Johnson's.' Whereas if a man spends a lot of time thinking about an apartment and decorating it, people may think he's a little queer, in one sense or another."

Perhaps because of her considerable fame or her easygoing disposition, Alison Lurie seems to me to be one of those few writers of the very top rank who is comfortable with her own importance but not in any way enraptured by it. She has spent thirty years writing about the foibles of feminists, social climbers, chauvinists, deluded dreamers, and maladjusted moralists, and she knows quite enough about the vagaries of human nature to laugh at them. She is philosophical even about reviews: "You have some good ones, some bad ones. . . . If you have a big success, the next book is going to get trashed, whatever it is, because people are tired of your name. . . . There's also the feeling [among critics] that 'we're not going to go on saying that she's good. If there is a writer that's constantly praised and only praised, [she] might get a swelled head and [she] wouldn't realize how dependent [she is] on us critics.' . . . Sometimes," she said, "they get it right. If you look at all the reviews a book gets, and not just those in the biggest circulation places, it balances out. If a book is good, people will see it, and if a book is not good, people will see it."

No anger. No diatribes. Just the comfortable, confident appraisal of America's best social satirist.

M.P.

BOOKS BY ALISON LURIE

NOVELS

Love and Friendship. New York: Macmillan, 1962; Avon Books, 1962.

The Nowhere City. New York: Coward, 1965; Avon, 1965.

Imaginary Friends. New York: Coward, 1967; Avon, 1986.

Real People. New York: Random House, 1969; Avon, 1969.

The War between the Tates. New York: Random House, 1974; Warner Books, 1975.

Only Children. New York: Random House, 1979; Avon, 1990.

Foreign Affairs. New York: Random House, 1984; Avon, 1985, 1991.

The Truth about Lorin Jones. Boston: Little, Brown, 1988; Avon, 1990.

NONFICTION

V.R. Lang: A Memoir. Privately printed, 1959.

V.R. Lang: Poems and Plays. New York: Random House, 1974.

[With Justin G. Schiller] *Classics of Children's Literature*. 1631–1932 Series. New York: Garland Publishing, 1977.

The Language of Clothes. New York: Random House, 1981, 1983.

Don't Tell the Grownups: Subversive Children's Literature. Boston: Little, Brown, 1990; Avon, 1991.

CHILDREN'S BOOKS

Clever Gretchen And Other Forgotten Folktales. New York: Crowell, 1980; Harper Junior, 1980; Mammoth, 1991.

The Heavenly Zoo. New York: Farrar, Straus, & Giroux, 1979.

Fabulous Beasts. New York: Farrar, Straus, & Giroux, 1981.

Amy Tan

AMY TAN lives with her husband, Lou DeMattei, and a Siamese cat named Sagwa in the bottom duplex of a post-Victorian row house on Sacramento Street in San Francisco. She and her husband, who is a tax attorney, own the building with the couple who live in the top unit. When I arrived she was baking cookies for our interview and for her writing group, which was meeting there that evening. We sat drinking tea in the comfortable living room surrounded by tangible artifacts of Tan's Chinese heritage, including photographs of her mother (like Tan, very beautiful) and grandmother. Tan is soft-spoken but articulate; she laughs frequently, both at herself and at some of the lighter ironies that have marked her life.

Our interview took place three weeks before the publication of *The Joy Luck Club*. Tan had sent me her page proofs so that I could read the book before our meeting. Within a few weeks of its publication the book was high on the best-seller list; seven months later, after being acclaimed by reviewers across the country, it was still there, and Vintage Books had purchased paperback rights for $1.2 million. While such success seldom comes the way of first novelists, few first novels are as moving, authentic, polished, and profound as hers.

The Joy Luck Club concerns four pairs of Chinese-American mothers and daughters, their often dramatic, interwoven experiences, and their complex mother-daughter conflicts. The mothers, all immigrants from China, meet weekly to play mah-jongg and give each other support; they tell their stories, and their daughters tell of their love/hate relationships with strong traditions that tie them to their parents and to a country they have never seen. While husbands and fathers play a role in the novel, the focus of intensity is the problematic mother-daughter bond, which, Tan says, is present in all cultures, but "separation happens in different ways in different cultures. The feeling is in Chinese culture that [the bond] can never be broken."

Talking about mother-daughter relationships in general, Tan referred to "the metaphor of the umbilical cord . . . which gets stretched over time; whether it's the mother or daughter who severs it or tries to pull it tighter, part of that is individual and part is cultural. In a Chinese family the mother pulls very tightly on the bond to a point where [the daughter] asks, 'Why can't I know about such and such?' and the [mother answers], 'Because I haven't put it in your mind yet.' The notion that your mother puts everything in your mind — the blank slate theory — is part of Chinese culture."

Tan sees a pronounced difference in American parents, who are "much more willing, when adolescence takes place, to give certain freedoms so children can learn independence and responsibility. Those freedoms were more difficult for my mother to give. As a result, the daughter then realizes the only way she can loosen the connection is to do something more drastic. My book doesn't have a sociological message about cultures, but this is my specific experience. The notion of never being independent from my mother was so terrifying to me that I went to extremes to sever [the bond]." Tan laughed when she admitted that "now I'm trying to pull it tighter again."

In many ways, Tan's own childhood could be a study in the tensions of cultural assimilation in the United States in the fifties and sixties. She was born in Oakland in 1952 to a Chinese father who was educated as an engineer in Beijing but refused an M.I.T. scholarship to become a Baptist minister. Her mother, who came from a wealthy Shanghai family, had left three children in China as the price of escaping from an unhappy arranged marriage. When she was growing up, Tan said, her parents "spoke half in English, half in Mandarin" and when she started school, her mother "continued to talk to me in Chinese and I would answer back in English." Her parents "came here for the large part so their future children would have a better chance," yet their Chinese traditions were apparent in "things that related to discipline or respect. I'd think, 'Gosh, I can reject that. . . . We're here in America.' " Tan said that "with assimilation you have a dominant culture and the underlying message is you have to reject your other culture." She said the schools also participated in sending this message, "not a didactic message, but when I grew up there were no courses about Chinese history or even about the United States's involvement with China during the war." Although Tan behaved like a thoroughly assimilated American child, she was in fact storing up memories, including stories her mother told her about her grandparents that would lead her eventually to *The Joy Luck Club.*

She wanted to write fiction from the time she won an essay contest at the age of eight, but "I was told that if you liked doing something, it wasn't worth pursuing." From the age of six her parents told her she would become "a brain surgeon because that's the most important part of the human anatomy. They also got a piano and had me take lessons from the age of five; they decided I would be a concert pianist in my spare time." It is tragically ironic, in view of her parents' ambitions for her, that when she was fifteen both her father and her older brother died within six months of each other of brain cancer. Their deaths began a strange odyssey for Tan, her younger brother John, and their mother. "My mother regretted that my father never really took a vacation and also believed that our house was diseased, so she decided to take us on an extended leave." After brief periods in New York, Washington, and Florida, "we took a boat to Holland with no idea where we would live." They had a list of English-speaking schools but could find no place to live in Holland or Germany; they finally found a haven in Switzerland, and Tan graduated from the Institut Monte Rosa Internationale after a year at the age of seventeen.

She then returned with her family to San Francisco, and after one year at Linfield, a Baptist College in Oregon chosen by her mother, transferred to San Jose City College and then San Jose State College because she fell in love and wanted to be with the man she married four years later. (It was at this point that Tan stretched thin her bond with her mother; they were estranged for six months after she left Linfield College and switched from pre-med to a double major in English and linguistics.) Tan received her M.A. in linguistics from San Jose State in 1974 and had begun a doctoral program at Berkeley when she realized, "I'd have to do something with my life, not just be a student, which was very fun and wonderful."

Tan's first job was working as a language consultant in a program for disabled children; then she took a job with the state education department. "I was at that time one of the few Asians in the field, the only minority project director in the country for the Bureau of Handicapped Children, so I was recruited to sit on all kinds of boards and go to hearings, but what bothered me was the idea that they would think that one Chinese American could represent American Indians, and blacks, and hispanics. Chinese Americans are very different from immigrants just coming from Thailand and Cambodia and Vietnam." So she left administration and "joined a friend who had a small medical publishing company"; eventually she became a freelance writer and a consultant to business corporations.

Of this period in her life Tan says, "It brought in good money — I never had to look for business — but I felt trapped. I'd get up in the morning and sit down and say, 'I hate it, I hate it,' and begin writing." She decided to do something for herself when her friends called her a workaholic because she worked ninety billable hours a week. "I at first went to a psychiatrist about this, but after he fell asleep three times during sessions, I decided I would try my own kind of therapy, so I studied jazz piano and tried to write something that I really wanted to write. I started writing fiction and went to my first workshop at Squaw Valley; I wrote a story which I never sent out, but someone [heard of it and] wanted to publish it."

When Tan wrote another story a year later, she was contacted by an agent. "I thought she was silly to want someone unknown. When I wrote another story she said, 'I think we're ready to sell a book'; I didn't pay much attention." Shortly after this Tan went to China; on the day of her return "my agent called me and said, 'We have an offer on your book.' I said, 'What book? What have you done?' I'd written only three stories. By the end of the week we had six offers." She spent a month closing down her freelance business and wrote *The Joy Luck Club* in four months. "I wrote from nine to six and took weekends off. I said, 'You have to get this done by a certain day because if you don't, this chance may go away.' It was so wonderful to be able to concentrate on fiction all day long."

Although she proceeded efficiently, Tan in fact went through a rigorous apprenticeship as a reader and writer of fiction between 1985 and late 1987, when she began the novel. Friends who were poets and writers gave her lists of books to read: "John Gardner's *The Art of Fiction*, Eudora Welty, Flannery O'Connor, Mary Robison, Amy Hempel." Tan met Amy Hempel through friends and said that Hempel "agreed to read my work and was very encouraging when I sent these horrible things to her. She gave me excellent advice for a beginning writer; she said, 'Think of everything you write as material you can always use later. Don't be afraid to cut just because you love something.' " Tan also read "all of Louise Erdrich and Michael Dorris's books. I read *Love Medicine* all one day and one night; then the next morning I started it again; it was so wonderful. I also got anthologies of *The Best American Short Stories*."

The writer Molly Giles, whom she met during the "intensely emotional, exhilarating" experience of the Squaw Valley workshop, earned her gratitude. "My manuscript was trashed; Molly Giles, who won the Flannery O'Connor Award that year, said, 'You don't have a story here; you have a dozen stories.' A lot of the stories she pointed out became part of *The Joy Luck Club*." After the Squaw Valley workshop Giles started a private workshop in San Francisco, which now meets at Tan's house. Tan said she couldn't have written her book without the group, that Giles is "the only writing teacher I've ever had." The members of the group, who at the moment are all women, read things out loud, a method that Tan likes because "you immediately get a real reader's response."

With some exceptions (such as Garcia Marquez), the majority of writers Tan prefers are women. "I see that Saul Bellow and Doctorow and Roth get a lot of recognition as the literary writers of America, and I'm sure they are wonderful writers, but their sensibilities are different. I don't get a sense of·identity with them. . . . Updike uses language wonderfully but doesn't hit at the emotional level." When asked if she saw general differences between male and female writers, Tan compared their techniques and effects to those produced by a movie camera. "Men pan the whole scene and describe a wide panorama; their world is larger, but the sense of intimacy is not there. In my fiction and that of many women, the focus starts close-up, then the world pans out." Tan also noted that "when men are close-in, their observations are cerebral, almost opinions — in men, the mind is connected to the brain. In women, the mind is connected to the heart, which influences the way they think."

The knowledge of Chinese women's culture that informs *The Joy Luck Club* is very directly connected to Tan's emotions and heart. Her mother often said to her, "I think you know only [a] little percentage of me." So Tan resolved, at a time when she thought that her mother might be dying, to learn all that she could about her. "Part of my writing the book was to help me discover what I knew about my mother and what I knew about myself." She realized that from her childhood she had heard "stories about fragments of things" and that her mother had "a natural narrative way of explaining things. When I asked how my great-grandmother died, she said, " 'One day your grandmother went into her mother's room (your great-grandmother was very sick) and cut a piece of meat off her own arm and put it in this soup, cooked it with some herbs, but the soup didn't work and she died that day.' " The explanations were "powerful images that stayed, and the stories grew from the images."

"I was surprised at how much I knew about Chinese culture," Tan acknowledged. Her friends, who thought of her as "very American" because she never discussed her Chinese heritage with them, asked her if she'd shown the book to Chinese people. Tan is pleased that "it's gotten good feedback from literary people from China and Taiwan; a woman who had come from Beijing ten years ago said, 'There are women in that book who are just like my mother.' I had anticipated being attacked by people finding it not authentic. It wasn't my intention to represent Chinese-Americans, but I'm glad [that I did]."

When I mentioned how many of the women in the novel suffered from arranged marriages, Tan said, "Some of our notions about arranged marriages and concubines are romantic; the myth says there is love later on." She believes that "it was really like slavery; women in China came from such hardship and such a loss of freedom. My mother still feels that she can never be rid of the burden" of her own experience and that of her mother, the widow of a scholar, who was "raped by a man who wanted her as his concubine." Dishonored, Tan's grandmother felt she had no choice but to become his concubine. "She was very unhappy but hoped to gain comforts to make things better for her children." However, after "she had a son and his second wife claimed that son as her own, she killed herself in 1926 by swallowing opium. My mother was nine years old when she saw her mother dying; she felt great shame to be the daughter of a concubine." Tan said her mother has for most of her life felt oppressed by unhappiness. She feels that "everything is cumulative; that if the sequence begins wrong everything is wrong; only in the past few years has she felt that she can be happy."

Since her grandmother's experience is found in *The Joy Luck Club,* I asked Tan if she had models for the main characters, four women with very different personalities. She said that she didn't have specific models, but "I think characters are subconsciously linked to things you know intimately. I have a headstrong side and a passive side; I think I took these different sides of my mother and myself and explored. I was very conscious of trying to understand my different character traits. When my editor saw me she said, 'I thought you'd be taller; isn't June five foot six?' Another reaction was how mean Waverly was; I thought, we are not our idealized self all the time." Tan said that the power struggle between Waverly and her mother was part of her own experience, too. "As a child I thought I had clever strategies for rebellion, but my mother had even more clever strategies."

When I asked Tan what she is working on now, she laughed and said that she is expressing "the male side of me. I was so afraid of being seen as a one-theme writer that I did something completely different. Men love it; women are not quite sure they're so fond of it." The novel is "about language" and began when Tan wondered what happened to Manchu, a language that is "actually dead, although not officially. Many of the words are onomatopoetic, the sound of horses galloping on sand, the sound of small birds. Within the words you could see a world that had disappeared."

The central character in the novel is a professor of historical linguistics. "Her favorite language is Manchu; she lives in her head. . . . A part of her personality lives entirely in the past." Tan identified the novel's theme as "loss and redemption through memory. . . . When a language dies a whole culture disappears." Tan's agent advised her that the book is "so different from what I've written that I might alienate readers. So it probably won't be the next thing I publish."

She is also working on another novel set in China at the turn of the century about "my father and notions of immortality." The novel opens with a young girl watching "her father, who had inadvertently killed an official by giving him what he thought was the elixir of immortality, held in a cage, a Chinese form of torture prior to execution." The father has attempted to turn his daughter into a boy by shaving her head; he wants to preserve "a spiritual tradition" in which the men of one generation worship previous generations. The girl then comes to the United States with its "different notions of immortality." (In my latest conversation with Tan she said that she had to drop both of these projects, at least for the present, because she told so many people about them that they lost their force in her imagination. She said she realized too late that "secrecy" is an essential ingredient of her method.)

In October 1987 Tan made her first visit to China (with her husband and mother) and met her half-sisters for the first time. Even though she knew herself to be different from Chinese living there, "I felt that in some way I belonged, that I had found a country related to me." She also found "all this family, after the isolation of my small family here." Since then a sister has come to the United States with her husband to live, and her uncle has visited. While other relatives showered him with American products as gifts, she decided to spend time with him and to speak Chinese, since she believes that American plenty "distorts old notions of respect."

Through writing, remembering, and renewed contact with Chinese culture, Tan has come to understand both sides of her heritage and the sometimes comic, sometimes tragic tensions between them. Her rich heritage, her brilliance, her total commitment to fiction, and the unique power of her imagination — "Someone said you hear words, but I always see things when I hear words" — make her a writer of great vision and even greater promise.

I saw Amy Tan twice after this interview, both times at Dominican College of San Rafael. In the fall of 1990 she gave a public lecture on the subject of different languages, describing how she made the transition from business writing to the novel by writing in her mother's dialect, a combination of English words and Chinese syntax. "I decided to write for myself and my mother," Tan said, and she knew she had succeeded when her mother said of *The Joy Luck Club,* "It's so easy to read."

Tan was principal speaker at Dominican's 1991 graduation ceremony, and probably the only commencement speaker in the country to describe the ways that success and celebrity can make you frightened — even give you hives. In the din of contradictory critical voices she temporarily lost her own voice, until the story of Pearl and her mother Winnie found *her*. In *The Kitchen God's Wife*, a Chinese mother and her Chinese-American daughter exchange secrets. The mother's secret is essentially a novel-within-a-novel, the saga of her marriage to a brutal man told against the background of Japan's devastation of China during World War II and the rise of communism shortly after.

Tan said that the honorary degree she received was really for her mother, who had been cheated because she never saw her daughter walk across the stage. After the ceremony she presented her mother with her doctoral hood.

The Joy Luck Club had not yet been published or reviewed when I first met Amy Tan, and I found her to be genuinely approachable and completely honest. Between that occasion and our following two meetings, she experienced tremendous commercial and critical success. *The Kitchen God's Wife* shot to the top of the best-seller list as fast as her first novel and many critics think that it outshines its predecessor, but I could not detect the slightest change in Amy Tan. Warmth, honesty, and humor are visible components of her essential self; her energy and superb storytelling skills are a matter of record. These traits are all reasons to hope that she has just begun.

K.U.H.

BOOKS BY AMY TAN

NOVELS

The Joy Luck Club. New York: Putnam, 1989; Ballantine/Ivy, 1990.
The Kitchen God's Wife. New York: Putnam, 1991.

Gloria Naylor

GLORIA NAYLOR, who always has to have "a little bit of sky," lives in a sunny cooperative apartment in upper Manhattan whose living room windows face the Hudson River. She works at an oak rolltop desk (the kind that most writers lust after), but only a foot or two away is the inevitable computer, and the boxes of continuous-feed paper are piled up nearby. The plumbers were there the day I arrived (is it comforting to know that pipes break even at Gloria Naylor's?), but we settled in to talk despite the bangs and the clanking.

Naylor is a woman with a formidable intellect and a deeply ingrained sense of personhood. She had recently returned from a fellowship at Cornell where she had the space and the time to relax after the considerable accomplishments of *The Women of Brewster Place, Linden Hills,* and *Mama Day.* We talked initially about a writer's use of memory and about identity. Naylor said that when "you think about the process itself, within the artist, what you are doing is trying to somehow give cohesion to the chaos that is all of you. You are taking the memory of your personal self, your historical self, your familial self [because] your writing filters through all of those things." For most females, she said, your "identity comes through connecting yourself to nurturing of some sort, to your body, and . . . when you write, the writing flow[s] through that identity. That goes back to the nineteenth century. . . . What has changed somewhat is *the way* women see themselves in relationship to the female *as body,* the female *as nurturer,* the female *as mother of the family.*" Now "you get literature that will sometimes rail against that" and that tries "to broaden the horizons of what [being a female] means. As long as we have woman defined [in the usual ways] in our society, as long as that must be my identity," she explained, "I can either accept it or somehow define myself against [it, because] . . . my art will indeed come through what it means to be a woman. And, what it means to be a woman, unfortunately, is a political definition, is a personal definition, and it ties me to my body and to what society has told me is my fate, whether I choose to see it this way or not."

A writer, Naylor continued, uses what "has been your living reality, consciously or unconsciously, and you articulate through that reality." Naylor said, philosophically, that she doesn't "think this is a bad thing because male writers . . . had a certain identity that they had to live with, and they [have] articulate[d] through" that identity. The point is, "We get marvelous perspectives of the world, and now, at least, [we are] getting somewhat of a forum for the women's view." What is important is that "we used to look at women's writings, or at any writing that had not been involved in the traditional — i.e., white, upper middle-class, male canon — and we would look for [the influence of memory or identity]." But these influences "exist in everyone — they exist in James and in Faulkner and in Hawthorne and in Irving and in Mailer." It is only "when the politics of 'Is this included in the canon? Is this American literature? Is this literature, period?'" occurs that we "begin to say, 'Well, how are women doing it?' My argument," Naylor said, "is that all artists do it — 'it' being articulating through our concepts of self." The concept of self "depends on where you are placed within a society because of gender, because of race, because of class, and I think that's fine because great literatures come out of that."

That concept of self is closely related to women's perception of space, and we talked about the ways in which the physical and psychological spaces in *The Women of Brewster Place,* for instance, seemed to grow smaller and more confining as the novel progressed. In each case, it seems to me, the seven women living on Brewster Place move from larger, more viable spaces to more limited ones. (The novel ends when the black women of Brewster Place revolt against their environment and, with the help of their neighbors, tear down the walls of the dead-end street on which they are trapped.)

But Naylor said that closed spaces emanate from "a whole web of circumstances." A woman's sense of space grows out of "the society in which you are born, and the way in which you are socialized to move through that society," and that movement, or the lack of it "determines who you are, how you see the big *you* when you look into a mirror." That is why space was used "intentionally in *Linden Hills.* [It] was to be a metaphor for that middle-class woman's married existence [as] she was shoved into that basement." Naylor said she "saw women having been shoved, historically," and that this woman does "uncover our history, and she does it the way that women have made history, and that is in a confined place. . . . She is able to break out and to claim herself" after her husband locks her in the basement for giving birth to a light-skinned child. "Not the way I, Gloria Naylor the feminist, would have liked her to claim herself. But she did at least say, 'Yes, this is me, I can affirm myself, and I can celebrate me,' if you call that a celebration." Celebration, she said, "is not quite the right word, but yes, she claimed herself and the repercussions were whatever they were."

Space and memory also play a part in *Mama Day,* a novel about Miranda (Mama) Day, a descendant of Sapphira Wade, a slave, who is the matriarch of Willow Springs, a small sea island off the coasts of South Carolina and Georgia. The novel is "history concretized. My parents are from the south, from rural Mississippi, but what impressed me when I went down to Charleston [to do research, was that] you walk around a city that has been contained architecturally and therefore you get a time warp. . . . I grew up around southerners and I know how provincial they are (and there's that old joke that southerners are still living through the Civil War)," but they "do indeed hold onto tradition, and all of that came together for me. . . . I said, 'My God, I'm walking on history, I'm talking to history, there is no separation in their minds often between one hundred years ago and yesterday.' " Willow Springs "was a living thing in their minds, and Mama Day was just sort of the most recent reincarnation, in a sense." Mama Day is an enchantress, but she is very much an earth-mother figure to her niece, Cocoa, a New Yorker; this novel is one more in a long list of books about mother-daughter combinations. I asked Naylor why this issue persistently recurs. Naylor said that in "finding out what it means to be a woman, you either accept or reject" what the mother represents. A mother's influence is "so strong, sometimes acknowledged, sometimes unacknowledged," that the mother-daughter conflict is "going to show up in books written by women. I don't see how it cannot. . . . I used to teach women fifteen to twenty years my junior, and the [issue is] still there. These women are going to go on and do things I never dreamed were possible for a female to do, and they are still struggling with what it means . . . to be a woman."

That gender-linked identity struggle is part of a larger struggle that is often linked to race. In Naylor's case, her identity as a black woman "came at Brooklyn College, which was the place that formed me. . . . I was twenty-five years old when I began college. I had gone off, hit the road . . . lived down south for a while, [been] a sort of street preacher . . . and at twenty-five I wanted structure because I had had the freedom, and I realized that I had no marketable skills." Brooklyn College "made me conscious of what it meant to be me — and me in all of my richness and specificity" because it was where "I first ran into feminists. I had never thought about who I was — I had other identities: I was Roosevelt and Alberta's daughter, and then I was a Christian, and then I was a switchboard operator; but I never knew, really and truly, what it meant to be a black woman. I did know what it meant to be black." By the time she reached Yale for the M.A., she was thirty-one and had already written one novel, so she "went for security because I thought, 'Well, I cannot make a living out of being a writer.' I think that was a very wise thing to think because the odds were definitely against me. So I said, 'Fine, since I love books, I'll go and get my master's in Afro-American Studies' because I wanted now to really deepen my knowledge about what had been awakened in me at Brooklyn. I'll do that, and then I'll go on and get my doctorate in American Studies. I'll get one of those high-class union cards, which is tenure, and I won't have to worry. What I was not prepared for was that the side [of me] that had started to grow while I was working on *Brewster Place,* the need to write, would really be that strong, and there was a clash. . . . I did not think I could do both [graduate work and writing] with the same amount of energy. . . . I found it difficult to always be thinking about how you take apart [a novel] and then having to shut all that out to just let the process evolve. Just the logistics of it! The work involved was tremendous. I'm one of those type-A personalities who like to do things well, and to do things well I read about 1500 pages a week for those seminars. So . . . it was the clash between what I wanted to do with my [literary] output and what they required of me to be an academic. And that's why I left after I got the master's. I was ready to leave after the first semester and come back to New York and go back to the switchboard because I had written *Brewster Place* while I was working on the switchboard and it paid well, the hours were flexible, and I had started *Linden Hills* the summer before I went up to New Haven. But I was able to work out a deal (after my first year) with the department, where if I just did the course work, did the papers, my thesis could be . . . *Linden Hills,* and that freed me up. After that I decided to leave academia alone and to just try my wings as a writer." She supported herself through "teaching and fellowships."

Naylor said that at thirty-nine she now understands many of

the ways in which she was formed by her childhood and "why my parents did what they did. They were trying to protect us from pain, and they took us up to Queens . . . to put us into a good school system. They never talked much about the racial problems that were going on in America, and I grew up in the sixties, mind you. I would hear it at school and see it on television, but we never got that sort of talk in our home: 'You should have pride in yourself because you're black, you should have pride in yourself because you're you, and never let anyone put limits on you.' You were taught to treat people as people and that sort of thing, which is all right, all very nice and good and well, but you grow up terribly innocent and eventually you are going to get hurt. So it is a matter of trying to ward off the moment when that would happen." Naylor spoke of her "niece and nephew who do understand the political ramifications of what it means to be who they are in America, so they are getting their pain and the disappointments and the frustration early. . . . They are talked to about why certain things happen, why people say certain things to them." I asked Naylor if she thought racial consciousness and pride brought with it an unhealthy separation of the races, but she said, "They have to go to school with children of other cultures, their stepmother is a woman of Italian-American [ancestry], the doctor who saved my nephew's life and has been his only surgeon since he was twenty months old is a Jewish man, so they have all their ambivalences," but "ultimately what we learn in this society is that there must be coexistence, there has to be." Now, she said, all people "face other cultures" on television and in magazines. "What they do when they filter that information is something else again, but they are aware of what this country is."

Gloria Naylor is now one of the six members of a committee that chooses the books offered by the Book-of-the-Month Club. That job requires her to have a sense of what literature has been and what it is now. I asked her, perhaps naively, whether a writer without the big agent or the powerful publisher had any chance of having her book chosen by the Book-of-the-Month Club. She seemed genuinely to believe that "it depends totally on the composition of the jury" and the choices depend on "the individuals and the chemistry of that particular panel." Naylor expects them to be "open and fair people who take their commitment seriously, and to look for . . . the best books that we have read." The problem here is "what is best to begin with." I was particularly interested in whether a woman without a powerful agent or a contract from a New York publisher had any chance of being noticed. Naylor replied, "Will you be disregarded matter of factly? Not today. Maybe once when they had all men on those panels, it's possible that it could have happened. Now, even some men who sit on these panels are sensitive enough to know that they may *not* know. Often a woman's voice will have *more* input because they want to do what's right and they are aware of their ignorance. But the bottom line is, good literature is good literature. I think that the people who make up these panels now are sensitive to gender, to race, to class, and to region. Region, believe it or not, is extremely important. I have heard that one time there was an eastern 'mafia' and if you were not an eastern writer, forget it. Now they will bring in panelists from the West or from the South to sit on these juries." I asked her if unknown writers had much chance of having manuscripts accepted by important publishers, and she said, "Publishers are out there looking for good writing. . . . The whole thing is what constitutes 'good.' "

Her most profound advice to writers is to "totally forget [about prizes] and to write their hearts out." They should write "with as much integrity as they can — to the story they want to tell, to the characters who entrust them with those stories. Try to use the language as beautifully as they can. When that's done [and here Naylor reminded me that "God said, after the seventh day, 'It is good' "], the writers will then be able to say 'It is good' [and] that is enough!" Naylor said that after she completed *The Women of Brewster Place,* she said to herself, "I did this!" She thought that "nothing would ever replace this feeling, and nothing has."

Naylor now plans to adopt two children. "I don't like the fact that I can live, totally gratifying myself, and live quite well, on all levels. My work nurtures me. My work gave me my sanity; it really did. But it cannot be enough. I think it is a matter of looking at the scope of my life and wondering how I can become a fuller human being."

There is much to be learned from Gloria Naylor. She is an

extraordinarily talented writer, a woman of conscience and vigor who understands the writer's commitment to her work and to herself. She said, with passion in her voice, that when she writes, "I want to be good, and *each time* I want to be good."

"If I could have created myself," said Naylor, "what would I come here as? I would come here just the way I came by happenstance; I truly would. Because I celebrate myself. I see so many strengths in being a black woman, so many strengths in being from a working-class family with a rural southern background, *so many negatives too,* for all of those things! But it gives me *Me*."

M.P.

BOOKS BY GLORIA NAYLOR

NOVELS

The Women of Brewster Place. New York: Viking Press, 1982; Penguin Books, 1983.

Linden Hills. New York: Ticknor and Fields, 1985; Penguin Books, 1986.

Mama Day. New York: Ticknor and Fields, 1988; Vintage, 1989.

Gail Godwin

TO REACH Gail Godwin's home in Woodstock, New York, I drove along narrow roads that wind and dip across streams and through tangled woods. Her home itself is the essence of elegant simplicity, a new but traditionally designed Canadian cedar house on top of a steep hill, its interior full of light and space. One room on the first floor is built around a rectangular pool where Godwin swims daily. We stopped in the kitchen, and while Godwin made tea I admired the spacious living room with picture window and cathedral ceiling. Two imperious blue-eyed Siamese cats named Felix and Ambrose followed us up the stairs. The cats left us drinking herbal tea in Godwin's book-lined study, which looks east down a hill dotted with tall white birches, their branches austere in the winter afternoon light.

Author of eight novels, two collections of short stories, and numerous articles and book reviews, Godwin is a writer with an immense readership. Among her most highly acclaimed works, *The Odd Woman* was nominated for a National Book Award, and both *Violet Clay* and *A Mother and Two Daughters* were nominated for American Book Awards. *A Southern Family,* probably the most universally praised of her novels, is an ambitious book about a family's complex and interwoven reactions to the violent death of their son and brother. It has recently won the Janet Heidinger Kafka Prize.

A journalism major at the University of North Carolina–Chapel Hill and for two years a reporter, Godwin said writing was for her "a way of life" and "a way of dealing with the world" long before she published anything. "I've always wanted to write; I've always written. Even as a young girl waiting for a boy to show up, . . . I would get to a point where I had to write something. I would end up writing fiction, making up a girl like myself, but then, as I told the story, getting away from that. I remember once I was so involved that when this particular boy did finally come by I was annoyed!"

Godwin comes by her profession naturally, for her mother was both reporter and fiction writer when Godwin was growing up in Asheville, North Carolina. (She taught as well, doing three jobs while Godwin's grandmother took care of the house.) Her mother is still writing and still an important person in her life: "My mother is sending me her journals now . . . as she finishes them. I'm seeing her as a person with her own center of gravity and I [also] see in her, more than ever, the little lost only child who felt that she never fit in." We spoke about the practice of sharing and/or publishing personal journals. "It's an adventuresome thing to do; it takes courage, especially if you tell the truth."

Godwin has drawn upon both family and individual experience in much of her fiction. She said that *A Southern Family,* based in part on a private family tragedy, was extremely painful to write, "but it was an act of healing, too, to force myself to go into all those different points of view, even the ones that were alien to me. I must have succeeded because in the letters I get readers like some of the people I had a hard time being fair to. Ralph and Snow were definitely the aliens, outsiders to me. I didn't particularly want to understand them, so I knew I had to make every effort to write from the way they felt it. It was an enlarging experience; I feel I can be more people now."

Six points of view are sustained in *A Southern Family,* six characters fully revealed through their most intimate thoughts and fears. "I can only do that about every other book and then I like a single viewpoint again. The multiple viewpoints make for a long book; you lose a kind of intensity that you get when you just focus on one character and, like Henry James said, have the whole world come filtering through that character. You get a certain pressure and intensity from the world having to narrow itself to get into that one opening. Each kind of book gives a different reward; I like to balance them."

Memory and dreams, important themes in all of Godwin's fiction, are in *A Southern Family* a way for Theo's relatives to come to terms with his death, even, in some sense, to reach him. Godwin observed that we all live to some degree in our memories: "What person in the world goes through life in a straight line? I'm sure as you drove up this driveway you were not totally in the present moment; you were all over your life, maybe in your dreams as well. I think that most people, whether aware of it or not, are never in one place or one time. We have this idea of a linear time imposed on us. That's why we have such trouble with concepts like eternity, heaven and hell, and all that. If you start looking at it, it's all here and now. And that's the kind of fiction I like to read." Godwin said that she doesn't "trust a book that just has someone living in the present instant; it's too simple, too simplified."

I remarked that in very few novels — most of them by women — do characters confide their dreams to each other, as they do in *A Southern Family.* "I let my characters express themselves through dreams because that will give a side to them that you couldn't get any other way. Then it's up to the reader to do the analysis, of course. Lily tells Clare that she has a dream that she's lying in a bed and there are all these nuns around her and they think she's dead, but she's not and she's afraid they're going to bury her. They say, 'Oh, she's a saint,' and then she's afraid if they know she's alive she won't get to be a saint anymore, so she just lies there. She's telling something about herself that she wouldn't be able to tell anyone [directly]."

Godwin said that perhaps women are simply more used to revealing themselves to others, making themselves "open to ridicule or attack. . . . Men have their carapace, their shell. It would be like riding into battle without armor, with your heart wide open. What do you have when you have these icons of Jesus? You have him baring this open heart, and that's what a dream is. Telling someone your dream is saying, 'Here I am, I'm not sure what this means, you may find something in there that will make you think me worse than I think I am.' It's a gift and it can turn on you. You're doing something very private and it can have more stingers than you know."

Godwin is an ardent admirer of the Canadian writer Robertson Davies. "There are the special men writing. Davies' people dream. They have a rich fantasy life and are all over their memories. I believe that John Fowles' people dream. We have male elements and female elements in us, and maybe some of these good men writers have more female in them." Godwin agrees that women count large among major fiction writers in America today. "Some of the best fiction being written — I mean real fiction, not this short stuff with no basement and no attic — usually it's a woman doing it."

All of Godwin's recent novels, including *The Finishing School* and *A Mother and Two Daughters,* have breadth as well as depth — of setting, of time, of numbers of characters. "I do have a lot of minor characters and they get their moment. A minor character might not have much to do with our day, yet when we look back, that person was a figure, an important sign of some kind. What makes fiction rich are all those hordes out there who each has a story and memory and dream. Of course if you put everybody's voice in . . . you'd have pandemonium."

As James Joyce did in *Ulysses*? I asked. "That's probably what he was getting at. Faulkner was getting at something similar [when] he said what he really wanted to do was get his whole world into one sentence. If you refine an idea enough or refine a sentence enough and try to get everything in it . . . all the allusions and connections . . . that's not a road that many people are able to follow. Faulkner was doing that in *Absalom, Absalom!* Joyce got interested in trying to get every shading of a word into the word itself, and then he found himself creating a language all of his own. When you get deep, you do start losing readers, but it's just a chance you have to take."

Godwin said that she was amazed by the vast sales of *A Southern Family.* "I was looking at it the other day; this book is hard. You really have to pay attention, and yet it's been on the bestseller list and it's right up there in the supermarket with these books that you don't have to pay attention [to]. It makes me worry. I'm very happy, but I wonder if people read it when they take it home or if they buy it because they think it's going to be something else." Either way, however, Godwin thinks more Americans are using their leisure time to read. "I don't believe the doomsayers who say people don't read any more, who say we've all become illiterate. I see more and more people reading and I see people in the kinds of occupations who wouldn't have been readers twenty years ago."

I asked Godwin about her new book, which is about "an Episcopal clergyman and his daughter. The mother runs away when the daughter is very small and she more or less becomes her father's parent; she doesn't have a childhood. She just takes it on herself to keep him going and he has these melancholy episodes when she has to keep up the front. They keep up a front — a good Southern couple — but it's hard. The girl's mother runs off with another woman and that makes it even more difficult in a small southern social setting," said Godwin with considerable understatement, "to have your mother run off with a woman."

Godwin is "writing about a kind of madness right now, a kind that interests me very much because I've had a lot to do with depression. The more I read about madness the madder I get because most of it's dumb and written in technical language. . . . People go mad because of things which happened in their histories, their own configurations. It's not much help to consult these boring, clinical, pop-psych works, so I'm just having to figure it out for myself. I've been having the father describe to his daughter what it's like. He calls it going behind the black curtain, and the little girl says, 'You know you don't like it behind the black curtain. Why do you go there?' He says, 'I don't go there; it's as if I'm wandering and suddenly I find myself behind it and I can't get out.' " Godwin says that this description works "better for me than to use the technical language, which resonates with no images."

I asked Godwin if she viewed her new book as a tragedy — as she does *A Southern Family*. "It'll be a redemptory book. I wanted to write a novel about a young woman of today who could be called a heroine; she had to be a person who had read and knew the myths of humanity; she couldn't be a 'valley girl.' I thought, 'I want to make a heroine, a twenty-two-year-old woman of depth today. What would she be like? What do we mean?' " The book, whose title ultimately became *Father Melancholy's Daughter*, was published in February 1991. The novel is a sensitive first-person chronicle of the emotional and spiritual growth of Margaret Gower, an intelligent, caring young woman growing up in a small town in western Virginia.

Thinking of the quotations from Emerson and Lawrence in *A Mother and Two Daughters*, I wondered if the leitmotif would be literary. "In *A Mother and Two Daughters* one daughter was literary; Cate taught literature, so she'd think that way. The characters in *A Southern Family* didn't think that way. In the book I'm writing now, in each chapter is something to do with the liturgy or the Bible or the Book of Common Prayer." Walter Gower, "Father Melancholy" of the title and an Episcopal priest, is a contemporary Christ figure who must confront challenges parallel to those in the life of Christ: abandonment, dejection, enemies to his ministry. Like Christ, he also has loyal and loving supporters whom he inspires. The focal character, however, is his daughter Margaret, whose spiritual quest reflects Godwin's own recent spiritual odyssey.

Godwin said that a year ago she started "going back to church . . . through the whole liturgical year. I see now what we've missed, losing our religion. I was raised as an Episcopalian in a good, small, Anglo-Catholic church; then I went to a Roman Catholic school run by nuns. There was always a festival of some kind. All these things go way back before Christianity, tied in with the seasons, the solstice, the equinox, pacifying the dark gods so you can have spring again. When you don't observe the changes and the seasons and all these events in our natural lives you're bare, you miss something, the fact that everything is connected with everything else. It's much easier, when you don't do any of that, to see yourself as the 'only lonely,' wandering in a Beckett landscape with not much text and not much furniture but garbage cans and an empty road leading to nothing."

I asked Godwin if she had a sense of going home when she returned to church. "I had to find the right church first. I first went to one that was so off-the-wall that I came home angry. Then I found a high church with all the beauty and formality and respect for God; it suited me fine." She said that churchgoing brings back a lot of memories, including "the prayers and the confessions. I was in a Catholic school from age seven to fifteen. I was Protestant, but our penmanship teacher — clever nun — made us copy the catechism, so I know it."

Our discussion of family memories reminded Godwin that her mother has been sending her pieces of her past. She showed me a magazine entitled *Love Short Stories* dated December 1945 whose cover showed a woman gazing passively through a heavily framed window. The magazine contained two stories by her mother; Godwin said they were good despite the rules and constraints of the genre. "You can almost hear her saying, 'Oh, hell, now I have to describe how she looks.' This is the scariest issue of all. Every story in it is about the men coming home. Every ad shows dress patterns, dolls, aprons."

Asked if she encountered sexism either as a graduate student or as a reporter, Godwin said, "I came along at a good time; women were being welcomed in graduate school with open arms. All my professors and supervisors were older men. When I was trying to write and publish as an undergraduate, I got a lot of rejections, but I think that's because my writing simply wasn't good enough; I hadn't pulled it together. . . . When I was on the newspaper in

Miami, all my bosses were men. They were patient, but I did finally get fired, but I deserved to be. I kept pressuring them to [let me] return to Miami, while they wanted me to stay at the outposts and get trained." She acknowledged, however, that "I may have been discriminated against and not even known it, because I am a very conditioned southern woman brought up to be gentle and not push myself."

Godwin said that "since we're on the male/female subject," she has noticed a weakness in women's writing style that she tries to guard against in her own. "Women tend to qualify more than men. They put 'perhaps' and 'I think' and use diminutives more than men. I had a professor in graduate school and when I would do that he would just write 'lady' in the margin. I had told him I wanted to watch that. I just started an essay about my mother with 'About seven years ago' and then realized that I knew exactly when it was. 'Seven years ago' seemed too blunt and too direct. Then there's this southern woman element: you don't want to come on too strong, to make people uncomfortable, to mow them down with your intellect, so you put up smoke screens."

I asked Godwin what writers she read as a child, and what writers she still reads. "As a child I read whatever was taught in school, mostly men — a lot of the romantic poets. Browning I liked a lot, the way he did so many points of view. He'd take a cast of characters and do the monologues from each point of view. That's probably where I first got the idea." She said that a book she picked herself in high school was "*Jane Eyre,* one of my all-time models. Adrienne Rich calls it (after Keats's quote) 'a vale of soul-making,' a tale about how a soul was formed. I love that kind of book." When working in England for the U.S. Travel Service, "I gravitated toward Henry James, D.H. Lawrence. Lawrence can do the undersides of people better than almost anyone, the unsocialized part of a person. 'The Virgin and the Gypsy' shows the way he did it . . . by equating people with certain animals. I loved George Eliot for sheer scope, Jane Austen for the same elegance as Bach. These are books I read over and over. I like Thomas Hardy for the way he does the animate in nature."

We noted that James, Lawrence, and Hardy were all fascinated by the characters of women. "Eustacia Vye and the woman in *Far from the Madding Crowd* . . . aren't a sawed-off Norman Mailer half-toned paper doll but a seething mass of humanity. Henry James also expressed the soul of a person through a female character — Milly Theal, too good to be true. Isabel Archer is one of my all-time favorites; I read that book about every three years. But about every ten years I totally change my mind about the people in it. I now understand that Isabel Archer could not have married anyone but Gilbert Osmond. He was just like her father, a charming, no-good man; the scene of the father with the little girl will attract her more than anything. Gilbert Osmond is her moon side, the other side of her; she'll go back to him and they will make each other exquisitely miserable."

Because of my unspoken belief that the character of Cate in *A Mother and Two Daughters* is at certain moments a woman's re-creation of Isabel Archer, Godwin's next words gave me the thrill of a hunch confirmed. "These books become a part of you. . . . I hope I can sometime carry Isabel on in some novel or other. . . . She won't be called Isabel." When I mentioned the many parallels between Cate's refusal of Roger Jernigan and Isabel's refusal of Lord Warburton, Godwin responded, "That's true, because the reader is saying, 'Go on, marry him, you won't do any better than this' — even I was. 'He won't jail you, he wants you to be yourself, he loves you' . . . so yes, I am carrying her on." I said what I found wonderful in the comparison is that whereas Isabel floundered after refusing her rich suitor, Cate went on with her life, reunited with Roger as her lover yet keeping her independence. We recalled the *toute ensemble* at the end of the novel, which (unlike *Portrait of a Lady*) has the classic structure of a comedy. "Roger's even there at the end with the alcoholic lady flirting with him. It's fun to write books."

Godwin has taught at Columbia University for several semesters, at Bread Loaf in Vermont, and at the Writers' Workshop in Iowa. When asked how she taught creative writing, she said, "What I like to do is have two courses. In one I teach good books and stories, how to read, what to look for. Until you can read that way, you don't know what you want to do with your writing, how to get effects. Then I work very much with the individual and . . . just see what's there to start with. Then I give assignments: imagine a person as unlike yourself as possible; imagine that person going to bed at night or getting up in the morning; put in every detail." Godwin professed profound admiration for good teachers. "If I teach well, I have simply nothing left when I finish. It's like being both a very good actress and a very good listener at the same time. Doing one or the other you get something back to sustain you; but doing both at once, you're simply drained. You don't even have a memory at the end of the day."

Her advice to young writers is to "pay attention" to the world around them. "It took me so long to learn to pay attention. I went through my teen years in a fog. I can remember being driven places and it was like a mist drifting by outside the window. I was living in Nat King Cole's songs and who-knows-what fantasies." We agreed that young people protect themselves by not observing, by living inside their heads. "When you start noticing, the world just comes falling at you. There's a part of Robertson Davies' novel *World of Wonders* where this old gypsy woman who tells fortunes explains to a young boy who's joined the circus how she does it. The whole book is worth it for these few pages. She says, 'It's a matter of watching people. Look at the way they walk in. Do they favor any part of their body? Look at how they sit, what they have on, what part of their body they put forward, what part they hold back.' You know too much if you really pay attention."

She said that it's equally important to observe places. "What we surround ourselves with makes statements. You can go into anyone's house and you're told almost more than you want to know. I went to a party this weekend. A man furnished his house with the money he made, quite a lot; I could write a novel about that man on the basis of what I saw in an hour."

I asked Godwin what contemporary women writers she reads. "I like Margaret Drabble and wish she'd write more. I like the way she does a complete treatment of interiors. Rosellen Brown's *Civil Wars* is a powerful book. . . . There's a great kitchen in there. My favorite book of Mary Lee Settle's is a memoir of when she was in World War II stationed in the English countryside. She drives her bicycle by an old tree every night until she simply can't any more because she feels such evil vibrations from it. So she asks someone who tells her, 'That's where they used to hang people.' The whole book has this extra dimension in it."

I asked Godwin if she herself believed in the "extra dimension," in the possibility of the kind of communication that took place in *A Southern Family* between Rafe and his dead brother. She said she has experienced it, that not long ago she asked a friend from the South who was dying of cancer to somehow let her know when the time came. On the night she died Godwin dreamed of her death, and the next day she told her mother that it had happened. Her strong sense of this dimension reflects her notion of time as layered rather than linear and her sense of the reality of things of the spirit, of transcendent categories in human experience.

Before leaving I asked Godwin why she has settled in Woodstock. She answered, "Circumstances mixed with desire. I was in England, then went to Iowa to study at the Workshop and got a Ph.D. while I was there. I met Robert and he taught at Juilliard." (Godwin has shared her life for some time with the composer Robert Starer, for whose music she has written four libretti.) "I didn't want to be in New York City — you can't think there — so we had to find a place where he could go in for his two days of teaching. Two hours away is the outer limit. The first place was Stone Ridge; I had never lived in the deep country before and there was so much to love. I grew up in the town of Asheville, not a metropolis, but I lived on a street with other houses and had never had the experience of just looking out the window and seeing nature. I've gotten so spoiled that I don't even want to see a telephone pole."

In Godwin's presence one feels courtesy that is not a veneer over personality but its essence — a sensitivity to others that is at her very core. The same sensitivity — to character, to place, to feeling — is at the core of her writing. At least twice during the interview she said, "It's fun to write novels." Gail Godwin is a writer at peace with her profession, herself, and her world.

K.U.H.

BOOKS BY GAIL GODWIN

NOVELS

The Perfectionists. New York: Harper & Row, 1970; Penguin, 1985.
Glass People. New York: Knopf, 1972; Warner, 1983.
The Odd Woman. New York: Knopf, 1974; Warner, 1983.
Violet Clay. New York: Knopf, 1978; Warner, 1979.
A Mother and Two Daughters. New York: Viking, 1982; Avon, 1983.
The Finishing School. New York: Viking, 1985; Avon, 1986.
A Southern Family. New York: William Morrow, 1987; Avon, 1988.
Father Melancholy's Daughter. New York: William Morrow, 1991.

SHORT STORIES

Dream Children. New York: Knopf, 1976; Avon, 1983.
Mr. Bedford and the Muses. New York: Viking, 1983; Avon, 1984.

Joyce Carol Oates

EVEN AN experienced interviewer looks forward to meeting Joyce Carol Oates for the first time with nervous excitement and trepidation; there is, after all, a halo of brilliance around Oates. No one on the current literary scene, male or female, so dramatically and consistently epitomizes excellence in such profusion, or writes, seemingly with ease, novels, poetry, short stories, essays, plays, reviews, and screenplays at such a formidable, somewhat intimidating, rate. At fifty-one, Oates, the Roger S. Berlind Distinguished Professor in the Humanities at Princeton, is the author of twenty novels, several plays, five collections of essays, eleven collections of short stories, poetry, and substantial numbers of reviews.

On reflection, the interviewer realizes that she has prepared herself to meet an autocratic, distanced, supremely confident, exemplary God-person — well-protected by questioning secretaries in an ivy-covered Fine Arts building off the fabled Nassau Street of Scott Fitzgerald's novels. Instead, she meets Joyce Carol Oates, a gracious, friendly, accessible, generous scholar dressed in a raspberry sweater and dark trousers. Oates is at work in a bookcase-lined office, unexceptional except for its extraordinary occupant. The sparsely-filled bookshelves hold copies of Oates's novels and books, in English and translated into various languages. A laminated wooden plaque with a poem by Stanley Kunitz sits on a shelf behind the Scandinavian sofa and chairs and, facing a wall near the uncurtained windows, is Oates's very large and uncluttered desk.

All of this is unremarkable unless you are one of thousands of Oates fans who has read *Marya,* her seventeenth novel, published in 1986, which Oates says is "a conflation of my life and my mother's." It is about a lonely, unmothered girl who grows up in upstate New York and eventually becomes a distinguished college professor and very famous writer. The novel traces her emotional and intellectual passage and contains one of the most intrinsically, if not overtly, violent scenes in contemporary literature. A disturbed janitor, for uncited but obviously malevolent reasons is secretly victimizing the still young, untenured professor by wreaking havoc on her emotional and actual space — symbolized here by her office. He rifles through her desk drawers, leaves his unflushed excrement in her office toilet, puts cigarettes out on her desk, lurks silently in the darkened hallways when she works late. *Marya* is chilling in its ability to reach the often-unspoken and amorphous fears of helplessness familiar to all women, and, at the same time, shocking in its singularity, specificity, and foreignness. "The novel," said Oates, "is really about power between the male and the female."

Suddenly, this interviewer gasps! In tree-lined, super-respectable, manicured, upper-class Princeton, we are sitting in Marya's office! "Yes," says Oates with delight, "it is this office. It was different when I first came here. . . . It was painted recently, maybe a year ago. It was very dark. And there's the restroom, the lavatory. We did have a janitor who was a strange man. When I would leave this office it would be late at night sometimes, and it was very dark and all the lights [out there] would be dark. I remember leaving this office and walking into that blankness out there, and in fact, there would be nobody there. But psychologically," the threat was ever-present. Much to my relief, Oates added quietly, "He's gone now."

Oates goes to this office twice a week and spends "very little time" on campus. She lives nearby in a house in the woods; the house in *American Appetites,* "in which the McColloughs live, is actually the house in which I live — with glass walls — so I am writing about my own house." It is intriguing to think of her, reed-thin and delicate as she appears, in "Marya's space" and in her Princeton office. To reach it, you walk up stairs and down halls that reek of the oil-based paints, turpentine, fixatives, and thinners that define all Fine Arts buildings, and through the disordered piles of students' paintings. It is somehow equally intriguing to imagine this author, who writes about fragmenting, chaotic, inner spaces, surrounded at home by glass.

Joyce Carol Oates says she is "very much a writer who is interested in class, in class consciousness, class warfare, you could call it, so I tend to see [experience] in terms of . . . economic power, or loss of power, or lack of power. Gender is part of it, but there is also the economic base." She comes "from a background that is 'working class,' I guess you could say, if you stretch it a little, so I am very aware that money is power and within that, the woman is always even less enfranchised — the woman [has] less power than the man." In that context we talked about the emotional and actual spaces of women, which Oates agreed were often closed, but she said she "tends to feel it is a matter of economic class too because money brings more power [which] brings more freedom." For her, space "is an economic issue because of the kind of background I come from." She mentioned that "some people, [women] friends of mine, upper middle class, are traveling as much and virtually as freely as the men. [Women] colleagues go to Europe or they go round the world by themselves. This was not a part of my generation and it would have been very amazing. So it is a different world and a different consciousness, with different degrees of affluence." In *Do with Me What You*

Will, Oates "actually structured the novel so that the woman's sections surrounded a man's section as if she was embracing him and he was contained within her. So though she seemed very passive, she had a strange stubborn strength. I think there's a good deal of strength in passivity and that activity or action of a frenzied nature sometimes is a kind of weakness. Being able to leave the space and go places can actually be a demonstration of weakness." I suggested that the "weakness" she mentioned comes from a dissipation of emotional strength and physical energy and is sometimes counterproductive, remembering here my own and my colleagues' often-frenzied trips around the country to conferences. Oates said, "We've had an American ethos of the male going to the frontier and leaving the confines of civilization and, in so doing, abrogating adulthood and being a perpetual adolescent." Women, we agreed, have always assumed that passivity and enervation were the same thing, and Oates reiterated that "they are not necessarily the same thing."

The spaces in Oates's novels emanate, of course, as they do for all writers, from memory, and from the transmigration of those memories into fiction. Oates says she feels a strong connection to "the places where I lived when I was brought up . . . to about the age of eighteen. Then, of course, I left home, lived a different kind of life; I went to college, got married, and we moved around. So I think it is the early formative years and the enclosure of the family" that provide the encoded pain, violence, and loneliness, or the well of security, love, and possibility, that feed the author's imagination. During the early years there is "a house and property, and the child's mind more or less branches out; there's the neighborhood and so forth. That territory that we claim with our earliest selves is somehow so deeply imprinted in the brain that I think anything else could go and you'd still have that; you'd still have this great reservoir of emotion. I feel [that reservoir of emotion] as a kind of love, and I think it is analogous to the feeling that most painters and visual artists have. They love what they are rendering. Other people may look at it and say, 'It is ugly, it is destructive, it's violent, how can you do this?' but when you are working with the material on that level, almost like a child's level, you are not judging. People often ask me whether I know these violent people or these terrible people . . . but to me they are people, and their violence is not more pronounced than the violence of nations, or so-called civilized people, or upper-middle class people. I don't see that at all. So I think that yes, the hauntedness [of memory] is certainly a part of my life as a writer."

"Joan Didion once said that 'the impulse for much writing is homesickness. You are trying to get back home, and in your writing you are invoking that home, so you are assuaging the homesickness,' and I think that is very valid. Some people have unresolved memories — something like ghosts in the psychological sense, and they can't exorcise them. Much of my writing is energized by that." Oates said she feels "very haunted" by her parents' early life, before she was born. Her mother was from a very large, impoverished farm family. Like Marya, she was given away. Also, like Marya's father, Oates's grandfather was killed in a tavern fight. Some of the early experiences in *Marya* are "my mother's. I joined my mother and me together in kind of a mysterious way. The novel is very much about mothers and absent mothers and a daughter who won't admit that her mother is absent from her life. [She] tries to be almost [autonomous] like a man . . . but then at the end comes back to her mother. It meant a lot to me to write it." Violence, sadness, grief, I suggested, are in the end what is violent, sad, and grief-making for you.

That haunted quality reverberates in *You Must Remember This* where "the girl Enid is also searching for a way out of the confines of her life." Her Uncle Felix, who rapes her and whose mistress she becomes, "does represent something different" from the increasing numbers of incestuous characters in contemporary literature. "He turns out to be the way out. I saw the novel as about both of them. Felix more or less loses his youth in the course of the novel, and Enid gains her maturity." The rape and ensuing sex "could have been an act that was crippling for her, and she does try to commit suicide. But then she becomes stronger. Felix is her father's half brother and is someone she is attracted to. Often in incest cases there isn't a reciprocal attraction but there *are* young girls who are very attracted to their own uncles, at least if their uncles are attractive. In most incest cases we have the sense of a person who is not attractive, forcing himself on someone who is not willing, but my novel is a little different because Felix is more attractive and does represent something different — he is beyond the small confines, the suffocating world that would have been [Enid's]."

Another kind of problematic connection and disconnection reappears in *Because It Is Bitter and Because It Is My Heart,* which Oates had just written. It is "about a girl who has a love-hate relationship with her mother . . . a very beautiful woman who drifts into alcoholism, [who] doesn't really know what she's getting into. So the crux of the daughter's life is dealing with the mother who, because she is an alcoholic, is also a liar, is also deceitful. Still, there's this love here, and the daughter sees the mother all the way through [until] the mother dies." Oates had finished it only "a few weeks ago and I am still jangling and frazzled and thinking about the deathbed scene." The novel is "not based on an experience with my own mother but on an experience with an older woman with whom I was close about twenty years ago [and] who drifted into alcoholism."

One of Oates's best novels is *American Appetites,* her "Princeton novel, the world of the intellectual, of privilege." I didn't put any university [in the book] but the world is like Princeton; it's a bit like the Institute for Advanced Study. I'm friendly with people who are involved with the Institute, and of course with the university, so I wanted to write about that world." The novel hinges on the inadvertent death of Glynnis McCullough, who is pushed into the glass doors of her house during a late-night quarrel after Ian McCullough's fiftieth birthday party. Oates said, "It's also a picture of a woman in her space, in the house, and [she], like many of us . . . like all civilized people, I think, [has] a certain common delusion. She felt that she owned and controlled that space — 'This is my house, my life, my world' — and she didn't." Perhaps "intellectually she understood, but emotionally she didn't understand how fragile it all was and how a tragic interlude could destroy everything." Bianca, the McCulloughs' daughter, "has to define herself in terms of the mother, and she has to define herself in opposition to the mother, in order to have an identity." Oates thinks "many daughters . . . are close to [and] love their mothers enormously but the love is so strong it has to be denied if they are to be two people. We know this is true because, when people get really very sick, they want their mothers — they regress. Bianca is going through that phase when she is designing herself. When the mother dies, [for which] in some buried, some inchoate way," she has wished, "then she realizes she loved her mother." The mother in some sense becomes a buried memory, and her death is the impetus for what happens to everyone in the novel. "When Bianca is . . . mourning for her mother she looks around and finds an old book of her mother's and finding that old book changes her life. She ends up going to Thailand, studying Buddhism; things her mother picked up and put down in the sixties she is going to pick up more seriously. Bianca becomes concerned with certain themes in the Tibetan *Book of the Dead,* which I had read and studied at one time." The book suggests that "the dead person still has a spirit in him or herself and that the dead are not really dead, so [the daughter] has this kind of confused, almost hallucinatory idea that maybe her mother, though buried, is in a sense not dead, is a kind of pervasive spirit that's always in the house."

The death of Glynnis is "the beginning of the end" for Ian McCullough, too. "He's got this new young woman and she loves him but he's fifty years old, he did love his wife, he's lost a daughter and his own father committed suicide; he's not that shallow a person [that he can] just forget the past. It is a golden age that [Ian and his friends] have lost and they don't even know why it has happened."

Oates and I talked about what she had, in a *New York Times* review of *Jean Stafford,* called "pathography," an "unfair" and "wrong-headed" view of a writer's life that makes it "a repository of illnesses and disasters and disappointments" and "whose motifs are dysfunction and disaster, illnesses and pratfalls, failed marriages and failed careers, alcoholism and breakdowns and outrageous conduct. Its scenes are sensational . . . wallowing in squalor and foolishness; its dominant images are physical and deflating; its shrill theme is 'failed promise' if not outright 'tragedy.' " This is the strongest and probably the best statement to date about those (usually male) biographers who "so mercilessly expose their subjects, so relentlessly catalogue their most vulnerable and least illuminating moments, as to divest them of all mystery save the crucial and unexplained: How did a distinguished body of work emerge from so undistinguished a life?"

Clearly a writer's intensely public work and the intensely private consciousness from which it grows are demonstrably separate entities that lose their demarcation in a pathographer's hands. This is particularly and increasingly noticeable when the writer is a woman who fails to resemble Snow White, Betty Crocker, Mother Teresa, or other icons of female expression to which women are often tacitly held. Stafford's life, which was irrevocably shortened and shortchanged by her alcoholism and the distorted vision that is often its product, is not the essential point. What are "charming" quirks and foibles in the lives of male writers are seen as the unacceptable marks of a deviant in the life of a woman who writes. The biographer separates the "life" of a male writer from the lives he creates, and assumes that those lives created by a woman are a reiteration and replication of her own life. And a "pathographer" distorts both the personal and the fictional lives of writers of both sexes, feeds on the agony of one to destroy the value of the other. Oates, who is herself an intensely private person quite used to the inane, trite, and invasive questions of some biographers, did all writers a tremendous service when she made this distinction and dramatically made the point that the "outrageous conduct" on which pathographers feed is finally less squalid and foolish and virulent than their own.

Joyce Carol Oates is a frequent target of reviewers and critics, many of whom seem unable to resist the opportunity to comment in a scornful and derogatory fashion on the prodigious nature of her writing. What should be acknowledged instead is that Oates can use every genre, that she publishes more frequently and has more to say than most of her contemporaries, and that she is, indeed, the first woman of letters in American life.

M.P.

BOOKS BY JOYCE CAROL OATES

NOVELS

With Shuddering Fall. New York: Vanguard, 1964; Fawcett, 1971.

A Garden of Earthly Delights. New York: Vanguard, 1967; Fawcett, 1969.

Expensive People. New York: Vanguard, 1968; Fawcett, 1968.

Them. New York: Vanguard, 1969; Fawcett, 1970.

Wonderland. New York: Vanguard, 1971; Fawcett, 1973.

Do With Me What You Will. New York: Vanguard, 1973; Fawcett, 1974.

The Assassins. New York: Vanguard, 1975; Fawcett, 1976.

Childwold. New York: Vanguard, 1976; Fawcett, 1981.

The Triumph of the Spider Monkey. Santa Barbara, Calif.: Black Sparrow, 1977; Fawcett, 1979.

Son of the Morning. New York: Vanguard, 1978; Fawcett, 1979.

Cybele. Santa Barbara, Calif.: Black Sparrow, 1979; Dutton, 1986.

Unholy Loves. New York: Vanguard, 1979; Fawcett, 1981.

Bellefleur. New York: Dutton, 1980, 1987.

Angel of Light. New York: Dutton, 1981; Warner, 1982.

A Bloodsmoor Romance. New York: Dutton, 1982; Warner, 1983.

Mysteries of Winterthurn. New York: Dutton, 1984; Berkley, 1985.

Solstice. New York: Dutton, 1985; Berkley, 1986.

Marya: A Life. New York: Dutton, 1986; Berkley, 1988.

You Must Remember This. New York: Dutton, 1987; Harper & Row, 1988.

American Appetites. New York: Dutton, 1989; Harper & Row, 1990.

Rosamond Smith [pseud.]. *Lives of the Twins*. New York: Simon and Schuster, 1987; Avon, 1989.

———. *Soul-Mate*. New York: Dutton, 1989; NAL, 1990.

I Lock My Door Upon Myself. New York: Ecco Press, 1990.

Because It Is Bitter and Because It Is My Heart. New York: Dutton/ -Abrahams, 1990; Plume, 1991.

The Rise of Life on Earth. New York: New Directions, 1991.

NONFICTION

The Edge of Impossibility: Tragic Forms in Literature. New York: Vanguard, 1972; Fawcett, 1978.
The Hostile Sun: The Poetry of D.H. Lawrence. Los Angeles: Black Sparrow Press, 1973.
New Heaven, New Earth: The Visionary Experience in Literature. New York: Vanguard, 1974; Fawcett, 1978.
Contraries: Essays. New York: Oxford, 1981.
[Ed.] *First Person Singular: Writers on Their Craft.* Princeton: Ontario Review Press, 1983.
The Profane Art: Essays and Reviews. New York: Dutton, 1983.
On Boxing. Garden City: Doubleday, 1987; Zebra, 1988.
(Woman) Writer: Occasions and Opportunities. New York: Dutton, 1988; NAL, 1989.
[Ed. with Daniel Halpern.] *Reading the Fights.* New York: Holt, 1988; Prentice Hall, 1990.

SHORT STORIES

By the North Gate. New York: Vanguard, 1963; Fawcett, 1971.
Upon the Sweeping Flood. New York: Vanguard, 1966; Fawcett, 1971.
The Wheel of Love. New York: Vanguard, 1970; Fawcett, 1971.
Marriages and Infidelities. New York: Vanguard, 1972; Fawcett, 1973.
Where Are You Going, Where Have You Been? Stories of Young America. New York: Fawcett, 1974.
The Goddess and Other Women. New York: Vanguard, 1974; Fawcett, 1976.
The Hungry Ghosts. Santa Barbara, Calif.: Black Sparrow Press, 1974.
The Poisoned Kiss. New York: Vanguard, 1975.
The Seduction and Other Stories. Santa Barbara, Calif.: Black Sparrow Press, 1975, 1976.
Crossing the Border. New York: Vanguard, 1976; Fawcett, 1978.
Night-Side. New York: Vanguard, 1977; Fawcett, 1980.
All the Good People I've Left Behind. Santa Barbara, Calif.: Black Sparrow Press, 1979.
A Sentimental Education. New York: Dutton, 1980; NAL, 1982.
Last Days. New York: Dutton, 1984, 1986.

Raven's Wing. New York: Dutton, 1986; NAL, 1987.
The Assignation. New York: Perennial/Harper & Row, 1989.

POETRY

Women in Love and Other Poems. New York: Albondacani Press,
1968.
Anonymous Sins and Other Poems. Baton Rouge: Louisiana State
Univ. Press, 1969.
Love and Its Derangements. Baton Rouge: Louisiana State Univ.
Press, 1970.
Wooded Forms (single poem). New York: Albondacani Press, 1972.
In Case of Accidental Death. Cambridge: Pomegranate, 1972.
A Posthumous Sketch. Los Angeles, Calif.: Black Sparrow Press, 1973.
Angel Fire. Baton Rouge: Louisiana State Univ. Press, 1973.
Dreaming America and Other Poems. Aloe Editions, 1973.
The Fabulous Beasts. Baton Rouge: Louisiana State Univ. Press, 1975.
Women Whose Lives Are Food, Men Whose Lives Are Money. Baton
Rouge: Louisiana State Univ. Press, 1978.
Invisible Woman: New and Selected Poems. Princeton: Ontario Re-
view Press, 1982.
Luxury of Sin. Northridge, Calif.: Lord John, 1983.
Wild Nights. Athens, Ohio: Croissant and Co., 1985.
The Time Traveler. Northridge, Calif.: Lord John, 1987; NAL, 1989.

PLAYS

Miracle Play. Santa Barbara, Calif.: Black Sparrow Press, 1974.
Three Plays. Princeton: Ontario Review Press, 1980.
Invisible Woman. Princeton: Ontario Review Press, 1982.
Twelve Plays. New York: Dutton, 1991.
In Darkest America: Two Plays. New York: Samuel French Inc.,
1991.

Diane Johnson

DIANE JOHNSON's house in the North Beach section of San Francisco is small but perfectly proportioned, with breathtaking views of city, harbor, Angel and Alcatraz islands, and the Golden Gate and San Raphael bridges from the wrap-around window in the living room. When I visited just after New Year's Day, boxes of Christmas ornaments sat on every table and chair. She explained, "I heard the garbage man coming this morning, so I flung everything off the tree and rushed it out. We're going skiing tonight, so I had to get it out."

Johnson's skiing partner is her husband, John Frederic Murray, a doctor and professor of medicine at the University of California Medical Center, San Francisco. Over the holidays she and Murray were surrounded by family, including Johnson's new four-month-old grandchild. "We have seven children between us and all but one are married or have a significant other. So there was a core group at Christmas that was simply enormous. When we sat down without friends or external people, it was at least a dozen at every meal." Their nest now empty, Johnson and Murray plan to combine this small house with the adjacent one and move into the city. When the children were home they lived in a larger house in Berkeley, and she rented an apartment in the city for writing; now she works in neither the Berkeley nor the San Francisco house. ("I always try to find a space out of the house to work in.")

In the various spaces that she has discovered or created since 1965, Diane Johnson has written seven novels, two full-length biographies, three screenplays, and upwards of forty essays and book reviews. She is also professor of English at the University of California at Davis, where her special field is nineteenth-century British literature. She is not teaching now, however, for she has a Strauss Living Fellowship from the American Academy and Institute of Arts and Letters. The generous fellowship gives her five years ("one of which is up, alas") for writing.

Johnson wrote her first novel — fiction is her favorite genre — while doing the course work for her Ph.D. and raising four small children. "When I started fiction, I didn't see it as a vocation, although at some level I took it seriously. I always knew that I was better at writing than at whatever else I was doing, that it was my best chance to do something. It's hard to conceive of yourself as a writer, so you await proof before you take that plunge and say, 'I'm a writer.' " In one sense the proof came early, when she immediately published *Fair Game;* but the fact that the novel was barely noticed led her to validate the process of writing by beginning again.

Persian Nights, Johnson's sixth novel, recounts the sexual, emotional, and political adventures of American Chloe Fowler in Iran just before the fall of the Shah. It received stunning reviews throughout the country; Rosemary Dinnage in the *New York Review of Books* called it "the best of her novels [with] the unobtrusively good writing, the gripping readability, the tension of the others, but with a broader, more expansive canvas." Johnson considers *Persian Nights* a political adventure novel. "I wanted it to contain all the elements a travel novel with a male protagonist would have. She has to sleep with a local person, hardly ever think of those at home, not tell them what she's done. At the same time it was about an American in Iran. The political point was about Americanness and not femaleness. . . . The CIA or whoever was supposed to predict what was happening in Iran."

The female protagonist of *Persian Nights* lives very much in the present, in the sensuality of her current lover, the sensuousness of Iranian flowers and foods, and the immediacy of the political tensions that surround all of the characters. From time to time she drops her children a postcard, but she never dwells upon the past or in sexual or maternal guilt. "In general I'm less concerned with the past than some writers, less interested in that post-Freudian view of fiction by which it had to explain present character and changes in character in terms of the past or, specifically, childhood — a rather deeply held belief of fiction writers in this century. I think fiction is more like a play in which the action is unfolding before us, so there isn't that much about childhood in my fiction."

We discussed the concepts of liberation *through* memory and liberation *from* memory, especially as they apply to women. "Memory is almost always the province of powerlessness. We think of old people living in their memories, people who can't be effective any more — or think they can't — and people who have met with a disappointment that represents an obstacle. Females have dwelt on the past as an expression of powerlessness. Not that you can't remember things, but memory loses its power over you if you have something else to do."

Johnson said that she differs from other writers in both experience and temperament: "My memory may be underdeveloped because I've never been analyzed. In psychoanalysis people learn to remember; their memories are trained. As a novelist your memory is trained in a different way; you depend upon your ability to remember something when you need it — it comes out of somewhere. Also, analysis presupposes that you are somewhat neurotic, that there is a particular problem which, if you get over, things will go better. Since novel-writing is essentially the same process as psychoanalysis, I'm not sure writers feel that particular need." We remembered that Freud, believing art to represent healthy sublimation, exempted artists from the need to delve into their pasts. "Writers often aren't psychoanalyzed and don't wish to mess around with the mechanism, whatever it is."

Johnson does not believe that women have a particular gift for preserving family memories. "Women do that, but men do it too. In my family a couple of male cousins are getting the family archives together. If women spend more time with the children, they will remember the things [that happen]. They are the only witnesses who can transmit certain things."

In Johnson's psychological terror novel, *The Shadow Knows*, the narrator spends most of her time fearfully within her apartment, protecting her small children from the real but unknown menace. In her other fiction, however, much of the action takes place outdoors and involves the kind of event associated with male writers — a bombing in *Lying Low*, a shoot-out in *Persian Nights*. Johnson believes emphatically that men still write more frequently than women about external space — "Their lives until recently were spent in external space and ours were spent at home." She pointed out that this large difference often obscures similarities, such as that between *Jane Eyre* and *Moby-Dick*, that Brontë's novel can be viewed as "the female version" of Melville's: "There's the Ahab or the Bertha Mason figure, the dark tyrannical captain, and a kind of disaster at the end in which the great figure is reduced."

We talked at length about the degree to which fiction is dominated by women writers. "It probably always has been that way; certainly in the nineteenth century there were a lot of good women writers who just haven't been resurrected — in England as well as here. I think it's something that women can do and fit in with their lives as women. [But] there's a history of great novels written by men; we can't belittle the male contribution to the novel." Johnson does not share the belief that the reason women have been so prominent as writers of the novel is its focus on private life. "Jane Austen was not writing about intimate private things but about manners. Her perspective was that of a social observer, kind of a male perspective. There also are male confessional novelists; think of those novels of Philip Roth."

We agreed that women now have a fair chance at being writers, even though society's generic image of the writer seems often to be a male. "It would be nice if the whole category could be abolished, but in the meantime it's as though there were two different sets of writers, the great writers, the great-writer stakes which the men consider that they're playing at, and [the] women [who] are somehow treated as a different category. No one thinks of comparing Eudora Welty and Saul Bellow." Johnson observes that reviewers often hold women writers accountable for the behavior of their characters. "I wonder if that's true for men? There's probably always some conflation of character and author. When we read Bellow, we say, 'Bellow's such a pig,' when in fact we don't know that he is."

The critics labeled all Johnson's early novels "women's novels," but they haven't done this with the last two, and "often men are the reviewers." She recounted an anecdote that shows a reversal of labels: "Recently a Frenchman who runs a bookshop with American titles said, 'Women aren't going to like Alison [Lurie]'s new novel much; women don't read Alison anyway. She's definitely a man's novelist.' That was the first time I heard a woman called a man's novelist." She said that of course women read Alison Lurie, but "he meant it as a compliment as well as an observation, since she isn't romantic."

We queried whether there are male traditions and male plots in the novel. ("What is a *male* plot? A plot is just a configuration of events. But I agree with you that there is a male plot.") I asked her about the influence on women's lives of certain novels by men, such as *Portrait of a Lady,* which were invariably present in college curricula of the fifties. "*Portrait of a Lady,* like all of Henry James, is no use at all as role model. For that matter neither are the works of George Eliot. You wouldn't want to turn out like any of the women in either Henry James or George Eliot. I always thought Isabel Archer was an idiot, but then lots of people in James — Strether, for example — are life-refusing. When I realized that I was always on the opposite side from Henry James I felt better about his works in general. Do you think James means you to feel that way?" Probably not, since he extolled renunciation as a noble human action.

Johnson's incisive comments about various writers reminded me that she is a frequent book reviewer for the *San Francisco Chronicle*, the *New York Times Book Review*, the *London Times*, the *Washington Post*, and the *New York Review of Books*. "I'm happiest writing fiction, but I do like to write essays from time to time if there's an interesting subject. I don't think that you should ask to review a book because then there aren't any surprises; it doesn't lead you into new territory. *New York Review* has always been good about proposing unexpected things. *Friendly Fire* is a good example; most people wouldn't have asked some woman writer to review a book about Vietnam."

Johnson may describe herself as "some woman writer," but her book reviews are brilliant essays on contemporary culture. *Terrorists and Novelists*, the collection of twenty-nine of her review essays published in 1982, was on the short list for the Pulitzer Prize for nonfiction. I asked Johnson how the prize is awarded: "There are two committees for the Pulitzer; there's the nominating committee that changes every year. . . . I've done it for both nonfiction and fiction; then there's the committee of the Pulitzer board, and they decide among the choices the nominating body gives them. The nominating committee chooses (it's very cumbersome) among books nominated by publishers and newspapers . . . so the *New York Times* can nominate its favorite among its reporters for journalism and Knopf can nominate among its books. So that's how it works."

Living on the West Coast is in general a disadvantage, Johnson asserts because "one just isn't in town. Publishing happens in New York. The main reviews are printed there and there's just so much that goes on over lunch. I don't think I myself have that much to complain about, but there are wonderful writers like Carolyn See who have suffered much more." She observes that to be in Los Angeles, as See is, may be a particular disadvantage because "then you get categorized as a Los Angeles writer as well." Because of the inevitable pressures, "I think it's very good for a writer to *not* live in New York, but when it comes to the logistics and the politics. . . . It's not mysterious; people who live around New York are more visible to New York publishers. It's not fair, but it's not surprising either." Johnson mentions that, although most California writers have New York publishers, "There are some West Coast publishers that are coming along, like North Point, that are producing some conspicuous books and moving into the market in a way that no West Coast publishers did before."

The screenplay is one genre that does not require an East Coast publisher. Few people know that Johnson wrote the script for the film adaptation of Stephen King's novel *The Shining.* She has written several others which, due to the vagaries of the movie business, may or may not be produced. "A couple of summers ago I wrote a film script for Volker Schlondorff, the German director, about this Mormon family of polygamists from Utah, who have just been recently in the news. . . . they have just been sentenced." She sums up the experience: "Film writing is slightly collaborative, which can be fun or can be horrid."

Johnson sounds genuinely excited when talking of her just-completed novel *Health and Happiness,* "a hospital novel about women and doctors, about the power structure in a hospital. It actually has a male main character as well as two women main characters." There are no women doctors because "part of my point is that the power structure of the hospital is male-dominated; I didn't want to blunt that point. There are women, but they're functionaries, volunteers, nurses, patients. If you had a woman doctor protagonist, she'd have to be concerned about this or that patient." She regards this fiction as primarily a "novel of manners," one for which she did some field research: "A few times I've gone over with John and hung around his hospital; also, I've been married to doctors for a good many years, so I had absorbed a lot."

Johnson's novels all have intricate, well-executed plots, and she is master of a wide variety of styles and techniques, varying from the fast-moving action of *Persian Nights* to the inner terror of *The Shadow Knows* and the subtle, swiftly shifting interior monologues of *Lying Low.* When I mentioned that the texture of *Lying Low* reminded me of *Mrs. Dalloway,* Johnson said she has studied and "been influenced by Woolf without (alas!) being able to imitate her. But I would if I could. I think that she has a much more poetical style."

Johnson is currently working on "stories or — not exactly — travel pieces set in different parts of the world." She travels with her husband, who is interested in Third World and international medicine. "I've been everywhere — China, Australia, Japan, Taiwan, Africa, South Africa. . . . We stay in one place about six weeks; things happen, and I have a few stories due to that. I'm not really comfortable with the short story, but I'll see what happens."

Johnson also travels to see her children, who "have married widely. One lives in France and one lives in Hawaii, one lives in Japan." Although she never created fictional portraits of her children because it didn't seem fair to make use of their experiences, she does "notice in my new novel there's a daughter who comes home from college. She's not like any of my own children, but suddenly there's a grown child, so I suppose they're creeping in suddenly." We observed that most fictional characters are composites of various people known by the author. "People rarely understand when it's them in a book and when it's not them. As a novelist, you get used to that." Even when they do recognize themselves, however, Johnson says that they don't seem to mind. "Perhaps they like it. Or their interior reality is so different from anything you imagine that they know when it's not them." We discussed the way writers generally use pieces of their own experience. "There's a bit about my first husband's family in *Loving Hands at Home,* and about my divorce in *The Shadow Knows. Loving Hands* was my bored housewife novel."

Although Johnson wrote regularly when her children were growing up, "I think I write better now that they're big." She says that while you don't exactly become more "skilled" as you write more fiction, "The tricks of the craft that you learn can save you from this or that mistake. At the same time each new fiction has some problem at its bottom that doesn't get any easier to solve — or maybe one always *makes* a new problem so it won't be any easier — a knot that needs to be unknotted to make it work on its own terms. With *Persian Nights* it was the foreign country and the ingredients of a male adventure novel, the shoot-out which for obvious reasons was hard for me to imagine."

Johnson works on these problems and does preliminary drafts of her work in her head. "I find knitting a good way of thinking about what you are writing because it makes you sit still and doesn't demand your best concentration." When ready to write, she either writes in longhand or uses "a little Canon electronic typewriter that is almost like hand writing because it makes no noise. It's like a keyboard to a computer, but you have paper in it." We go into the next room so that Johnson can show me this elegant typewriter which is small and light enough to fit into a suitcase.

She tried putting her last novel on the word processor but was disenchanted. "I couldn't find anything once it was there, so I don't know that I'll do that again." Although she doesn't do that many drafts of her work, she does move chunks of prose around — and found this a challenge with the word processor. "I was always having to scroll through everything. . . . I made the mistake of opening different documents for different chapters." She said she spent so much time "meeting the demands of the machine that it became about the machine instead of what I was writing."

Writer, teacher, and critic, Johnson has thought deeply about the present and future of the novel in America. "I think it's moving away from the deeply internal, interior confessional mode to a more plotted mode." The new mode will be "more traditional with regard to events" but not necessarily more traditional in style. "Experiments with language will continue, but there may be fewer soul-searching explorations of childhood, more novels of manners. The success of *The Bonfire of the Vanities* is a good example."

Johnson welcomes this trend because it carries "the potential to make us a more rational, examining society; and also because the others have begun to seem a little repetitious and self-indulgent. I'm not sure that particular writers will or should do this, but I hope fiction as a whole will." She also notes that sometimes individual writers relinquish the confessional mode after one or two novels. They have "a couple of things that are immediate, whether their childhood or their divorce; once you've written about that, you have to go on to something else. We may yet have from Mary Gordon a very observed novel of manners."

When teaching nineteenth-century literature, Johnson assigns several novels by women, including *Jane Eyre* and *Pride and Prejudice*. She says that both male and female students enjoy the novels, but "girls have read *Jane Eyre* already and can appreciate how rich and mature it is." She occasionally encounters sexism in the classroom and in the world, and "it always surprises me, because you just think things are getting better. But I think things are getting better." A determined supporter of women, a writer of powerful intellect, Johnson has done her share to make things better. We can rejoice that her own plans are to "just keep writing."

K.U.H.

BOOKS BY DIANE JOHNSON

NOVELS

Fair Game. New York: Harcourt, Brace & World, 1965.

Loving Hands at Home. New York: Harcourt, Brace & World, 1968; Ballantine, 1972.

Burning. New York: Harcourt Brace Jovanovich, Inc., 1971.

The Shadow Knows. New York: Knopf, 1974; Pocketbooks, 1980.

Lying Low. New York: Knopf, 1978; Fawcett, 1988.

Persian Nights. New York: Knopf, 1987; Ballantine, 1988.

Health and Happiness. New York: Knopf, 1990. Chatto & Windus, 1991.

NONFICTION

Lesser Lives: The True Story of the First Mrs. Meredith. New York: Knopf, 1973.

Edwin Broun Fred: Scientist, Administrator, Gentleman. Madison: Univ. of Wisconsin Press, 1974.

Terrorists and Novelists. New York: Knopf, 1982.

Dashiell Hammett: A Life. New York: Random House, 1983; Fawcett, 1988.

Susan Fromberg Schaeffer

To INTERVIEW Susan Fromberg Schaeffer in her black and white house three blocks from Brooklyn College is to enter an enchanting world filled with dollhouses; pink, green, and ruby Depression glass; angels; green velvet sofas; stained glass church windows; overstuffed bookcases; and polished, treasured Victoriana of all kinds. All of this is background for an extraordinarily intelligent critic and writer (she wrote the first Ph.D. dissertation on Vladimir Nabokov at the University of Chicago), dressed in chartreuse leather boots, nine silver rings, and turquoise earrings that match her billowing artist's smock. She is protected by Sam, surely the smartest (and largest) German shepherd in New York, a some-

In memory of Nan Nowik: May 14, 1941–January 13, 1988. A shortened version of this interview was published in *Belles Lettres*, May/June 1988:9.

what incongruous presence on a curlicued Victorian settee, and her "crazy, vicious, demented, fearless" black and white cat, Foudini (named after a similarly grouchy and assertive magician on "The Lucky Pup", a TV show before which Schaeffer insisted on eating her childhood dinners).

Schaeffer works in an L-shaped attic room, reached by narrow, winding steps. Tucked into a corner is a rose-colored, taffeta-covered "fainting couch" and an ancient floor lamp with a pleated pink shade. Her writing table faces a window overstuffed with geraniums. There are pictures of Ted Hughes, the poet, among others, many cans and bottles of diet soda, and the (here) invasive but omnipresent word processor familiar to all of us. The adjoining Victorian study of her scholar-writer husband, Neil Schaeffer, is dominated by a high-tech exercise bicycle. Schaeffer, who is best known for *Anya, Madness of a Seduced Woman, Love,* and *Time in Its Flight,* has just completed a thousand-page novel about Vietnam called *Buffalo Afternoon.* This seemed, initially, to be a surprising topic for an author often pigeonholed as a Jewish-American novelist, even though her other two recent novels, *Mainland* and *The Injured Party,* are about Brooklyn writers and teachers of no discernible religious or ethnic background, and both *Madness of a Seduced Woman* and *Time in Its Flight* are about Protestant New Englanders.

Schaeffer's novels are dominated by the powerful force of memory, often in the form of ghosts. In different ways, so too is the work of Toni Morrison (*Beloved*), Carole Maso (*Ghost Dance*), Jayne Anne Phillips (*Machine Dreams*), the work of Didion, Mary Lee Settle, Oates, Erdrich, Virginia Woolf and a growing list of women writing fiction in America and elsewhere. Ironically, when I asked Schaeffer how she thought memory functioned in fiction by women and whether it was indeed a synonym for ghosts (perceivable or otherwise), Schaeffer revealed that the narrator of *Buffalo Afternoon* is a "South Vietnamese girl, still in her teens, who is already dead when the novel begins and is therefore, technically a ghost." Schaeffer used her narrator to give the novel a "wider context than it would have had if [she] had included only United States servicemen," and to underscore her belief that

"Vietnam was more than a war. It was," she said, "about the corruption of a generation, of motherhood, of children, of American ideals, innocence, and renewability" and most poignantly about the sense that "some things," as soldiers in this war correctly perceive, "can never be made right again in this world." This narrator ghost stands for "the corruption both of the next generation and of the ability of the land to bring things forth," and she is a haunting reminder of "what was lost and of how much was lost," both for the victims and for the victimizers. The novel ends with a dance where other dead characters — a brother, grandmother, and grandfather — return as ghosts, underscoring again the interwoven strands of memory and the past. The ghosts serve as connectors between the living and the dead and as "reminders that the dead aren't really dead, that life continues in the hereafter exactly as it does here." This is a view that Schaeffer does not share in her own life, but which "seems to be my view when I write fiction." There are, says one of the characters, "still library fines in heaven and an overdue book doesn't stop being overdue," and "people have the same complaints in heaven as they had on earth."

Schaeffer explained that she used a medieval, structured dance as metaphor because the dance allowed her to reinstate the now-dead characters, to show "that life did not begin and end with the war." There was, she said, "a life before and there will be a life after." Schaeffer says that *Buffalo Afternoon* "emphasizes the futility and destructiveness of letting your life be eaten up by events that happened in one small segment of time, no matter if enormous and of horrific proportion, because the ultimate perversion, and an unnatural act, is to try to stop the process of time." And useful ghosts "show that it can't be done." Ghosts and dreams, she added, are essentially the same. "Dreams are," in fact, "psychic ghosts."

Schaeffer researched this novel in Thailand, which she says looks much like Vietnam. She spoke about the "water buffalo which are omnipresent in Asia," about the spirit of the water buffalo which pervades the consciousness of her narrator, and about how the Vietnamese sheltered buffalo in and under their houses and built protective bunkers for them during the war. The buffalo sustained whole families and the loss of an animal was, therefore, more dangerous and damaging than the death of a child. She spoke of the water buffalo with extraordinary sympathy and affection.

Schaeffer seems an ironic candidate for an animal lover, product as she is of Brooklyn, the Long Island suburbs, and urban Chicago's Hyde Park. (Her mother says she "was born saying, 'Take me to the country!'") But Schaeffer contends that there is something "wonderful about animals"; they are almost "prehuman, with their own opinions," and, unlike many of the characters in her novels, "they are constant, always the same." You can, she noted, "count on them." This view, that no thing or person is totally reliable and unchanging, pervades her first novel, *Falling,* and reasserts itself strongly in the two related novels, *Mainland* and *The Injured Party*. In fact, Eleanor, the female protagonist in *Mainland,* writes a grade school essay that consists of one line: "Nothing remains the same," the "first truth Eleanor came upon on her own," and one for which she is severely reprimanded by both family and teachers. That essay suggests the chaos and fragmentation which many women in Schaeffer's fiction experience. *The Injured Party*'s Iris Otway is suffering from a mysterious illness, but the novel is more profoundly about sight and insight, seeing and perceiving. Eleanor has premature cataracts, and she is fighting also for insight into her own life.

Schaeffer acknowledges that "depression and isolation are much more feminine than masculine" and that these emotions account for the enclosing and often entrapping configurations of space in her novels. "Women under stress," she says, "hole up, tunnel in under blankets, almost as if they are drowning, while men, whether they want to or not, are programmed to go out." The female character in *Buffalo Afternoon* operates from mixed internalized messages. She wants the house, husband, children — all associated with space as nest — but as soon as she finds herself safely ensconced in New England, far from her familiar Brooklyn milieu, she feels encaged and imprisoned. "This woman," said Schaeffer, "has no talent for open space."

The lives of Schaeffer's fictional women often seem dominated by the interruption of daydreams and the dreams of night. When I asked her why she thought so many women writing fiction used dreams, she said that "dreams are a repository of memory and a tremendous source of truth." Memories "reappear in dreams, which are preservers; the unconscious preserves in dreams what the conscious life loses." As she says in *Anya*, "memory is a form of reality after all." In *The Madness of a Seduced Woman*, Schaeffer's most popular novel, the character's "psychic life is established in a dream," and in other novels there are repeated instances of "sleepy, twilight dream" states where extra rooms, rooms that lead to open, freeing spaces, magically appear. Most centrally, dreams are links back to family and to ghosts.

Schaeffer talked about why the husbands in both *Mainland* and *The Injured Party* seemed to be peripheral, shadow figures. "Actually," she said, it is the "fictional women who are removing them from the stage" because "the women are involved with the puzzles of their own lives," and the husbands "actually care too much," and "know them all too well." It is the "strangers" (John Stone, Iris's college sweetheart in *The Injured Party,* and Toh, the Chinese student in *Mainland*) who lead the women either backward or forward in time to facilitate a rapprochement with the present. The husbands become "irrelevant," and Schaeffer noted that some "people [read critics here] were not too happy about this." As Schaeffer and other women have deduced, "even when someone is married, they really do have a life of their own. Life can take over and fill the space, which of course happens in men's lives regularly. Their work takes over and they forget that there is anybody else on earth. The same thing happens with these women. And men reviewers detested this; they did not like it one bit."

According to Schaeffer, the whole idea of suffering, when it is women who are suffering, is generally disparaged in reviews. The implied question is, "What is this woman complaining about, if she's not an Ecuadorian peasant?" At this point in history, "it seems as if there are only approved forms of suffering. If you want to complain and 'carry on,' you have to be a citizen of Nicaragua or El Salvador or South Africa, and then you can complain all you want." But Schaeffer's characters (and women generally) have experienced the continuing hostility which is pointedly directed at their pain.

I asked Schaeffer if she thought women writers got a fairer, truer reading from women critics. She said, "Men aren't riddled with the various [feminist] theories"; they have their own pet theories and certain sets of presumptions and assumptions, but "women can be much more aggravating than men, when they are aggravating." The "expectation, on my part, is that another woman should have a head start in understanding something that I've written, because I'm a woman. Then, when they sound like mechanized dolls and instead of being Barbie dolls, they've become dolls that say, 'Women should look at things in such and such a way,' and you find prescriptives falling out of their mouths like stones, it is absolutely horrifying. Men have not cornered the market on obtuseness and opacity."

The whole dilemma of reviewing is one that has obsessed Schaeffer. She says that she does not approve of "practicing writers reviewing one another. If everyone reviewed for major newspapers under a pseudonym, we would have very different book review sections." She makes the point that "it is superhuman not to expect, if someone's book is poorly reviewed, that all their friends and relations are likely to be anxious to return the favor when the reviewer writes his or her next book, and the repercussions can take quite a long time to die down." Schaeffer wishes "there was a community of reviewers who were not themselves writers whom you could count on to be somewhat more objective." She added, "Some people think this is a naive idea, that there is no reason to assume that these reviewers would not be corrupted as fast as everyone else," and that they might court favor with one writer or technique or angle of vision over another. In an early, positive review of her first novel, *Falling,* the reviewer applauded Schaeffer for condemning the "dollhouse as a symbol of female oppression." Schaeffer "loves and adores dollhouses," and starts building and furnishing a new one when she is working on a book. This review reminds her that it is less annoying "to be scolded for things you have done, than to be praised for things you haven't said or written." We discussed the fact that all published writers are aware of a puzzling phenomenon: reviewers often insert details into the review which are not in the novel, although Schaeffer protested that this "doesn't happen to men so much." Reviewers, in her opinion, don't "feel as free to investigate the personal lives of men and drag it into reviews" because they "will be taken out behind a building and kicked in the mouth." There is, she suggested, probably "an underlying assumption that if a woman is going to expose herself in public, she deserves what she gets. Nobody inquires about the relationship between a man's latest marriage or affair and what's going on in his book, but this is a regular, chronic, reflex action when you read reviews of a woman novelist." The underlying message is that no woman could be inventive enough to imagine anything that doesn't hinge heavily on the details of her own life.

When Joyce Carol Oates published *Lives of the Twins,* written under her pseudonym, Rosamond Smith, it was reviewed by Schaeffer in the *New York Times Book Review.* Oates wrote to ask if Schaeffer was herself a twin. She is not, but she feels that all "writers are perpetually obsessed with doubles" and in some sense they are all twins, since they are themselves, and, to some extent, either by intention or invention, one of the characters in the novel. I suggested that all novelists are triplets — themselves, the fictional characters, and the characters as usually misread by the reviewers.

Susan Fromberg Schaeffer is a writer of wit, intelligence, and perception. She writes about familial disenchantments, identity crises, the intervention of memory, and the struggle for insight. Women readers in particular should pay close attention not only to her answers, but to her questions.

M.P.

BOOKS BY SUSAN FROMBERG SCHAEFFER

NOVELS

Falling. New York: Macmillan, 1973; NAL, 1974; Ivy, 1991.
Anya. New York: Macmillan, 1974; Avon, 1976; Ivy, 1991.
Time in Its Flight. New York: Doubleday, 1978; Pocket Books, 1979.
Love. New York: Dutton, 1981; Pocket Books, 1982.
The Madness of a Seduced Woman. New York: Dutton, 1983; Bantam, 1984.
Mainland. New York: Linden Books/Simon and Schuster, 1985; Bantam, 1986.
The Injured Party. New York: St. Martin's Press, 1986; St. Martin's Press, 1987.
Buffalo Afternoon. New York: Knopf, 1989; Ivy, 1990.

SHORT STORIES

The Queen of Egypt and Other Stories. New York: Dutton, 1980.

POETRY

The Witch and the Weather Report. New York: Seven Woods Press, 1972.
Granite Lady. New York: Macmillan, 1974.
Rhymes and Runes of the Toad. New York: Macmillan, 1975.
The Red, White and Blue Poem. St. Paul: Ally Press, 1977.

CHILDREN AND YOUNG ADULTS

Alphabet for the Lost Years. San Francisco: Gallimaufry, 1977.
The Dragons of North Chittendon. New York: Simon and Schuster, 1986.
The Four Hoods and Great Dog. New York: St. Martin's, 1988.

Marge Piercy

MARGE PIERCY lives in Wellfleet, Massachusetts, a town of winding streets, summer flowers, and tangled woods, bordered on the east by the National Seashore and the Atlantic Ocean and on the west by Cape Cod Bay. She lives with her husband, the writer Ira Wood, and four lively cats named Dinah, Oboe, Colette, and Jim Beam in a traditional-style house on a wooded promontory separated from the town by a marsh. We conducted our interview at a table on the closed-in porch of her very lived-in house; Piercy sat at the head of the table, radiating the energy and intelligence that are projected in photographs of her, while her assistant worked at the computer in the next room and the cats jumped into her lap and onto the table at every opportunity.

Many readers of this prolific and versatile author (ten novels, eleven books of poetry, a collection of essays, and a play co-authored with Ira Wood), who grew up in inner-city Detroit and is closely identified with radical movements of the sixties, are surprised to find that she lives in a small New England town. Piercy explained, "I moved here in '71 from New York because I was very ill. I couldn't live or work." A smoker since the age of twelve, she said that "stopping smoking wasn't sufficient because New York gives you about two or three packs a day just breathing. I moved here fleeing from the city" and "discovered I liked living here. It was nothing like I expected it to be."

She now has her health back, "except for a touch of hay fever" and appreciates Wellfleet as a community where "you meet people in very different jobs and economic situations than you might meet if you lived in the city, where you might tend to stick to your own class. There's [also] more age-mixing here." Politically, "the Outer Cape is quite liberal; Wellfleet always votes Democratic." Piercy and her husband are deeply involved in community and state affairs. She is "a public official in Massachusetts, a double Dukakis appointee" to the Massachusetts Council of the Arts and Humanities and to the State Arts Lottery Council. She had just completed a lengthy session evaluating grant proposals before my arrival and noted that "both [appointments] take a lot of time." She also recently "did a benefit for Mass Choice, the pro-choice group in the state" and was "active in starting the NOW chapter on the Cape." She is "also very involved in a Jewish group on the Cape, Am Ha-yam, a group that puts on services, holiday observances, speakers, and discussions for Jews on the Outer Cape. We [recently] organized a rainbow sign service on the themes of nuclear and ecological destruction."

Possibly because her father wasn't Jewish or possibly because Judaism was not "rammed down my throat — my brother went to Hebrew School; I didn't" — Judaism was always something special for her, "something I wanted more of." When I asked whether it had strengthened her feminism and criticisms of the establishment, she answered affirmatively. "Feminism, a strong ecological consciousness, it all ties together, feeling political and religious. It's not one simple grid you impose on reality, but one consciousness meshes them, though not always seamlessly. Even the contradictions between the values are rich."

A complex web of values also informs Piercy's huge literary achievement. We discussed her two most recent novels, *Gone to Soldiers,* an epic interweaving the experience of ten characters during World War II, and *Summer People,* which Piercy defined as "a moral tale about people, artists, and their patrons." *Gone to Soldiers* was a runaway bestseller with smashing reviews; Piercy acknowledged that "my publisher pressured me to write a sequel," but instead she wrote a completely different kind of novel. *Summer People* "has a small compass and place" and is focused on the inner lives and relationships of a small group of artists in a small town. Piercy sees as central to the book the question of "what people want, does it issue from their work or does it issue from the media, are the images [they pursue] programmed by the society?" It is a moral book in that all the characters must bear the consequences of their choices; those who choose false images suffer heavy penalties, whereas those, like Dinah, who follow an inner vision and care about others earn at least tentative happiness.

Piercy has a systematic approach to writing a novel: "No matter what genre I'm working in I start with theme and work out the architecture and then spend a lot of time with the characters. People identify strongly with different characters. I make a dossier for each. I write out my autobiographical impulses in the poetry; what interests me in the fiction are the lives I haven't led, the choices I haven't made." She noted that "a useful gift for a novelist is being able to enter other people's experiences," although "characters based on one person seldom work."

She became excited when discussing the fundamental nature of fiction: "I see fiction as being about time and choice. . . . The stuff of narrative is time; it's *then* and *then* and what happens *then;* that's the basic question in fiction. The movement may be circular; it may be in epicycles, it may go back and forth, but it's about time — past, present, and future, parallel time. Other spaces in fiction are like other times." She sees her own fiction as also emphasizing choice, "the ability to say yes and to say no, to shape things, to make choices and accept their consequences."

When I asked her if — like some woman writers — she had

more difficulty doing male than female viewpoints, she said no. "I started early in my career with the male viewpoint and weaned myself off it, and then it wasn't hard to go back to. I had a brother and I've known a lot of men very well. [But] I wanted to see the world from only female points of view for a period of time."

Although Piercy's work sells well (her collection of poetry *The Moon Is Always Female* sold 50,000 copies), selling books in the millions is not her highest priority: her refusal to write a sequel to *Gone to Soldiers* put her "back to midlist again." The publishers and "the big chains like Waldenbooks make that decision before a book is published." She believes that fiction in America is in trouble: "It's hard for it to survive, given the marketplace. New York is a real obstacle to fiction. The sensibility of the New York publishing houses is a tremendous obstacle to fiction. What editors like and want to read and what people in the rest of the country want to read — the heart of fiction — are very different. It makes it hard for younger writers and anyone who does not write blockbusters to get published. The growth of the chains is frightening."

Piercy expressed surprise when I mentioned that many West Coast writers feel their distance from New York City and the people who review books as a keen disadvantage. "Why? Do they imagine that you deal with them? Go out to dinner with them? When I've met them, we insult each other. There's no old boys' network that includes me. In the seven years I lived in New York I managed to insult most powerful people I met. Here I don't have to deal with them." I recalled that some of her recent books — even the novel *Fly Away Home,* which earned the highest praise from most reviewers — were negatively or ambivalently reviewed in the *New York Times Book Review.* Piercy replied, "Since 1973, the only one of my novels well received by the *Times* was *Vida.* I think that they are threatened by my politics in general, especially my feminism. They almost invariably assign a minor reviewer to cover my books."

When I asked Piercy at what point in her life she knew she was a writer, she answered definitively. "When I was fifteen, my parents moved into a house where I had a room of my own and a door that shut. From the time I started, I had no other ambitions. It took forever to begin. It was impossible to publish serious fiction about being a woman in the late fifties and early sixties. I broke into print by writing about childhood and male characters." We talked about the immense difficulties that confronted women writers in the period of the "feminine mystique." Piercy pointed out that, despite the obstacles, "Muriel Rukeyser and Adrienne Rich went on writing; they didn't just try to please men. Rukeyser is tremendously underrated for the size of her talent; I dedicated *Early Ripening* to her."

Piercy reads a lot of fiction, "mainly contemporary" at this point in her life, and "probably more women than men. I like Toni Morrison a great deal; I think she's a giant. I like Joanna Russ and Maxine Hong Kingston. I like the short story writers Jonis Agee and Colleen McElroy." Piercy likes Margaret Atwood, "her poetry even better than her fiction," and Gloria Naylor. "Carolyn See is a very fine novelist." Piercy also has recently read a lot of cyberpunk, a genre that "extrapolates the present into the near future" rather than inventing a completely different universe as science fiction does. Cyberpunk is being produced right now primarily by men.

Most of her favorite male writers are "Latin American or Eastern European, like Stanislaw Lem, or science fiction writers such as Samuel Delaney and William Gibson." She believes that "North American fiction hasn't assimilated the advances made in Latin American fiction" and cited "Manuel Puig's use of pop culture" and writers such as Garcia Marquez and Luisa Valenzuela, who write "more politically, less realistically, with a conscious assumption of mythology, a conscious sense of place, a richness of economic and linguistic awareness." There is, however, a group of black North American writers — Toni Morrison and Sherley Anne Williams, among others — who "seem to have assimilated what the Latin Americans are doing."

When asked whether women write differently from men, Piercy answered as one who has thought about the question: "In a book by a woman, rape won't be fun and women won't be simpleminded. There are women who do the chic violence number;

Jayne Anne Phillips writes like a man when she writes about miners. When she writes about people she knows, she writes like a woman." Piercy believes that women writers in general, "like Joanna Russ, are concerned with violence in a more real, ethical, troubled way."

When I asked whether women rely more on memory than men, she at first demurred. "You can't claim that for women; Proust has a patent on memory and so does Joyce." She went on to speak of memory as a storehouse of experience: "You have to train yourself to remember; everything is in there if you can get at it. It's never all available to you. Your mind is a cantankerous old computer that doesn't remember how to access the old files. There are learned ways to access it; there's a discipline by which you can recapture it."

I refined my question about memory: "Do women writers create characters such as Daria in *Fly Away Home* who are more defined by their memories? (Daria believes her husband is still a good man who loves her even when confronted by massive evidence to the contrary.) Piercy answered that Daria is "too captured by memory when the novel begins. She hasn't noticed that her memory is no longer the present, which I think happens to women. Women in bad relationships often live for the past that will never come again. Men will look up and say, 'Who is that fat creature across the table?' " and simply leave, whereas "a woman will say, 'I remember when he told me how much he loved me' and 'I remember our beautiful vacation,' etc., and keep expecting the good times to return."

I recalled that, in contrast to Daria, memory was empowering to Jacqueline, the young Jewish Parisian in *Gone to Soldiers,* whose determination as a fierce Resistance fighter was built upon her memories of the Nazis rounding up her family. Piercy responded with an astute observation: "None of our capacities are empowering or weakening in themselves; it depends on how we use them." She illustrated with two other characters from the same novel: "Oscar has to learn to place himself and connect with his own history to stop behaving like an idiot, to connect action and consequence; for Louise, letting go of memory for a time is empowering. When she becomes a war correspondent, she lives in the present." Piercy stated, "Throughout my fiction I've been concerned with memory as I've been concerned with choice — in the broadest sense."

Gone to Soldiers is profoundly feminist in its rendering of the crucial, often life-threatening roles played by women in World War II. Our conversation turned to contemporary feminism and the women's movement in America. Piercy said that the movement "ran out of energy for a time. However, the fear of losing legal abortion has provided an infusion of money and new bodies; women who had not done anything politically have been galvanized. Membership of feminist organizations has risen and there are big demonstrations again." She believes that the reasons for the decline of the movement in the eighties are economic and media-related. "The nuclear family doesn't exist for a lot of women; it's a myth of women's lives." Piercy also cited "the reduction of the working-class standard of living; in the sixties you could survive on a part-time job; now you need a full-time *and* a part-time job for the same buying power.

"If you look at what's working on women now, you have these [economic conditions] and the increasingly powerful media. [On] fifties and sixties TV, the images of women were passive but physically attainable. The models of the forties had boobs and asses and bellies. Now you have [images of] competent women which are physically unattainable, unless a woman has four to six hours a day to work out. You have tremendous self-hatred and a sense of failure. There's a correlation between income level and how much you can resemble that image; if you have enough money you go to a plastic surgeon and carve yourself into it. The older you get the less you look like that. I love Roseanne [Barr]; her humor has nothing to do with her weight; she is sexy, not the butt of jokes."

Piercy told me she worked for feminism within Judaism by being "involved in a siddur project, a prayerbook for Reconstructionism. Reconstructionism tries to deal with sexism. There aren't too many serious writers at this time who have put in time on something intended for weekly use by people; I've rewritten forms of a number of prayers; it's the opposite end from writing more personal poetry." When I asked her to what degree this work is parallel to rewriting of Christian prayers ("Our parent, who art in heaven"), she said that "some of us aren't comfortable with the parent-child relationship as a paradigm for holiness. We're trying to produce something truly relevant. Part of Judaism is that you're supposed to use your mind as well as your heart and faith; it doesn't make sense to pretend that you don't know what you know. I probably have more in common with liberal Catholics (at least, pro-choice ones) than with extreme Orthodox Jews. I'm sure there are feminist Buddhists somewhere, too."

Piercy said that she is "too much" involved in public life right now, in part because of her belief that artists are "all part of the same economic and social web and have the same obligation to vote and recycle as anyone else. To pretend you aren't part of the society makes you stupid again."

Through an expenditure of energy that approaches the heroic, Piercy maintains both high artistic productivity and active involvement in society. "I get up at five or six and go for my walk [four miles] and work until mid-afternoon. I knock off around 2:30 or 3:00. In first draft I tend to work a shorter day. In later drafts I can work a very long day, as it's less exhausting. I print out four drafts at least, but [even the first one] isn't really first draft. You are revising it all the time." Piercy is the most computer-sophisticated writer I've ever met; she uses not merely a word processor but also the computer's other capacities. "I run data bases. I keep financial records — bookkeeping — on the computer. I write everything on it — poetry, prose, even grocery lists. I compose on the computer; I couldn't give up the control." She has worked on a computer "since the IBM PC came out, either '82 or '83. It wasn't adaptable to hard disk, so it went in the closet. Now I work on a compact with a hard disk."

When Piercy received the Sheaffer-PEN/New England Award for Literary Excellence at the end of May 1989, she read from her poem "The fecund complain they are not honored." While the poem is about *all* writers with high productivity, it is also a self-description: "The driven work. They get up like Sylvia / Long before dawn. They write in buses. / They write in the laundromat while clothes / flash by, and somebody steals their socks. / They write on computers if one is there; / If not, they write in pencil or crayon." The poem ends, "When the driven die / their real inner stone reads: you did / a little piece of it, a little piece." Readers of Marge Piercy might disagree, believing she has already done more than a "little piece" of that work dictated by her conscience, her integrity, and her artistic genius.

K.U.H.

BOOKS BY MARGE PIERCY

NOVELS

Small Changes. New York: Doubleday, 1973; Fawcett, 1985.

Woman on the Edge of Time. New York: Knopf, 1976; Fawcett, 1985.

The High Cost of Living. New York: Harper & Row, 1978; Fawcett, 1985.

Vida. Hastings-on-Hudson, N.Y.: Ultramarine Publishers, 1980; Fawcett, 1985.

Braided Lives. Hastings-on-Hudson, N.Y.: Ultramarine Publishers, 1982; Summit, 1987; Fawcett, 1988.

Dance the Eagles to Sleep. New York: Fawcett, 1982.

Going Down Fast. New York: Fawcett, 1982.

Fly Away Home. New York: Summit, 1984; Fawcett, 1988.

Gone to Soldiers. New York: Summit, 1987; Fawcett, 1988.

Summer People. New York: Summit, 1989; Fawcett, 1990.

NONFICTION

Parti-Colored Blocks for a Quilt. (Poets on Poetry Series) Ann Arbor: Univ. of Michigan Press, 1982.

POETRY

Breaking Camp. Middletown, Conn., Wesleyan Univ. Press, 1968.

Hard Loving: Poems. Middletown, Conn.: Wesleyan Univ. Press, 1969.

To Be of Use. New York: Doubleday, 1973.
Living in the Open. New York: Knopf, 1976.
The Twelve-Spoked Wheel Flashing. New York: Knopf, 1978.
The Moon Is Always Female. New York: Knopf, 1980.
Circles on the Water: Selected Poems. New York: Knopf, 1982.
Stone, Paper, Knife. New York: Knopf, 1983.
My Mother's Body. New York: Knopf, 1985.
Available Light. New York: Knopf, 1988.
The Earth Shines Secretly: A Book of Days. Cambridge, Mass.: Zoland, 1990.
Mars and Her Children: Poems. New York: Knopf, forthcoming.

PLAYS

[With Ira Wood]. *The Last White Class*. Trumansburg, N.Y.: Crossing Press, 1980.

Carole Maso

SØREN KIERKEGAARD, the Danish existentialist, said that it was his task to create difficulties everywhere. Since I am absolutely sure that he died in 1955, I can only assume that his spirit was mightily at work in New York City on the scheduled interview day with Carole Maso at her apartment in Greenwich Village. The customary drive from northern New Jersey took an hour (instead of the usual twenty minutes), the West Side highway and Riverside Drive (which run parallel to each other) were, even more than usual, crammed with hostile, kamikaze drivers. All the streets around the Museum of Natural History, never a driver's paradise, were blocked off and encircled by a noisy collection of ambulances and police cars. It was only later, much later, that I realized even long-time commuters from New York/New Jersey/Connecticut could still be surprised, even amazed, by the panoply of spontaneous and manmade disasters that are a natural component of life in the not-so-fast lane of the Big Apple. It was on the six o'clock news that I heard about the manhole covers which had somehow managed to fly out of several New York streets that day, pick up velocity, speed, and power, knock several fire escapes off the sides of buildings, and, as a concomitant gesture to incivility and stress, back the traffic up to Philadelphia.

The traffic problems were not the whole of it, however, since I (who have been taking the Fifth Avenue bus to the Village for twenty years), somehow managed to get on the wrong one, leaving me with a ten-block run through Washington Square Park to Maso's apartment, which was, needless to say, on the third floor (no elevators). The tape recorder (battery-less), which had worked perfectly for five interviews, proceeded to function not at all in Maso's apartment (electrical wiring by Christopher Columbus), in spite of much sympathetic meowing by her giant cat, Fauve. The Italian coffee house, to which the interviewer and the writer repaired (after a helpful hand from an intelligent salesperson at Crazy Eddie's who understood tape recorders and their vagaries), started its daily airing of opera records, at full blast, five seconds into the interview. This may be the only tape in existence on which Rigoletto rants, Pearlman questions, Pagliacci cries, and Maso explains, all at the same time. And one tape like this is probably enough.

This unwinding of efficiency was somehow more acceptable when the Vassar-educated author of *Ghost Dance* and *The Art Lover* said that her "interests are in the mysterious and in things that can't be explained and can't readily be put into packages and aren't tied up and neat — because that's not how I see the world; I also see it very large."

We talked at length about the genesis of *Ghost Dance*. This first novel is profoundly about memory, and about Christine Wing, a bejeweled and bewildered poet, "very definitely a ghost . . . very much alive, and very much in the mind of Vanessa," her daughter. The novel, she said, is also "about the difficulty of loving a difficult woman . . . and the consequences you pay for loving," and about "breaking through silence," specifically the silence of Christine's husband, who "is so silent, so withdrawn, that [Vanessa] makes up everything he won't tell her." As one of the characters says, "If loquaciousness and vivacity had been demanded of my father in order for my mother to produce great work, he would not have been capable of it." Maso said, "The novel is about formal, inaccessible parents [since] I was interested in working with an unreliable narrator. Because her parents gave [Vanessa] so little of the so-called facts, she [was forced], from her selective memory and great powers of imagination," the powers she "inherited from her mother," to "invent her own life from nothing." Vanessa is a woman who "feels very self-invented." "My point is that every single [woman], every day, does this, and it's a very beautiful and strictly human impulse."

What people do she said, "is rehash over and over again the last time they have seen someone who is now dead." The central scene in the novel, where Vanessa and Christine meet in Grand Central Station in New York, "is the last time she sees her mother and it keeps playing over again. . . . She tries to find a way through that obsessiveness, that attention and diligence, to make this handful of images resonate and come to light." "In the days to come the world would continue to empty itself of color until finally, by the time my mother was handing her suitcase to my father at the top of the stairs, I would barely be able to see her at all, she would be so lost in white. This happened many times through the years of my childhood. The lake would gray and flatten into a pale square. The red-winged blackbird flying across the blue sky would lose its shock of red, its feathers would fade, and the white sky would devour it" (38–39).

Maso said that she "started *Ghost Dance* when I was so young, twenty-one, that I didn't know then what my concerns were, or what my obsessions were, and I had to write in order to find out. For the first three years after I was out of college, I just wrote. One day an image appeared before me and that was of a very beautiful woman walking through the snow. Her feet are bright red and she has no idea that she feels cold. And I said, 'What's wrong with this woman?' and 'Where are the people who love her?' and 'Where is she going; what's happening?' and for three years I started writing around this image. I started writing about what might be going through her head, from her point of view, about how she acquired family members and lost them," and about "her friends who stayed" and those who didn't. "I found that my obsessions and concerns started to assume shapes, began to grow arms and legs and to become people. They weren't people I knew, but of course I knew them intimately. I began to think that every character in the book was me." These characters were both real and invented, like the woman in the snow. "It was three years' worth of work, writing on faith."

Since *Ghost Dance* is also a novel profuse with the images and symbols of Christianity (the Wing family and ascension, the god-head in Christine's name, ideas of purity and absolution inherent in the snow and in other expressions of whiteness and virginity), I asked Maso about the connection between faith, imagery, symbolism, and this novel. "I was very aware after a while [of these images]. I saw the religious imagery running through it, but I didn't consciously set out to do that [even though] I was brought up very religiously as a Catholic, and I'm still very much a religious person. There were times," for instance, "when I would just pray to have the strength to be able to see what the book was about. I had faith that if I just kept writing, what the book was about would emerge," and "after a few years I looked at the mass of material and I could see threads: 'Oh, this is a concern,' 'this is interesting,' 'this keeps emerging,' " and "I started to make some formal decisions about how to proceed. . . . Finally I realized it was the daughter's story, in fact; it wasn't just this woman in the snow's story." Maso stressed that although the religious symbols emerged from her childhood, and that "some people think the book is very, very dark (which it is), . . . it is also very light," and that she thinks "the struggle in it is a struggle for faith, for the transforming powers, for the human spirit to endure despite constant suffering, constant setbacks." She said that she is "a very severe editor who can't have anything there that is there gratuitously. I felt these symbols were there for specific reasons, and if they were not working, they couldn't stay."

Maso and I discussed what seems to be a strong determination on the part of some critics to believe that what women write comes from their own lives. Since *Ghost Dance* is at least in part about a daughter's struggle to extricate herself from her mother's memory, I asked her if she found this autobiographical angle of vision invasive or disheartening. "I can answer those questions very directly because when my family read the book they were quite relieved not to recognize themselves. They said, 'This is not our family.' My mother is not a poet, my father is not that father, [and] I am one of five children [from Wyckoff, New Jersey]. None of the details is taken from my life, but it is emotionally autobiographical. It's my concerns, my obsessions, but when somebody assumes that this is my story, I say, 'Do you think my life would be so structured and artful that I could just translate it to the page and make it work?' I think many writers do do that and that it doesn't work. Some writers are too attached to what happened; you can smell it out in the book" when they use realistic events that do not contribute to what Maso calls the "structural beauty" or the "integrity" of the novel. "It's fine to use the details of your life when you can, [but] with most young writers the problem is that they have no sense of the work as a whole, of the work as a musical piece." Many writers agree that "nothing that goes from you to the page is ever the exact same experience anyhow because you're transforming it, you're writing it in symbols . . . and making choices out of your whole life about what to put in."

One of the continuing metaphors in this novel is the dance and, in a very poignant and evocative fashion it is a metaphor for the separations and reunions that mark the entire family, for the connecting and disconnecting with which all of the characters are obsessed. Maso said that "somebody once did a paper on *Ghost Dance* and counted the dances . . . and there are twenty or more dances in the book: the mother and the father when they first meet, the grandmother on the lawn, the father doing a dance on the cruiseship . . . dance after dance after dance." The metaphor of dance, I pointed out, is also related to configurations of space. Maso said that "dancing for space, imaginative dancing for space, is what the Indians [in the ghost dance ritual] were doing. They were totally deluded into thinking that if they did this dance they would be saved and they would thereby gain more actual, physical space. . . . I realized," Maso said, "that the book was not only about the disintegration of a family, but also about the disintegration of a country. [Vanessa's] memories were of specific sorrows in the American culture as well as of [her own] specific personal sorrows, and that the personal and the public [sorrows] were intertwined. . . . Because of capitalism running amok in very terrible ways, it seemed to me that she had to reinvent the entire history of the country through memory and through imagination." She was trying to "be at peace with her family and her private sorrow but also with her greater sorrow."

Maso talked about how much energy a novelist needs to make money and to write. She realized "early on" that she could not work at a variety of jobs — proofreading, waitressing at Lord and Taylor's, teaching fencing — and come home at night to write, that she "simply did not have the energy to do both." Her system has been to work at a nonwriting job, accumulate some money, go off to an "affordable spot," and write for as long as funds permit. She does not do reviews any more because she is "a person who can only read and respond" to the work "and whatever I say is always held against me. What I write" she said, "is only my pure reading." There are some dangers associated with this point of view, however. Silence on any level "engenders in the artist" a combination of "protection and entrapment," as a recent rereading of "Death in Venice" reminded her.

The most moving part of this interview evolved from Maso's discussion of Christine Wing and what the writer called "the sorrow of women, the tyranny over women [which is empowered and reinforced] in subtle ways. Society," she said, "is fed an image of what a woman is and what a woman looks like, and what a woman should be, and it is reiterated over and over again until you think that beauty is enough." Maso reminded me that Jack, Vanessa's lover, says that "you think a stranger can come in here and tell you what to do and how to live and that is the myth of the oppressor. You are fed this and then you take it in and then you believe it." Christine Wing "takes these confines with her" and finds an "expansive space" only when she is creating.

One senses that the implicit and important message of *Ghost*

Dance was underscored in Maso's words to me: "You have to get to the point where you can open up the memories so you can get the spaces you can live with." In a world of minimalists, Carole Maso's layered, textured, intricately woven words release the often tightly locked memories, and the emotionally loaded spaces, of the careful, intelligent reader. She is one of the most gifted younger novelists writing in America today.

M.P.

BOOKS BY CAROLE MASO

NOVELS

Ghost Dance. Berkeley: North Point, 1986; Harper and Row, 1987.
The Art Lover. Berkeley: North Point, 1990.

M.F.K. Fisher

ON THE ROUTE from San Francisco to the ranch in Sonoma County where Mary Frances Kennedy Fisher lives, a thin November sun revealed soft purple hills and small vineyards, their stakes entwined with leaves of deep red or pale green. Fisher's home, located just beneath the main house of the Bouverie ranch, is approached by climbing a gentle slope through California brush and bits of volcanic rock from the eruption of Mount St. Helens. My knock was answered by a handsome young man with a shock of dark hair who introduced himself as Chris, "the grandson," and took me to Fisher, a slender, strikingly beautiful woman of eighty-one with silvery hair and high cheekbones, dressed in a black jersey and long red skirt. From the bedroom/study where the interview began we looked out on a hill with a vineyard and a tall red belfry in front of a stone ranchhouse.

Temporarily unable to walk because of a back injury, Fisher sat in a lounge chair and invited me to sit on her right in her leather wheelchair. Her desk, books, and papers filled one end of the room to my left; a large calico cat bounded through the room at regular intervals.

After one phone call for Chris and another in which Fisher rescheduled a lunch date because of a filming crew about to descend upon her house to do a story on her, Chris brought me a cup of tea and Fisher expressed a few reservations about the interview. First, because one writer once claimed that she was born in Nome, Alaska, and another that she was born in Savannah, Georgia, she would like to see a transcript of the interview. (Fisher was in fact born in Michigan, but has lived most of her life in California and in Europe, with twenty-two years in France and Switzerland.) Her second concern — "I'm very indiscreet. I say 'O God' a lot" — was simply stated. Her final concern arose from my statement that we are interested in "configurations of space" in writings by women; she said this sounded "esoteric and weird." When I explained that women writers often define characters in terms of their homes, rooms, and other "spaces," she responded, "Sex and food and shelter, those are the three main things in life. We really can't live without them. Some people try to, but they don't. If you were terribly cold all day you wouldn't want to eat and you wouldn't want to have sex."

To say that sex, food, and shelter are major themes in most of Fisher's sixteen books is true, but crudely put. Fisher is perhaps America's best anthropologist and historian of food and its rituals and attendant pleasures. Food in her writings is always tied to work (fishermen and farmers and vintners) or love, the nurturing love of the parent teaching her child to make gingerbread or the harmony of food shared in friendship. There are recipes in her books, but they are there "like birds in a tree — if there is a comfortable branch" (from the introduction to *Serve It Forth*).

In addition to writing about food, Fisher has written a novel and dozens of short stories, a history of folk medicine, an autobiography of her childhood called *Among Friends,* travel books, a book on winemaking, and a translation of Brillat-Savarin's *The Physiology of Taste*. Her writing has captured the spirit of places as exotic as Paris and Marseilles, as sleepy as Whittier, California, as beautifully serene as Napa; but she always writes not merely about a place, but about her own subtle, observant, richly nuanced relationship to that place. Much harder than citing the themes of Fisher's work would be to discover a theme on which she has *not*, in a lifetime of professional writing, discoursed with grace, intelligence, and wit.

Fisher said that she wrote "from the time I was four. It was my way of screaming and yelling, the primal scream. I wrote like a junkie; I had to have my daily fix. The stuff I wrote fifty years ago is as good or bad as the stuff I am writing now. I became more sure of my craft, but I was a good craftsman from the very beginning. I can't hold a pen or type now, which is one reason I'm rather frustrated. I can and do dictate, but it's not the same. I'm forcing myself to use cassettes, but they're not the same either."

She currently spends her afternoons going over her unpublished journals and fiction. "See that end of the room, all those papers. We dug all those up. . . . They are journals and novels and stories. A friend is going through them with me. We've rescued about five books and have more to go. They are really good stuff, I hope. I can read them but I can't read what I've already printed."

Fisher is a "fifth-generation journalist." Her father, the son and grandson of printer-writers, bought the daily paper of Whittier, California, in 1912 and edited it for the rest of his life. Writing in Fisher's family was as natural as breathing. "No one encouraged me — we all wrote." From the age of seven she presented petitions to her parents in writing, the first a plea for an end of dosages of castor oil; the second — signed by her sister, the hired hand, the cook, and even the ice man — a petition against her mother bobbing her hair in imitation of the dancer Irene Castle. The fact that Edith and Rex Kennedy "took our manifestos very seriously" must have helped convince Fisher of the power of the written word.

Fisher's parents emerge in her autobiography as rational, sensitive, and highly principled people. Her mother "went to a ladies' finishing school in Kenyon, Ohio, when it was the hotbed of radical liberal Episcopalian thought. She was mildly suffragettish when she went to London. Her rich relatives wanted her to come out, to be presented at court. Only a few American girls did back then, unless they were to be married into English aristocracy, like Mrs. Astor, or to marry Italian counts. The Italian and English wanted the money and we wanted the titles. Mother didn't want either, [but] she went off to England to be presented to the queen. They got all ready to send back the pictures of this beautiful American girl; the one they sent was of her chained to the iron gates of Buckingham Palace with some leaders of the suffragette movement like Mrs. Pankhurst and Mrs. Sanger. So she lost caste . . . she was not presented at court at all."

Fisher's household consisted of her parents, her maternal grandmother, and four children, three girls and a boy, of whom she was the oldest. As Anglo-Irish in a predominantly Quaker town, she and her siblings were subjected to much teasing and prejudice, but their stable, loving household enabled them to offset the miseries known to children of any ghetto. "A lot of people think that I liked my father better than my mother and that's not true at all. . . . In fact I preferred my mother. Maybe I talk more about Rex than I did about Edith, but I liked them both very much." She told a story about roller-skating on the bumpy sidewalks of Whittier. "Did I talk about how I used to try to collect my skin? I lost so much of my legs on the sidewalks, which were put directly on the roots of trees [which] kept on growing. I went dashing back to mother once, streaming with blood down one knee, and said, 'Mother, where's that pillbox?' She said, 'Why?' I said, 'I have to go and get my skin.' I found some of it and tried to put it on, but it wouldn't stick so I came home. She loved having children. It was her best job."

I mentioned my surprise, in reading *Among Friends,* to find how relaxed an attitude toward the human body her parents conveyed to their children. "She and Father were both what we now call broad-minded. We did talk very freely and casually. One time I thought I heard my little brother crying (he slept in my parents' room) and sneaked into the bedroom, and I realized father and mother were making love so I just disappeared. I was kind of embarrassed, but mother said, 'That's all right.' Years later my mother asked me whether I realized what they were doing and I said of course I did and it didn't bother me a bit. One night I went into their room stark naked to get a handkerchief, thinking they were asleep. The next day Mother told me that Father had said that I was growing up and my breasts were like half-apples." Yet they were strict about social conventions regarding language. "There was a backyard language and a table language and I erred by saying *turd* at the table."

I asked Fisher about her grandmother's impact on the family. "Like all Victorian middle-class ladies, after she got too old for childbearing, she embraced the church, the Protestant church. . . . You don't love anybody but God. You don't love peanut butter or anything. She wasn't lovable, but she commanded respect and admiration. We had steak and watercress when she went to religious conventions and we gabbled away. She believed children shouldn't speak unless spoken to. I wondered profoundly why I didn't cry when grandmother died."

I asked whether she cried when her mother died. "We were taught not to show any emotions much, except Mother did. Stiff-upper-lip school, terrible, awful — I never raised my kids that way. We bit our tears back . . . we were stoical. We behaved well, but not too well. Oh God, I cringe at some of the things I've done." I reminded Fisher that she is always generous to her family, that she nurtured her younger siblings and her aging parents in addition to her own two daughters. (Before her back injury she had planned to take Chris, who graduated this spring from the University of Oregon, to Marseilles for Christmas.) Generous is "what I'd like to be." She remains close to her two daughters and her three nephews, the sons of her sister and closest sibling Norah. "We were both single parents so we raised her three boys and my two girls together. They are all very dear to me."

Although Fisher wrote from the age of four, she was in her twenties before she realized that writing might be a source of economic support. "I didn't really earn my living until my first marriage in the middle of the Depression. That was when I became almost militant about being poor. We worked as a team, my husband and I, cleaning houses on Laguna Beach. We lived there all year round. And I got thirty-five cents an hour and Al got fifty cents because I was a woman, you see. And he didn't work very much because he was writing the great American novel. I did all his work and mine, and it made me so damn mad to get thirty-five cents an hour. I did it all because it never occurred to me to write."

Fisher became a professional writer in the late thirties, earning most of her income through writing for magazines. ("The books I wrote for fun; I never earned any money from them until lately.") She had a problem with writing for magazines, however, for she felt compelled to "bend certain ways. I wrote for the *New Yorker*, and I was very happy *not* to write for the *New Yorker*. When I wouldn't bend once, I learned to bend. Bill Shawn, the editor, read every word everyone wrote for the *New Yorker*. He would make a faint pencil line with a teeny square in the margin with the initials W.S. and a teeny question mark. And I'd say no or yes. He would question the position of a word in the sentence, so I would think more before I'd put a word on paper."

Other magazines required more dramatic forms of "bending." "Years ago my agent sold a story to the *Ladies Home Journal*, mostly sold in the Midwest. The schoolteacher in the story had a glass of sherry before dinner. They said, 'No, no. A teacher in the Midwest does not drink.' So they changed it to milk. I said, 'Damn, I can't do this. She wouldn't drink milk before dinner.' I needed the money very badly, but I told them absolutely not, I can't do it. My agent said, 'What the hell difference does it make? It's a good story.' So that's a compromise I learned I can make, but I don't like to." She enjoyed writing pieces for the California Automobile Association because they gave her freedom: "When I didn't have to bend, I just said, 'Whee!' "

Fisher's family was not impressed by her prolific writings, nor did they understand why she had a byline when writing for magazines. "Now newspaper editors sign their own stories and editorials, but in father's time they didn't." She remembers a family dinner when "I asked casually, 'How did you like my last book?' It must have been my seventh. Mother said, 'We saw that book, didn't we Rex? It was very nice.' He said, 'Yes, I think it's around somewhere.' I said 'God damn it!' There was a hushed silence and father said, 'You may leave the table.' I slammed the door and began to laugh and then everybody laughed." But "they still didn't remember the book or take it seriously. My father wrote 2,000 words a day for sixty-five years at least — he was working on a paper when he was nine or ten. If there was extra space, Grandma turned out a sonnet. You never signed anything. Then I signed myself. O dear. But I had to earn a living."

Fisher had taken several phone calls ("Not this week, dear. Monday'd be marvelous. Come and have lunch with me. I have to go to work at two.") and received a visitor during our morning interview, a neighbor who stopped in to bring her a bouquet of large yellow mums. Chris then summoned us to lunch, helping his grandmother navigate the wheelchair into the kitchen/living/dining room, a large room with enormous windows that open onto distant mountains on two sides and a descending slope on the third. As Chris served us a light gourmet lunch that began with ginger broth followed by brown bread, cheese, and pasta — and of course wine — Fisher told the story of the building of her house in 1970. "I knew I would live here for the rest of my life. I sold my house in St. Helena for $25,000 and gave the architect [her friend David Bouverie, who invited her to build on his ranch] the check and said, 'Goodbye. I want two rooms and a big bathroom.' When I came back the house was almost built. It's a terribly selfish house because it doesn't have any bedroom for anybody but me. Have you seen the bathroom?" I had seen the enormous bathroom with its huge tub, plants, and long counter. "I don't believe in the American idea that a bathroom should be a nasty little hole. We spend a lot of time in the bathroom doing our hair and our nails." I thought of the descriptions in *Among Friends* of Fisher and her sister as little girls playing in the bathtub of their Whittier home while their father stood naked humming and shaving.

As we chatted over lunch Fisher's image of herself as writer became clearer. Although her short fiction is brilliantly crafted, she does not think of herself as a fiction writer. She related that during a period of boredom in school "I started to fabricate stories. I got rid of all of them so that when I finally had to write a novel I couldn't. My husband and my publisher said that every writer has one novel in him or her, but I didn't have a novel in my system, so I invented a character who's the exact opposite of me, the eternal bitch, destructive, cruel." (Jennie, the central character of *Not Now But Now* is a beautiful, elusive woman who travels through time and social class, seeking selfish, often material satisfactions.)

Fisher is puzzled when people describe her as a cookbook writer. And she is right, for her books are in fact reflections upon the rituals of eating, essays on the cuisines of various times and places. Asked if men have written broadly and intelligently about food, she named two classical writers from ancient Rome before realizing that I had the present in mind. "Lots of homosexuals now write very well about food. Elizabeth David writes well, too, although her recipes are sometimes hard to follow because she assumes everyone knows as much as she does about the methods and techniques. She's the kind of intuitive cook who tells you to mix ingredients until it feels right," I recalled Fisher's own essays on wonderfully vague Elizabethan recipes. "One of the Elizabethan recipes I loved said in making a sponge cake you put your elbow in the oven, and if it burns it's time to put the cake in instead of your elbow."

When I confessed that improvising usually leads me into culinary disaster, Fisher acknowledged the value of precision in a cookbook. "Julia Child is a case in point. If you follow her exactly, word for word, you can't possibly fail. If you know nothing, you can follow her and produce a beautiful thing. A lot of people say, 'I'll just skip this or that' and they fail. I can't follow her exactly because she bores me silly. I now use Mrs. Rombauer's *The Joy of Cooking* and Julia's two books. If I had to have just one book I'd have *Joy*. I have several editions; now they're into microwave and deep freeze." Fisher does not have a microwave because of concerns for safety, but "My daughter, who is a stage manager, uses one because she always has rehearsal or try-outs. She takes off one day a week or every ten days and cooks all day and puts it all in order. She has everything ready, and it's all good food, no preservatives."

As we were finishing lunch with exotic chocolates, Fisher took the fifth phone call since my arrival. "That was Judith Jones in New York. She's going to Provence. *Omni* wants to interview me about the cities of the future. My view is very dim. Judith told me that the *Omni* people were quite prepared for that."

The topic of cities and the upcoming California election with the AIDS disclosure proposition on the ballot led us to contemporary issues. "I have two tickets to the Nutcracker Suite and [the money is] to go to AIDS through the church. The Catholics and the Episcopalians, the stuffiest churchs in the world, are doing the best work for AIDS. I was Christian and Episcopalian, but I don't like to be labeled as such. Neither do I have AIDS, but I've been tested for years because I took a batch of bad blood which a woman died from. Nine people got the same batch. That would make an interesting story. Nobody died except this one woman, who was a deaconess in some Pentacostal group. She said 'I have AIDS' long before anyone had even heard of it. She died in 1984, in the worst possible way, and her church quite properly made a great heroine of her. So we were all tested every few months, then every six months. Now we're clear. Most people are unbelievably ignorant about AIDS. Somebody told me the other day to put newspaper on the toilet seats. I said, 'Who are you and where have you been?'"

M.F.K. Fisher knows who she is and where she has been. With a past rich enough to live in, she has chosen to live fully in the present. She was preparing to vote in the upcoming general election, having reached decisions on the complex propositions for which California is famous. "I'm a Democrat and usually vote straight ticket. I'll vote no on [the cigarette tax] because, although I don't smoke, I defend the right to choose. I was not in favor of Prohibition; nobody voted it in."

Her social calendar, kept by her phone, must rival that of Barbara Bush. And who would not seek out the company of this woman? Her dialogues during phone conversations revealed both wit and courage: "How are you? I have a brace on now. . . . The doctor said it was to remind me so I wouldn't have to go to hospital again, and I said, 'It's very expensive . . . this is the second time around. . . . Why couldn't you put a string around my finger?' He said the more it cost the more I'd remember. I wish you'd come and sit for a while. The 15th? I'll mark that down right now. Let's have lunch together. . . . I don't cook now but my grandson's here." I was reminded of Fisher's own borrowing from Alexander Pope's translation of Homer for the title of one of her books: "Here let us feast, and to the feast be joined discourse, the sweeter banquet of the mind."

K.U.H.

BOOKS BY M.F.K. FISHER

NOVELS

Not Now But Now. New York: Viking, 1947; North Point, 1982.

NONFICTION

Serve It Forth. New York: Harper & Brothers, 1937; North Point, 1991.

Consider the Oyster. New York: Duell, Sloan & Pearce, 1941; San Francisco: North Point, 1988.

How to Cook a Wolf. New York: Duell, Sloan & Pearce, 1942; San Francisco: North Point, 1988.

The Gastronomical Me. New York: Duell, Sloan & Pearce, 1943.

Here Let Us Feast: A Book of Banquets. New York: Viking, 1946; North Point, 1986.

An Alphabet for Gourmets. New York: Viking, 1949; North Point, 1989.

The Art of Eating [includes *Serve It Forth, Consider the Oyster,* and *How to Cook a Wolf*]. Cleveland: World, 1954; Vintage, 1976; Collier, 1990.

A Cordiall Water: A Garland of Odd and Old Receipts to Assuage the Ills of Man and Beast. Boston: Little, Brown, 1961; North Point, 1981.

The Story of Wine in California. Berkeley: University of California Press, 1962.

Map of Another Town. Boston: Little, Brown, 1964.

The Cooking of Provincial France. New York: Time-Life Books, 1968.

With Bold Knife and Fork. New York: Putnam, 1969; Putnam, 1979.

Among Friends. New York: Knopf, 1971; San Francisco: North Point, 1983.

[With Judith Clancy] *Not a Station But a Place.* Synergistic Press, 1979.

As They Were. New York: Knopf, 1982; Vintage, 1983.

Two Towns in Provence: Map of Another Town and a Considerable Town. New York: Vintage, 1983.

Sister Age. New York: Knopf, 1983; Vintage, 1984.

[With Lynn Newberry] *The Food Book.* Goodheart, 1986.

Dubious Honors. San Francisco: North Point, 1988.

Long Ago in France; The Years in Dijon. New York: Prentice Hall, 1991.

TRANSLATION

The Physiology of Taste, by Jean Anthelme Brillat-Savarin. The Limited Editions Club; The Heritage Press, 1949; Knopf, 1971; Harcourt Brace Jovanovich, 1978.

CHILDREN'S BOOKS

The Boss Dog. Limited art edition. Covelo, Calif.: Yolla Bolly Press, 1990; North Point, 1991.

Francine Prose

DISCUSSIONS AMONG feminists about "having it all" are pre-
dictably passé and increasingly take place among women who
have not tried to balance work, family, money problems, publishers, vacuuming, laundry, correspondence, writing conferences,
eating, and carpools without going crazy. But if there *is* one
candidate among short story writers and critics who are women
who can be said to actually "have it all," my nomination would
be Francine Prose: Harvard University (summa cum laude), author of *Household Saints, Bigfoot Dreams,* and *Women and Children First,* wife of "a genius cook . . . the Mozart of cooking,"
mother of Leon and Bruno, daughter of two doctors including a
mother who "used to get up at five in the morning and bake Julia
Child tarts with frangipani pears and then go see patients all day,"
and owner of a charming house on seven acres in upstate New
York, a cat named Geronimo ("because the kids used to pick it up

and throw it"), and three computers, and winner of a Fulbright Fellowship to Yugoslavia.

Francine Prose and her husband, Howie Michels, a sculptor and painter, left New York City in 1978 because she "didn't want to raise a kid in the city and schlep a stroller up five flights of stairs. The rents were going up and we wanted some place where we could work and be left alone." At first, she said, "it was rough, living on $10,000 a year, but now life is "fabulous, wonderful . . . we can have lunch. We have a sort of peculiar marriage; we're almost never apart. . . . I love it. For whatever reason, it functions beautifully." Michels, who was "great when the kids were small," would trade off child care; "he took the children from nine to one" while she took the one to five shift. She discovered when the kids were small that "if I strapped the kids into car seats . . . the little one would fall asleep and I could talk to the big one." Her husband said, " 'What a great idea.' We ended up driving eight hours a day. We put 10,000 miles on the car in one year and we never left the county." Now the boys are in elementary school, and Prose and Michels use the car for transportation instead of babysitting.

When they left New York City in 1978, "the city was still glamorous, and people thought we were crazy to live in the country with two kids. Now most people I know would love to get out. My horror is that when I get back to the city all my friends will have gone completely 'luxe' and will be living in designer lofts [in Soho] with glass brick" walls. Prose admits that she "missed the city for the first three years," but now they drive in for readings and to see friends and are more than happy to be at home in the woods. "In a strange way," she added, "it's harder to insulate myself" in the country. "Sometimes, in fact, if the phone doesn't ring for three days, I think 'Oh, my God, I'm out here, I'll be here forever, and the phone will never ring again. . . . No one ever reads my work.' There are days when I'm going nuts, answering machine or not, and as other people have probably told you, people will pay you for anything but to write, and people are always calling you up to ask you to teach this course for no money, or judge this contest for no money, but not for writing."

Since Prose seems so happy doing it, I asked her why women write. Is it some kind of a childhood disease that they don't get over? "It's fun," she said. "I can't imagine not doing it." It's more than genetic. "It's what you get rewarded for," and each novel or collection of short stories is a different experience. *Hungry Hearts,* for instance, "was a really peculiar book to write because it was the only one where the whole plot, except for one large chunk in the middle, came to me in about twelve hours. I said to Howie, 'Does this seem like a good idea for a book?' We went on to two in the morning. . . . It was almost like taking dictation. I really heard their voices . . . it came so quickly. Sometimes when writing a book you write yourself into a corner, you make a wrong decision . . . but there was none of that." When she finished the manuscript, "It was almost like the characters, [based loosely on members of her family] had died again — and that the world you have created disappears. . . . I hope I get another one," she said wistfully, since "many writers do talk about hearing a voice."

When I asked Prose if she thought she had to write about her childhood to "get it out of the way," she said it was "coming out in the short stories" but she would not want to write a novel about her childhood. "It was a Brooklyn childhood. . . . On the weekends I'd just go to the city and hang out. . . . It's not a novel." And "what I tell students [about biographical material] is that any time you change anything, even a name, it changes everything." Sometimes, as a writer friend said to her, "You have a day that seems like a gift, and she wishes she could spew it out, but it's not that way." Prose, an experienced teacher who is often a writer-in-residence at universities across the country, says "the most depressing conversation" she has with students, about using their own experiences as material for fiction, is when she hears "the 'you had to have been there' excuse for the story not working: 'Well,' students say, 'of course you don't understand it, you weren't there' or the equally horrifying announcement that 'it may have been all right for you to live on people's couches and live on no money . . . but my generation is not interested in that . . . we want money from the beginning,'" and they "all think they are going to go into writing and make 100,000 bucks the first year. Why do they think I'm here if it's so easy?"

Like every woman I have interviewed, Francine Prose had something to say about what we called the *People Magazine* approach to writers — the current emphasis in biographies of women writers, and in reviews of their work, on pathology and personality. I asked her what, if anything, women who write could do about the syndrome epitomized by the Shirley Jackson and Jean Stafford biographies and about the current tendency to treat writers as celebrities. "The reality," continued Prose, "is that there are more and more contracts for big bucks, and once the stakes are real, then all the rest goes along with it. It used to be completely a joke because nobody was making any money. Now some people are making some money. It's like painting, which is most corrupt. The art world makes the literary world look pure. Why? Because the stakes are higher. You can sell a painting for 250,000 bucks and do another one the next day. And also because the rich are so much more directly and explicitly involved." Alison Lurie's latest novel, *The Truth about Lorin Jones,* which we had both recently read, deals exactly with this problem.

Prose seemed an obvious choice to talk about the usually enclosed spaces of women, since she herself lives in the luxury of open space. She said that the use of space in fiction "is about the spheres of people's lives and how they get circumscribed. . . . It's not accidental, it's not biological, that women tend to write about the family, the garden, and men, for whatever reason, feel free to write about seafaring and wargoing. That's about the life you live. Jane Austen was not going to write *Moby-Dick*."

The women in Prose's own fiction exist within defined, limiting spaces as well. "The woman in *Bigfoot* is working in this hole of an office and living in an apartment that's not much better. All the women in the short stories [in *Women and Children First*] are very much in their houses." The woman in *Household Saints,* which was written in upstate New York, is locked emotionally in her husband's butcher shop or in the memory-laden space of her mother-in-law's apartment. She mourns her dead baby by huddling under the covers; her bedroom is a dark prison cell where even the geraniums die. "It's much more than your [own] physical space," said Prose. "It's how you feel in the world. Men have that sense of entitlement . . . that the world is rolling out for them. I see it in my kids; the world is there for them. Women, for many obvious reasons, don't have that." In her own life, however, she was luckier than most women. Because of her mother, "it never occurred to me that you couldn't do what you wanted to do. Only when I went to college and women started to say, 'How was it growing up with this kind of a mother,' did it suddenly seem odd to me. When you are a kid, your family is the norm. I just thought that was what you did." And "it's a terrific advantage," we agreed, to know early that there's a "life" beyond "life," and that mothers are knowledgeable, multifaceted human beings.

Prose accomplishes this for her young sons by taking them along when she teaches at colleges across the country. "Everybody comes. That's the rule. I don't go unless I can bring everyone. . . . We went to Alaska — there was a writing conference at Fairbanks. It doesn't get dark, so the kids didn't sleep for two weeks!" Before this arrangement she "found that I blew my entire paycheck, no matter what it was, on phone calls. I called them three or four times a day." When they went to Salt Lake City "some people were building a Mormon church nearby and there was this huge dumpster where they were throwing cardboard out. Howie got a hot glue gun and filled our living room with a huge cardboard sculpture from the dumpster." Now her sons have such a clear sense of Prose's professional life that "the little one . . . says, 'I am now going to give a reading of *The Cat in the Hat*'" and the family has to sit still and listen. Clearly, Prose's children do not value the "normal" life in which women, including writers, have so much invested for its presumed safety, and they are unaffected by "all the disaster movies that are going to happen which run through my head."

One of the reasons Prose likes to take the whole family, in addition to not spending all the money she earns on phone calls, "is that I still see female students being told, 'You have to choose to be a writer or have a family,' and it's just bullshit; you don't. You can aim for what you want and if you don't get it, you don't get it," but if you don't aim, we agreed, you don't get anything.

All of this was underscored at her recent twentieth-year reunion at Harvard, where a former mentor reminded her that "women graduated in the middle and never at the bottom or the top." Since Prose graduated very much at the top of her class, this underscored again the invisibility of women. "Harvard now has 50 percent female undergraduate enrollment, which is spectacular; the most obvious shameful surface inequities have been corrected. But not that much has changed in the rest of society, so why should we expect it to change in the bastion of traditional education?" She was struck by the uncomfortable epiphany she had while talking to Matina Horner, former president of Radcliffe, at lunch: she had had few if any female professors or section heads at Harvard and "you can't help thinking, 'Oh, my God. What did this do to me?' " and to all the other women who were educated in a male-dominated fortress devoid of role models. This is a particularly poignant memory for Prose, who was trained as a medievalist and is acutely aware of the Bodo effect, Bodo being the most common name for the common man (and woman) in the Middle Ages. She understands the significance of insignificance in the lives of marginalized people, fictional or real.

For the last several months Prose had been working on a novel, but she put it aside to write short stories — because "you get that powerful, emotional hit in three weeks. . . . It's wonderful." She thought, " 'I'm never going to write a novel again.' Then I reviewed Muriel Spark's *A Far Cry from Kensington* for the *Washington Post* [ironically, reviewed by this interviewer at the same time for *Belles Lettres*] . . . and I started to write another novel within days of finishing my review. Now [she thought], 'I remember why someone would write a novel.' " We agreed that the miracle of Muriel Spark is that her novels contain not one extra word, and that "her women are so resilient, funny, and smart. They have interesting inner lives but a sense of humor about themselves." Prose's favorite Spark novel is *Loitering with Intent,* and she added, "Her villains are great!" Spark's novels always have at least one demonic character who is insufferable but captivating in diabolical ways, and in *Loitering with Intent,* he is the particularly revolting Sir Quentin Oliver.

Prose has something in common with Muriel Spark. Critics of

Spark are always asking, "What's the point? What *is* her point?" but of course Spark aficionados know that the *point* is the point. Reviewers of Prose's work depend on words like "kooky," "wacky," and "quirky," all labels she detests. For *Women and Children First*, "the critics got it," 'it' being "whatever it is I am trying to say." Happily "in short stories you have more than one opportunity to get 'it.' " She "was less lucky with *Bigfoot*. . . . Face it, there are ways in which women's fiction isn't taken as seriously; you'd be crazy not to see it, not to admit it. There are lots of male writers who have complete psychopaths in their work and it's always taken seriously. . . . A woman who's funny," like the woman in *Bigfoot,* "is always labeled 'wacky,' 'kooky.' [But] it's about a woman trying to survive in New York City with a kid, and she has a sense of humor and it makes her suspect; it makes the book suspect." Prose is one more writer who understands that so-called pathology in women is treated in extraordinarily different ways from so-called pathology in men.

I asked Prose about the obligation and responsibility of memory to women. She said that "the idea of Alzheimer's scares [writers] more than anything else [because] memory is the storehouse of material," and that "for every women writer I can think of, I can think of a male for whom [being trapped in memory] is equally an issue. . . . Kafka was as bound by his family and shamed by memory and obligation as any woman. I don't think memory is particularly female; I think it's a certain cast of mind, and for God knows what reason, it's often a cast of mind that makes women become writers." This comment addresses the central issue of this collection of interviews: what is it exactly that makes women write, that energizes the human psyche into channels that are both powerful and painful, regenerative and recalcitrant? In the case of Francine Prose, the writer, one senses that this is a case of a powerful intellect combined with an oblique angle of vision about human experience that has so far produced work that is both unique and poignant. When you listen to her in her country kitchen, which, like the living room, foyer, and bathroom walls, is covered with hundreds of primitive, eerie, and evocative papier mache masks, that assessment is underscored. Francine Prose does have an oblique angle of vision about the vicissitudes of ordinary experience. But that vision, which is both foreign and familiar at the same time, is an intriguing reappraisal of the clayfootedness of household saints, the ephemerality of dreams, and the precarious safety of women and children in American life. "Writing," she said, "is something I get rewarded for," but it is equally true that her particularly modern novels and short stories reward her reader in ways that are contemporary, revealing, and true.

M.P.

BOOKS BY FRANCINE PROSE

NOVELS

Judah the Pious. New York: Atheneum, 1973.
The Glorious Ones. New York: Atheneum, 1974.
Marie Laveau. New York: Berkley Publications, 1977.
Animal Magnetism. New York: Putnam, 1978.
Household Saints. New York: St. Martin's, 1981.
Hungry Hearts. New York: Pantheon, 1983.
Bigfoot Dreams. New York: Pantheon, 1986; Penguin, 1987.

SHORT STORIES

Women and Children First: And Other Stories. New York: Pantheon, 1988; Ivy, 1989.

TRANSLATION

[With Madeline Levine]. *A Scrap of Time* by Ida Fink. New York: Pantheon, 1987.

Alice McDermott

THE CAB driver's monologue assured me that I was in Southern California. While driving me to Alice McDermott's home in La Jolla, he described in friendly and elegant detail his vast collection of movie star memorabilia. McDermott herself, when I met her, clearly did not belong to the celebrity-conscious set residing in this sunny coastal suburb of San Diego. In fact, she and her family were preparing to move to Bethesda, Maryland, where her scientist husband will teach at Georgetown University. McDermott, who grew up in Elmont, Long Island, has freckles and an easy Irish laugh; more important, she has the vision of life filled with passion, loss, and irony found in the greatest Irish writers. The author of two widely acclaimed novels, *A Bigamist's Daughter* and *That Night,* as well as a number of short stories, McDermott is feminist and very quick, a brilliant writer and stylist whose novels are dominated by the voices of women with layered, textured, and complex minds.

While McDermott's mother tended her baby daughter, we talked in the living room. McDermott, who also has a three-year-old boy, showed me her study, which looked over the back yard and was cheerfully arranged with books and a word processor. We talked about the problems confronting writing women and other working women with small children. "Even if you manage the getting away, and even if you have a couple hours while you're there [in your office or study] where it feels great, there is still the guilt or obligation waiting for you. It's going to take more than a few generations . . . to change that kind of thing. It is taken for granted now not only that you can but that you should do it all." She believes mothers are put in a no-win position: "If you were really serious about your job, then you wouldn't take that day off because your children are sick. But if you really loved your children, then you would never leave for that job with them sick at home. There is no sense that they [work and children] are of equal value."

She pointed out that when a writer takes time from her work for her family, it is impossible to measure what is lost. "You can't say that if I had been able to work two more hours yesterday, I would have written the most brilliant scene of my career, but I didn't, so I don't know that I could have. Maybe we need to start complaining more again. I don't think women are getting enough credit. That's why I think it's so amazing and twice as wonderful that women today are writing the best stuff. The exciting fiction, it's from women, and a lot of them are women with families. Not that it takes anything away from them if they are not, but it's where the stuff is coming from. The work should be judged on its own, but a nod to what went on to produce it wouldn't hurt."

McDermott herself is the product of a Catholic elementary and a "very progressive" Catholic girls' high school whose nuns she admired immensely. Religion had an impact on her consciousness as a writer through the symbols and "the metaphor of Christianity" and through its "concern for the inner life, or even the spiritual, which was immediately legitimized. That part of your life is as essential, obviously more essential in most cases, than anything else." That belief in the importance of the inner life "helps you to make that leap that says, 'Well, I'm going to spend my life making up these stories about nonexistent people's inner lives.' "

Part of the complexity of McDermott's characters' inner lives consists in their explorations of personal memory. She believes that memory is an ordering faculty, "a way to put things together," and sees parallels between fiction and memory as creative processes. With memory "there are things left out and things enhanced or changed. . . . That's where the parallel [between fiction and memory] is — that you can get almost anything you want to out of it if you manipulate it the right way, if you add enough speculation and imagination to the events as you know them." When I asked whether women writers use memory differently from men, she said, "I think that male writers do tend to have more happening on the surface, in the world. . . . When you think about Bellow and Updike especially, I think you can really see that the characters are sort of bustling about, driving around Chicago, buying gold and investing, that sort of thing." She acknowledged that she hasn't "come up with a character who is doing anything interesting while he or she is bustling around. If I did, maybe I would write about the bustling. That 'stuff of the world' stuff is just not compelling enough, it's not really the heart of what we're getting at."

McDermott says that she simply does not enjoy describing characters who are always on the move, that getting them from place to place is boring. What she wants to do with her characters is "sit them down over a cup of coffee, or have them alone at night, or get them to a point where they are lying in bed thinking. . . . But in the meantime I have to get their teeth brushed and get them in their pajamas. I lose interest. There is just not enough to surprise you. It's easy to lose the energy that you need for a long piece unless the characters are surprising you and showing you something new every week or even every month or every other paragraph, however often it comes."

McDermott is always guided by what keeps her interested in her own fiction. When I mentioned the nostalgic narrative voice of *That Night,* she said, "I'd been working on something else. Ideas kept sneaking into that novel. The characters would stop in the middle of a scene and start talking about their childhood, and I would sort of have to slap them around and say, 'No, no, no, don't get nostalgic on me; this is not what this is about.' I thought I'd better write something about this and write it out." So she took the theme of nostalgia and the "voice of someone looking back" and created *That Night*. I told McDermott that the narrator reminded me — as does the entire novel — of *The Great Gatsby*, in which Nick's voice and attitudes are important, although he is not the center of interest. She responded, "I remember at one point thinking very seriously, well, if someone else, if Gail Godwin or Mary Gordon was writing this book, there would also be a parallel story of what has happened to this narrator. Maybe I should do that. [But] I didn't care what happened — I want that voice, that's all I want from her. It was essential to my whole interest in the story, although she is not really essential to the story itself, the plot."

Thinking of the erosion of traditional values — marriage, family, religion — that is striking in *A Bigamist's Daughter,* I asked McDermott if the narrator of *That Night* expressed the longing for stability and permanence associated with the suburbs in the late fifties and early sixties. She said that what she finds compelling is "not so much the fact of the impermanence but . . . the effort nevertheless again and again to make something permanent. It's the effort that really interests me, but of course there is no way of expressing that without showing what the goal is, or what it fails to be." She sees her fiction "in a much more positive light than most people do." Although her characters often fail, "they are trying. The trying is what is fascinating to me."

McDermott has recently started a new novel. "I'm not quite sure what it's all about even, but I said to my editor a couple of weeks ago, 'I think the whole novel is going to take place in four rooms, is that okay?' " When I told her of our interest in the spaces of women's novels, she said, "I was thinking about that very thing. . . . The landscapes [of men and women writers] probably are different. Women's ground is the room. That's where the women dwell, that's their whole realm."

McDermott's still untitled new book is "probably more about

what's lost and what's forgotten than what's remembered. I'm dealing chronologically with more time than I've ever dealt with, maybe fifty or sixty years." She likes the new challenge of the long time span. "It's much freer for me to make things up as I go along, more than I've done with the other two, which were more limited to their time and place." The characters are physically confined, however, "limited to four rooms so far, and they never get out of them." The action is "really internal," and what she is working on now is voice. "It's kind of a rush of voices right now which is what made me go to Virginia Woolf to see what you do when that happens."

McDermott has learned a lot from Woolf's *To the Lighthouse* because "there is an interior with not very much happening. Just that rush, it's almost just a breathless rush of images and yet that control is just so absolute, it's fabulous. I think that the insides [of her characters] are so wonderfully revealed; they seem to creep up on you. It just seems to arise — suddenly you seem to know those characters, [wondering] how did that happen, I know them inside and out. She's wonderful."

McDermott wasn't taught any women writers as an undergraduate and only started reading them in graduate school, beginning with Gail Godwin. She now reads women extensively and especially admires Louise Erdrich, partly for the "kinds of things she does with just the voices, the lead-in characters. The thing I think I admire most about her is the narrative control, the way she can bring a story through time, from one place back to another place without lots of space breaks."

I mentioned that she and Erdrich are part of a new generation of women writers who are integrating their lives as writers with raising children. The mother of a blond three-year-old boy who wandered into the room from time to time and an infant who woke up during our interview, she had a lot to say on that subject. "I think this is something that women writers alone have to deal with. There is still that sense that 'it's very nice that you're writing your little stories but you really shouldn't neglect your children to write those stories. I mean, what's more important?' . . . Men don't have to do that," she said emphatically. "If they choose to put their pens down and go look after the kids, it's because they feel like doing it. I've said a couple of times that any book review I ever write of another woman, I'm going to call her up and say, 'Where were your kids when you were writing this novel?' I'm going to put that in the review, whether it's a good review or a bad review. 'This novel was written with the laundry going, somebody knocking at the door, and the school calling. Please keep that in mind.' "

Three years ago while teaching creative writing at the University of California at San Diego, McDermott discovered a course called "The American Novel from 1940 to the Present" that had twelve male writers on the reading list and not one woman writer. She wrote the instructor a note saying, " 'I'm just wondering why you didn't include any, and if you don't know about any I'd love to talk to you about it.' He never replied. A student of mine was in his class and I pointed it out to her. She said, 'Gosh, you're right' and she asked the instructor. He said that he was trying to find books that really reflected the times more than women writers. He didn't know, when it came down to it; he absolutely didn't know. I was so upset about that for so long. From America, 1940, the women's movement to the present, if there is one time in the history of American literature when you damn well better include some women writers," it is now.

Despite this experience, McDermott enjoyed her teaching at UCSD. "I arrived with all my East Coast prejudices that they were all too blond and too good looking to ever really be serious about anything, and I've been really proven wrong. There are some wonderful writers. They're not reading much, but they want to know who to read." She assigned writers like Alice Adams. To a student who admired only Stephen King she said, " 'If you'll give me a chance, I know I can find someone who can knock your socks off.' I gave her *Love Medicine* [by Erdrich] because there is the drama, and there is enough fantasy and gore, and there is the voice. And it's very accessible and some of the characters she could relate to personally. . . . At the end of the quarter she began to change her writing and to realize that . . . it might be more interesting to find out about the character [rather] than to have a driverless truck run the character over."

McDermott said that she was always writing as an adolescent

but never thought of becoming a professional writer until her second year in college, when she took a nonfiction writing course from Paul Briand, to whom *That Night* is partially dedicated. "I wrote a nonfiction piece; of course I made up the whole thing; my fiction was claiming me even then. After he read my paper out to the class, he called the day afterwards and said, 'Well, I've got bad news for you, you're a writer, you are never going to shake it, you're a writer.' I didn't know it, but I knew it." In a tutorial with Briand, "I would bring a draft in and I would sit in his office and really go over it word by word: 'Why this word and why not another, and how does this sound?' He was rather flamboyant. He would say, 'God damn you, McDermott, God damn you, another comma. What the hell is this?' It was the first time that I saw [writing] as a profession and as something that takes time."

After college "my parents were telling me 'Okay, you want to write,' but they were very worried about it. You know, 'Why don't you go to Katherine Gibbs and brush up on your typing and learn shorthand, and then you can become a secretary in a publishing house and then at night you can write your stories?' " McDermott tried working for a year and writing at night but found it very difficult. "Nobody to show your work to, nobody to say it's a good and healthy thing that you are doing." So she took a two-year master's program in English with Writing at the University of New Hampshire, where she had a good experience both with teachers and with colleagues. "We used to call it the hunting and fishing school of writing because of the male writers. One of them in particular, Mark Smith, was a wonderful writer, one of these people who isn't read enough. He was very helpful to me because I went through the first year at UNH and had not submitted a story. Then I got into a conference with him and he said, 'You're not taking yourself seriously. You can't giggle and be coy. I'm not going to take it. You've got what you need to be a professional writer; I expect you to do those things that a professional writer has to do. This is your career.' That was the second time that . . . I'd been caught. I started sending things out."

McDermott published several short stories and taught briefly at UNH before starting a novel. When she and her husband moved to Manhattan, she started *A Bigamist's Daughter*. "When I had 100 pages of it and I had spoken to Mark Smith a number of times and told him that I was making my first effort, he said that he was going to write to Harriet [her agent] and tell her that I'd be by soon with something. I gave her the first fifty pages and the first couple of stories that I had published and she called me up and said, 'I want to see everything you've ever written. I want it all; whatever is in your files, give it to me.' And then when she read the next fifty pages, I went down and met her at her office and she said, 'Would you like a male editor or a female editor?' I thought, 'If you can find a living editor who is going to do anything with this book, who cares?' It was about two or three weeks . . . she had it sold."

Unlike many of the writers we interviewed, McDermott had words of praise for the world of publishing, especially for her agent and her first editor at Houghton Mifflin. "You hear all these horrible stories about how nobody wants to read a [first novel]; my experience hasn't been that way. There are a lot of schleppy editors; there are a lot of schleppy anything, but there are a lot of good editors and good houses who are just waiting and who are willing to take the risk. I had 100 pages and no more, and I had never written a novel before."

When asked whether she thought returning to the East Coast would be good for her writing, McDermott was ambivalent: "I think there is something positive about being there. . . . People read more. There is a sense [that] what you are doing is more important. There is not that sense here at all, [but] there is some benefit to that, too. When I published *That Night,* there wasn't any sense of, 'Boy, everybody's paying attention to the *New York Times Book Review,* aren't they?' It was very easy to keep it all in perspective. The UCSD bookstore didn't have any copies of the book when it came out. [Then] I went back to New York to do some signing. At first it was a really wonderful surprise to hear people say 'Oh!' [but] I would get very distracted if that happened all the time. I don't publish that often, so I don't think I have to worry about that."

McDermott looks forward to the day when she can devote

more time to writing. "I remember reading an Anne Tyler thing about how she gets up in the morning and packs lunches and prepares dinner, and at eight [o'clock] she goes into her writing room and doesn't have to come out again until four. Someday that will come; that is ahead for me." We all have reason to look forward to the time when McDermott can follow that schedule. Meanwhile, we enjoy the perfectly crafted and envisioned fiction she has completed.

K.U.H.

BOOKS BY ALICE McDERMOTT

NOVELS

A Bigamist's Daughter. New York: Random House, 1982; Harper & Row, 1988.

That Night. New York: Farrar, Straus, & Giroux, 1987; Harper & Row, 1988.

Rosellen Brown

"I HATE leaving home," said Rosellen Brown. "I have a good time dropping into people's lives, but when I go away I can't wait to come home again. So I never add another stop along the way. I'm so rooted that when I did a self-portrait [for Burt Britton's *Self-Portrait: Book People Picture Themselves*] my head was planted in a flowerpot that was hanging in a window. My artistic nature is not freewheeling," she said with a hearty laugh. "It's sort of, 'sit down every day and work.' " This sounds like the kind of conversation you'd have while sitting on the porch swing of a clapboard house in New England, but in fact it took place over tacos and enchiladas in a noisy, cavernous Mexican restaurant in Harvard Square. Brown, who has lived in Houston for eight years and spends the summers in New Hampshire (where she used to live), was in Boston for the weekend.

Rosellen Brown is the author of *Tender Mercies* and *Civil Wars*, but we talked at length about her first novel, *The Autobiography of My Mother* (1976), the story of a New York civil rights lawyer, Gerda Stein, of her disaffected, flower-child daughter, Renata, and of a young granddaughter, Teresa (nicknamed Tippy), who dies tragically in a waterfall after letting go of her grandmother's hand. There was, she said, "a very surprising ghost who stood behind me for the conception of the mother" and "the book started with a voice that I heard. I'm not insane, and it was not a hallucinatory voice, but it is as close as I've ever come to hearing someone speaking in my ear. I was in New Hampshire on a rainy day, doing a bit of very primitive weaving, some kind of simple repetitive action without much thought involved, and I heard the speech that became the mother. It was a woman with a German accent . . . and I became fascinated with her. Later, when I thought very hard about it, I realized the voice was that of a man I knew, not a woman. My husband and I had taught at a black college in the 1960s" because "I had been a Woodrow Wilson fellow in graduate school [at Brandeis] and the Woodrow Wilson people sent letters to all their fellows (don't you love that word for women?) and asked if we would like to go and start Honors programs in various disadvantaged colleges — mostly black, but not all, mostly southern, but not all — and we went for our interviews in Mississippi in the summer of 1964 when [Schwerner, Goodman, and Chaney] were missing.

"There was an incredible man [in Mississippi] who was a German Jewish immigrant who had fled in 1938, leaving his whole family behind; they wouldn't [leave]. He'd been a judge in Germany, but he started again, got a doctorate in the sociology of law, and had been teaching for twenty years in this little black college. He was extraordinary, and his vision of the world was incredibly optimistic, not pessimistic as you would imagine, given his background. He had seen that what the world was capable of was so horrible that he gave himself over to a belief in the Constitution, to the constraints on 'natural man,' and became a proponent of American law. I realized that when I heard the voice speaking to me, I was hearing the voice of this man, Ernst Borinski, talking to me (as Gerda in the book talked), about how *reason is all*. She would take the cases, as all civil liberties lawyers will, of the most horrible people because [she believed] . . . we can constrain the worst impulses of people by a system of laws and the Constitution." But "he knew, and Gerda knew, deep, deep down, that that was not, in fact, the case. Some even more profound accident can end up unseating reason. Terrible things can happen and you can't control them. So the book started with an intellectual idea, and a voice, and a character." But Gerda "was not as wonderful as Ernst, who was a loving and funny man. I look back on that with some regret. I made her a cold and difficult woman and I wish I hadn't. I think if I wrote the book now I would write something much less forbidding. I'm not sure why I did that; it came out that way. I had no idea what would emerge while I was writing that book. It was a book written with a paper bag over my head because I hadn't any idea of how to write a novel at that point. How anything coherent emerged from it eludes me to this day. . . . I had started the book a million times, and I didn't know then that that is how all my books are written. It takes me a year or two simply to figure out where I'm going. I thought it was such a botched birth that I couldn't [believe] that what was emerging was making any sense."

This idea — that life is still open to the irrational, in spite of a given individual's devotion to order, rationality, and justice — permeates the work of Rosellen Brown, who says that her themes are "exile, alienation," and the sense of loss and displacement that characterizes much of the twentieth century. She is "not altogether sure where my own sense of unassuageable exile comes from, or which paradise I think I've been kicked out of. I suspect a certain restlessness and sense of never being quite at home comes not from some cosmic angst but in part from my having moved around a lot as a child. . . . People always love to help me out by suggesting that I must have been an army brat or some such, but it was only the coincidences of my father's work life that happened, for example, to start me out being born at the Philadelphia city limits, in a manner of speaking, only a few weeks before my parents moved us after living there for ten years. That kind of thing kept happening. . . . For whatever reason, my parents had rather casually broken the ties that some people never will, for job or geography, and left family and friends more than once to begin again somewhere. I have to wonder if my preoccupation with 'those who belong somewhere' and 'those who don't' began with the sense of being the new girl a few times too often, and being a little too shy to do it very well. . . . Add to the mix the fact that we've lived in places where being Jewish, in search of a Jewish community at the same time we've wanted to belong to the community-at-large, has added layers of discomfort and isolation, and you've got good grounds for a persistent if modest itch of alienation."

Even the symbols that find their way into Brown's work are touched and changed by her angle of vision. Water, for instance, which is often used by writers to signify absolution and/or rebirth, is here often the source of tragedy and catastrophe, and is coupled in her work with a sense of the inexplicable. *The Autobiography of My Mother,* for instance, ends with a child falling *into* water, and *Tender Mercies,* the story of a marriage in which the wife is accidentally crippled by a motorboat that is piloted by her husband, arises *from* the water. Brown said the event in *Autobiography* is "so horrific that people have told me they've turned away from it rather than face it straight." In the novel on which she is now working, she "was trying to figure out how to kill off a casual character and my first impulse was a drowning. Then I said, 'No, enough is enough.' So there is no water; there is fire in this one; we're changing elements."

She started writing *Tender Mercies* "when my agent said, 'How come you don't write very much about men and women together?' " But "you can't write a novel about marriage with a capital M. I needed *a* marriage and then I remembered a [concert pianist] I knew who had had a terrible accident in the Hudson River. She had been put back together again but with some of the pieces missing. (Here's where the strange alchemy comes in: why do you choose what you choose, to make into your element?). . . . This is the part of writing a book that is most interesting to me when I've contemplated it in myself or in others: How does that spark happen in which there's a connection made between some large thing that you want to do, and the specifics that are going to pull the vehicle?" And why are there "two kinds of writers: the ones who write action where [the events] happen before your eyes, and the ones who write aftermath — what happens then? What are the reactions, the responses" to the events? In Brown's case, "*Tender Mercies* starts after [the fact because] there is a downward arc in *Autobiography* and I wanted it to be rising in the other. I really wanted to write about what people go on loving about each other" after someone is so seriously disabled that she can't *do* much. And the voice had to be "cool, not sentimental" because "it was such a sentimental topic."

Both novels "started accidentally from stories I knew" about "real people." The genesis of *Autobiography* happened "at a party at Erica Jong's house. I overheard a story of someone who was walking with a child, who lets go of that child's hand, and the child disappears. I published a story about it and several people said to me, 'I'd like to know how they got to the edge of that precipice, with that child.' So I went backwards from the ending, which is a terrible, terrible idea, much too restricting. I'll never do it again. I caution everybody: never start with an ending! It was like *An Appointment in Samarra:* my characters *had* to get there."

Brown, like many of the writers in this collection, said she is "superstitious . . . disaster-ridden," and aware of the fact that she can "still be overtaken by some catastrophe beyond imagining." (See interview with Francine Prose.) She writes from a sense of "sheer terror" and in "the hope that if I write [these stories] down, they won't happen. . . . I'm trying at least to buy off the evil eye [by] throwing red meat" at it ("mixing metaphors [since] I don't suppose the evil eye eats red meat").

Part of this anxiety is expressed in her use of emotional and physical spaces which, in her novels, are often limited. Characters like the severely injured woman in *Tender Mercies* are caught in physical immobility, immured in a kind of dangerous emotional quiescence, and surrounded by silence. That character depends on an inner, often unexpressed dialogue, which is designated by italics. Brown acknowledged that "there's a dichotomy between what space means in my own life and what it means in my head and in my books. I realize that in my work houses play an extraordinarily important role. Yet if you came to my house you'd be very disappointed. I don't give it a great deal of thought (and surely don't spend much on it); it's not beautifully furnished. We're the kind of people who move into a place, work very hard for two days, put up all the pictures, and then we forget about it. It's *not* a negligently kept space, but I don't make it a significant part of my own life. What's fascinating to me is that in all of the novels I've had a very clear picture of the houses and rooms. For instance, in *Cora Fry* (a book of poetry), the character is hemmed in by the narrowness of her horizons. This is space 'inside out.' For someone who is confined in a small space, in a small town [in New Hampshire], to be thinking about light years is to be thinking about the farthest distance she can construe from where she is in her little house, on her little road." The "poems are about enclosure" because Cora Fry "wants to escape into a larger life," and it is Brown's "single exercise in trying to feel what it's like to *know* where you belong — to resist it, maybe, but to know it in every cell. Just about everything else has had as its implicit, if not its stated, theme the tension of 'outsiderhood,' and even though not a single line is strictly autobiographical, I know where the preoccupation comes from. (I should add, by the way, that as a way of life moving on gets to be a habit every bit as profound as staying put.)"

Brown's forthcoming novel has a similar theme, and she says "this is the one in which I put a lot of Yiddish-speaking, Russian-Jewish immigrants in a field in New Hampshire and wait to see what happens. These people are part of an experiment in idealistic farming," which was a nineteenth-century social movement, though it did not actually take place in that state. But, as Brown says, "I know New Hampshire so I put them there." It is not such a "funny coincidence that we, beginning almost one hundred years later, were busy turning soil in New Hampshire and feeling somewhat ill at ease in a place so very Christian — benignly so, most of the time, but certainly not an easy place in which to feel unself-consciously at home." This novel "started from a vision, similar to those John Fowles and Joan Didion have described; a strong image: I saw these black-hatted, black-coated, bearded types with a beautiful woman standing in the long grass. I know where I got her picture from. I had been reading some books about pioneer women and I saw a picture of an incredibly beautiful young pioneer woman standing outside of a sod hut, God knows where, and there was a cradle. . . . You had to say to yourself, 'What will happen to her after a few years out here. She won't look that way any more.' The drama was that my characters come here, they get off the train, and they have no shelter and no food. They have only what they could bring with them, the candlesticks and the down quilts — which is one thing if you were going to Rivington Street [on the Lower East Side of New York, where many immigrant Jews lived], but it doesn't put a roof over your head when you are in rural New Hampshire." The novel is in part about "the lust for a house, a way of belonging, on the part of one woman" who "wants to be like those farmers' wives who have houses."

I asked Brown if she had a title, and she said that her "really literary daughter can't stand the title, which is now *The Angel of Forgetfulness,* which is from a midrash," the rabbinical commentaries and notes on the Scriptures, written in the form of stories between the beginning of the Exile and c. 1200 A.D. The midrash says we are almost "born knowing all there is of Torah, but just before you *are* born, there is an angel, called the angel of forgetfulness, who snaps his finger over your lip and all of your knowledge vanishes and that's why [Jews] have to spend all of their lives learning Torah. Unfortunately forgetfulness," she says, "really sounds like you've lost your glasses and you don't know where you put them. . . . If it weren't for Milan Kundera, [I'd call it] *The Angel of Forgetting.*" The novel is "really about what you don't know, how you are always missing the information you need to reconstruct history or penetrate the mind of another."

This is a concept to remember when you are interviewing twenty-eight disparate and complicated writers and trying, in fact, "to penetrate the mind of another" person in a relatively short amount of time. In Brown's case, however, you come away wishing that she lived down the street, because she is smart, articulate, intuitive, and honest. You can easily picture her in New England, where she plans to move some day because she thinks Houston has been "really fine and a good move, [although] a little 'alien.' But 'do I want to be buried there?' " The conflict about rootedness and her sense of exile remains. "This summer, for example, my husband and I were at Bread Loaf, where we had a very good time. But when the director asked me to teach there again next year I could feel the old habit kick in: Do I repeat an experience and deepen into it or do I go somewhere else, indulge my curiosity, learn another way?"

Since considerable effort was made to have this collection be geographically representative, I asked Brown what it was like to be a writer in Houston, Texas. "All I want to say about writing here is that, for all we may lack in a place like this of the absolute end-of-the-line sophistication of New York City, one of the compensations (besides the pleasantness of the interaction of writers who don't compete with each other, who are pretty genuinely supportive and concerned for one another) is that I think there are certain real distortions in the perspective of the East Coast writer who really does see the map like the famous *New Yorker* cartoon, all undifferentiated, nearly nonexistent — defined, in a sense, by what it's *not* — once you've crossed the Hudson. The air of superiority to a nation of 'provincials' out there is — what's not too strong a word? — dismaying. Irritating. And occasionally amusing in its own provinciality. We've suffered some outrageous condescension at the hands of visiting writers who can't believe we really choose to live here (though many have appreciated the genuine virtues of the place), and in the end I can't help thinking that people who like to imagine themselves as curious, open-minded, flexible — which writer doesn't? — but who can't live for six months, let alone permanently, more than a mile from Zabar's will never understand America or the needs and desires and pleasures of ninety percent of the country. I don't want to sound self-righteous about it but I have to say I think the best thing that's happened to American writing in the last fifteen years or so is the decentralization of a good many sources of income and employment for writers — NEA grants, poets-in-the-schools, even writing programs, about which I have other misgivings — so that people can live all over the map . . . and manage to do their work far from Hollywood and the Village and the Upper West Side."

Like many writers, Rosellen Brown does not "trust mechanical things." During the interview she asked me several times if I thought the tape recorder was working, since "something always happens" when she is interviewed. Does it go without saying that when I returned to New Jersey, and listened to one of the tapes, not one word had been recorded? But everything that Rosellen Brown said, and all of the images and questions that her conversation evoked, were indelibly imprinted in my memory.

M.P.

BOOKS BY ROSELLEN BROWN

NOVELS

The Autobiography of My Mother. New York: Doubleday, 1976; Ballantine, 1981.
Tender Mercies. New York: Knopf, 1978; Penguin, 1986.
Civil Wars. New York: Knopf, 1984; Penguin, 1985.

SHORT STORIES

Street Games. New York: Doubleday, 1974; Milkweed Editions, 1991.
[et al]. *Banquet: Five Short Stories.* Great Barrington, Mass.: Penmaen Press, 1978.

POETRY

Some Deaths in the Delta and Other Poems. Amherst: Univ. of Massachusetts Press, 1970.
Cora Fry. New York: W.W. Norton, 1977; Unicorn Press, 1988.

NONFICTION

[et al.], eds. *The Whole Word Catalogue: Creative Writing Ideas for Elementary and Secondary Schools,* rev. ed. New York: Teachers and Writers Collective, 1972, 1975.

Carolyn See

CAROLYN SEE's house in Topanga Canyon north of Los Angeles is surrounded on three sides by canyons deep and wide enough to contain whole forests and whole sunsets. In her novel *Golden Days* she described her first visit to the site: "The house sat out on a wide raw crescent of cut and fill. That half moon of dirt hung, just hung there in the air, over another one of those astonishing cliffs above nowhere. Across the chasm . . . were stones the size of skyscrapers. Due east, a wilderness of bougainvillea and eucalyptus, sage, rosemary, mint, and a couple of blazing yellow acacias." By the time of my visit, the dirt had been landscaped into gardens, but it was the view over the chasm that compelled me — dense trees, immense rocks, and distant tiny horses on a dude ranch, with ranchers' voices carrying over the miles of blue sky.

Sitting in the sunny living room of her house at the top of the world, Carolyn See is a neat, attractive woman who embodies in her conversation the wit, animation, and profundity that characterize her writings. Her novel *Golden Days* is a stunning, daring book; beginning with hilarity, it evolves into a deeply serious vision of American society and one particular family before and after a nuclear holocaust. See, who was born Carolyn Bowland (Richard Edward See was her first husband), is also the author of three other novels (*Rhine Maidens; Mothers, Daughters; The Rest Is Done with Mirrors*) and a study of pornographers and the pornography industry called *Blue Money*.

I told See that I considered *Rhine Maidens,* a novel about a comically bitter, interfering, and energetic mother, to be a brilliant farce. She told me that "*Rhine Maidens* is about throttled female energy with no place to go so it turns to destruction; *Golden Days* is about male energy and science gone mad." *Golden Days* earned rave reviews from such different voices as William Buckley, Jr., and Betty Friedan, who wrote of it, "If such a heroine can be so truly imagined here and now, she might embolden us to save ourselves."

We discussed the fact that her fiction, long respected on the West Coast, has only recently become nationally known and is still underread in the East. She explained that she became a writer "with such ignorance. I was on the wrong coast, I was the wrong age, the wrong sex at the time, and then I did nothing whatsoever to rectify that situation, so that my first novel, *The Rest Is Done with Mirrors,* had a printing of [only] 2,000 copies." (Together with her other novels, it had just been reissued in paperback.)

By "rectifying the situation," See means going to New York, meeting the right people, being smart about marketing. "It's because I don't want to move away from here; I do go back to New York a lot but it took me a long time, plus there's the family stuff. I try in my mind to put my books and my family exactly on a par." She mentions Diane Johnson and Joan Didion, writers who built national reputations from the West Coast. "They're in another ball park and they deserve to be, and someday I will be, too. But it's taken me hell's own amount of time. . . . I figure if I live to be eighty I will have made some impression."

See had just won a Guggenheim to complete her next novel,

Making History, and her visibility has increased markedly in the last few years. "I'm on the National Book Award Committee; I'm on the board of the National Book Critics Circle; I do a lot of editorials now that get national attention. But I was a slow learner. I didn't know anything about how the world of lit worked. If you read Alison [Lurie]'s first memoir, she's in the center of it, she's in the heart of infinity from the very beginning. I was around her, but I was . . . stupid, did a lot of things in a vacant way." As an example of acting "in a vacant way," See cites her move to Topanga Canyon in the sixties. "Tom [Tom Sturak, her second husband] and I moved up here because we came up here on a day like this, but that meant we were an antisocial couple. There are a lot of people who won't drive up here or drive up once. It has ramifications down the line."

Despite her slow start, See feels that, like most writers, she is fundamentally a lucky person. "We're doing exactly what we want. How many people in the world do that? We're totally living our first choice, not our second choice. I might want to be younger or weigh less or not have my car break down, but you're already home free — it doesn't matter in a big way." A teacher of creative writing at UCLA, See tries hard to inspire her students but also to disabuse them of romantic notions about writing. "I tell my class, 'If you try it and fail, that's better than saying, I could have written it if I hadn't married Harold.' For the seven years I was married to Tom my belief system was, 'You only write when you're unhappy, and I'm happy; therefore, I don't have to write.' So I lost seven years of my writing life doing other stuff." (See and Tom Sturak were divorced in 1967.)

See doesn't think of herself as "a lady novelist. I don't want to write women's novels. I don't like *Mother, Daughters* because I think it's the most standardly womanish novel, and I want to write the way Diane [Johnson] did in *Persian Nights* and *Lying Low.* I want to be able to take on these larger subjects." Yet See is sometimes regarded as arrogant for taking on these traditionally "male" subjects. "Why should people listen to me? Who the hell am I to say I want to write about male power and nuclear energy and war, and, for the next one, the female . . . energy that runs through the universe. People edge away from me. Who wants to read that stuff? It's too pretentious, too fancy. I think I'm closer to Carlyle and Darwin. If I were in the nineteenth century and I were a guy, I'd be writing essays that no one would want to read."

We agreed that people are just beginning to take women writers who work with large ideas seriously. "I think they will down the line; it's beginning, with Margaret Atwood, with the fact that people did read *Golden Days*. But it's hard. I see it in my classes every single semester. It takes two or three weeks for the guys in the class to get it. Here's this middle-aged lady who's bossy and opinionated and sure she's right. [My ideas are] not lady-like material."

When I asked whether she believes that women are writing the exciting American fiction today, See observed, "I review a lot of writers, once a week, men and women. Men writers are in a trough between waves waiting for the next thing to happen to them. At the 1988 American Book Association convention the readers were Raymond Carver, Richard Ford, David Leavitt, Joanne Leedom-Ackerman, the president of PEN, and me. Joanne did a car chase through Central Park with blood and horses and buggies. Carver was the star, but he was dying. The guys wrote teensy tiny things about three people discussing their divorce — things that in the old days would have been thought of as women's subjects. Women wrote about crashing big subjects. Now women in this burst of euphoria see they can take on the world. Men are at the end of a long breath and waiting for the next breath."

I asked See whether she believes that women are the preservers of family memories. "They have to be because men are out hustling and making their names." We also agreed that many men believe that only that which is public and/or political is historically important. "We watch the soaps and the news, and the soaps are news for the ladies. The women have to record the family memories because the guys are too stupid to do it."

We agreed that many women fiction writers (Morrison in *Beloved,* for example) have recently expanded their fictional worlds to include phenomena such as parapsychology, ghosts, and communion with the dead. See asserted that "men are not going to write about that stuff. . . . It goes back to the Romans who owned the world; the Christians had to go to a better world. Why should Updike concern himself with anything beyond himself? Why should the Jesuits concern themselves with God when they have the Jesuits?" She cited a contemporary example of the male refusal to credit the spiritual power of women: "The Virgin is now appearing to a whole class of kids in Czechoslovakia; she sees them and they see her every day. The priests are saying, 'This is bullshit.' Some bureaucrat in the Vatican said about this, 'I can't stand these pious women.' He's got his office and his desk; he's got it aced. These guys don't care because they are stuck with, 'My dick is so long and red and it's such an amazing sight'; that's where they are."

See noted that women and the poor "may have invisible power. We are trained to think of power as having a corner office, but if you're in the backyard on acid, that's power but the world doesn't recognize it. There's a terrific new book by Paula Sharp about a woman who's got a bunch of kids. . . . She starts seeing the women who've lived around her and they start having a wonderful time. She ends up on the road after throwing away her house and furniture, but she has the power to love other people and make other people love [her]."

We adjourned to the first floor for lunch, which See produced with an efficiency that seemed magical to me. The main course was chicken with a delicious sauce. When I asked, "How did you do this chicken?" she said, "You go to the deli counter and say, 'Give me two of those.'"

See lives with John Espey, a distinguished Ezra Pound scholar and professor emeritus of English at UCLA. He figured prominently in our discussion of the huge lag between American scholarship and what people are reading. "John is part of this project that has been around for many years, *Sixteen Modern American Writers,* high-powered scholarship, a critical bibliography, now being updated. Sixteen pictures on the cover. Fourteen white guys, James Baldwin, and Willa Cather. And John is the kindest man on earth, not a swine, I can really say that after fifteen years. He's smart, I tease him about it and finally he sort of gets it. They aren't locking women out; they're locking themselves in. He says, 'Oh, my dear, but you can't leave out Robert Frost.' It's sweet and ludicrous and dopey. Fourteen white guys looking stupid. I don't know who some of these guys are. But the nice part is that women's novels are selling like crazy," so "it's just funny."

Suddenly See thought of something: "Do you know about our Monica Highland novels? My daughter Lisa See, who works for *Publishers Weekly,* and John Espey and I were all broke, so we decided we would start writing big popular novels for intelligent people to read in airplanes. So we wrote *Lotus Land* and *110 Shanghai Road,*" and "they make a lot of money. We're fooling around with [big questions] — how can we redeem our world, how much power does the individual have? In these books the characters have unlimited power because they can do what they want. They aren't romance novels but historical novels full of action: births, deaths, weddings, parties."

I asked about the logistics of these undertakings. "We all sit down and do the outline together — scene by scene; we have it all clear. That takes a couple of months." She showed me maps and family trees used to keep characters and places straight. "Then we talk about it. Then one of us starts out writing. Lisa puts it on the word processor. When we all have a hard copy we start from the top, reading out loud with our notes. We all notice different sets of things. With *110 Shanghai Road* they flew out an editor who didn't approve of it. He said there's too much extraneous knowledge, like what kind of underwear people wore in 1880. We told him, that's what you need in this kind of book."

See said that the process is entirely different from writing a serious novel. "You have to remember how old everyone is, what they look like, where they've been, where they've lived. One day we realized we had a fifty-five-year-old pregnant woman. We had to go back and see what happened when we took off years, and world history won't move, so you have to move your characters." She added that the actions of the characters are more idealized than in serious fiction. "They have a lot of panache and elegance; they always know the right thing to do without forty-eight hours' lead time."

At the moment the Monica Highland team is working on a book about baby farming to be called *Precious Cargo*. "We are pushing into page 500; we have these two women locked up in a room. We had to do a lot of research on baby-farming; we know all about the financial setup." One hero is "a nice New York Jewish guy in the book who went to Yale drama school who is like Clint Eastwood and wants to live in the Old West. He has a horse named Trusty and a helicopter named Twister." The bad guys will be vanquished at the end of the novel; in the meantime, the writers must devise a way for the two women to escape from that room.

I asked See about her own family background. "My dad was a hard-luck boy; his mother killed herself; his father drank himself into an early death." Her father's brother died from an infection received on the first day he worked in the sewers. "It's the working-class ethic of disaster; disaster is what you expect. My mother had a brother who beat their mother; she nursed my grandmother to her death from TB. She had a dark view of men. They were married until I was eleven and then my father went off to pursue his career — getting married and divorced — until he became a pornographer. He left my mother with enormous responsibility; I recognized that women have no training for getting along in life when I was left in the same position. Guys are socialized to get the car started, box each other on the arm."

See said that her father became a pornographer because he was "intelligent but frivolous and dopey. Allegedly my grandmother killed herself because of [her husband's] weird sexual demands; she left a nasty, passive-aggressive note. My father was fourteen at the time. His pornographic novels are about the weirdness of the sexual rules and the terrible guilt built into sex. That was his calling; he was giving his mother a good talking to — 'Just lighten up, this isn't such a big deal.' See said that her father mocked the genre even as he wrote it, doing "trapeze tricks and giving baroque twists to the conventions. Every porn book has an animal scene. In his first book, a nineteenth-century Victorian novel, the animal is a seductive lady sea lion who takes the man into the deep, and he experiences unbelievable pleasure."

See explained how she was rescued financially by defending pornographers in court in the 1960s. "I was divorced at the time [with Lisa and Clara, her two daughters] and one year we lived on $3,000. There were dark days when I thought, 'I have to get on welfare,' but I never thought, 'I have to go out and get a job.' We weren't together then, but John was testifying for *Tropic of Cancer* and *Tropic of Capricorn;* it was the year of the landmark trials. For my dissertation I had read a lot of soft-core Hollywood novels, and I was called in as an expert witness to defend 'the redeeming social value' of *Lust by Friends and Neighbors,* a pathetic little book."

The defendant's lawyer had promised her $50. "After the trial the lawyer tore up the check and wrote another for $100 and said, 'You are a genius, little lady.' For two years I went out to little courtrooms all over L.A. and made $250 a day. I could pay the bills. If my testimony went into the next day the prosecution had to pay. Everyone would get the giggles — even sad convicts in court — because our language has a sexual base to it that you don't notice until you talk about pornography. In *Blue Money* I tried to write about it as a business. The chapter on Harvey Peters, that's my dad."

See's current novel, *Making History,* is about the complex forces of creation and destruction in the universe. At the climax of the novel is an accident caused by a suicidal woman "who is not melancholy but just furious. She drives through Georgina, the safest street in L.A., perfect domesticity on the Palisades, as fast as she can, goes over the grass strip and drops on two or three cars on the Pacific Coast Highway and takes out about a dozen people. This happened about ten years ago."

I asked whether the idea for the book began with this event, or with an image in her mind. "I know the beginning and the accident scene and the end. It will end with the good guy having some heavy-duty mystical experience with arcing lights across his head . . . he feels better, but he doesn't know why." See believes that "nobody knows how to describe that stuff yet; we don't have the language; it's unclassifiable. We live in the world bumping into things without a way of noticing; it's like egg whites folded into the batter of life." She wondered how the ending of the book would be received. "Is this too weird? Will they lock me up, laugh at me?" No, I said, because it will be good.

See attributes many of the good reviews of *Golden Days* to her own position as book reviewer for the *Los Angeles Times*. "My first novel, *The Rest Is Done with Mirrors,* got terrible reviews. I loved *Golden Days,* but other reviewers in the country had something to do with its good reviews. By then I knew a lot of people. You've got to be mean to somebody, and it's better to be mean to somebody you don't know. If you give a good review to everybody, you're in trouble." See recalls that "I only became conscious of reviews when I got to know Alison [Lurie] and Dinny [Diane Johnson]."

For professional writers, See said, "I can't overstate the importance of something like the size of the first printing, the distribution. One of Dinny's books got swallowed up by a trucker's strike. We spend a lot of time with our Monica books; we say hello to everyone in the warehouse. It never gets easier; it only gets harder as you see how much more there is to do." She believes that, with few exceptions, "women are ignorant of commerce and marketing. The trick is to market and remain distinguished." See cites two women who have done both: Alice Hoffman and Louise Erdrich. Alice Hoffman "wrote *Illumination Night,* a beautiful, stunning book, and then a best seller called *At Risk* that got mixed reviews. She's very intelligent about how she sells, who she talks to. So is Louise Erdrich; her husband Michael Dorris does a lot of promotion for her — a good guy."

We concluded our conversation back in the comfort of the living room. In response to my question "Where do you work?" See says, "I work there — you notice how you're sinking into the couch — or sometimes here. I work with a piece of paper and a black pen. I write out my reviews and phone them in." She avoids the typewriter and the word processor almost entirely, writing out her fiction and sending it to a typist. As for her schedule, "A perfect day is to write two hours, work in the yard two hours, and write ten pieces of mail, that's all I want to do. It never works out that way — or not often."

I talked with See just before the appearance of *Making History,* a compelling and ambitious novel integrating mystical and religious ideas with realistic scenes of international high finance and family life in southern California. See says of the novel's hero, "Jerry is like Ahab with a good disposition. He wants to go out to perfect the world, but it is not available to be perfected. It is a random universe; you can accept it on its own terms or go nuts. Nobody's safe. The Christians have the father and son, a little bureaucracy to take care of everything, but it doesn't work. If there *is* a God, she's the goddess of birth and destruction."

In its message for contemporary society, the novel is "a continuation of *Golden Days.*" Most of the action takes place in America and Australia, the two continents most affected by immigration, because it explores "what it means when waves of people slap against each other. The world won't work the same way it did because things have changed. This is not a polarized society with good men and bad guys. Men are still meeting and building missiles that look like big red dicks but there is nothing to conquer. Look at the same six white guys walking around the White House, looking stupid. They *say* they're ruling, but what are they ruling? This incredible immigration is part of stuff not digested or recognized by people living through it."

See wrote *Making History* with the support of a Guggenheim grant, and we talked of her struggle for recognition and for financial solvency. The secret is "one thousand words and one charming note a day for the rest of your life. Every day you send out one note to a writer or editor. Never say no to a conference. You help as many writers as you can because that's correct — you're straight with the universe." About the start of her career, See said, "I had read a lot, but I didn't know anything." So she made "a conscious decision to get to know how the machine works. First you join the National Book Critics Circle; then you run for office; then you get on the Board. Then you say, 'this is the engine.' I've been supporting myself as a writer for about thirty years. It's fairly easy if you do magazines and reviews."

See believes that female and ethnic writers are "the good working writers now with the great ideas. John Updike and Philip Roth were really interesting forty years ago. Now they're . . . 'important,' not new." As an example of "a new voice," she cited Gus Lee; "*China Boy* . . . [is] the most amazing book. Traditional lit as we know it is just about bankrupt."

Carolyn See belongs to a small group of writers with brilliance to understand and imagination to render the world as it chooses either destruction or global integration. Combine these qualities with compassion, humor, and fast-moving action and dialogue, and you have fiction of breathless daring and power, a voice for a new millennium.

K.U.H.

BOOKS BY CAROLYN SEE

NOVELS

The Rest Is Done with Mirrors. Boston: Little, Brown, 1970; Fawcett, 1990.

Mothers, Daughters. New York: Coward, McCann & Geoghegan, 1977; Fawcett, 1989.

Rhine Maidens. New York: Coward, McCann & Geoghegan, 1981; Fawcett, 1989.

Monica Highland [pseud. — with John Espey and Lisa See]. *Lotus Land*. New York: Coward-McCann, 1983; McGraw-Hill, 1986.

———. *110 Shanghai Road*. New York: McGraw-Hill, 1986; Bantam, 1987.

Golden Days. New York: McGraw-Hill, 1987; Fawcett, 1987.

Making History. Boston: Houghton Mifflin, 1991.

NONFICTION

Blue Money: Pornography and the Pornographers. New York: McKay, 1974.

[with John Espey] *Two Schools of Thought*. Santa Barbara: John Daniel & Co., 1991.

Laurie Colwin

AS I APPROACHED her apartment in a Chelsea townhouse, an energetic take-charge woman with a huge, gray plastic trash bag in her hands looked up and said, "Are you Mickey? I've just got to get rid of the garbage. Come on in." So began my interview with Laurie Colwin, author of *Home Cooking,* subtitled *A Writer in the Kitchen,* part memoir and part cookbook; the novel *Family Happiness;* several collections of short stories; and the much-admired *Happy All the Time,* in which Misty Berkowitz, the archetypal New York outsider, the "only Jew at the dining room table," first appears.

Colwin, her husband, and her daughter, Rosa, live in a part of New York City largely devoid of glass and steel monsters, in a neighborhood where you can still sit over a cup of coffee at the local grocery/candy/deli; the newspapers are in Italian, Greek, Spanish, and Russian, and the buttered bagels are still fifty cents.

On a sunny day you can picnic on the tree-filled grounds of the General Episcopal Theological Seminary of New York, which faces Colwin's front door.

Entering Colwin's apartment is similarly relaxing. The living room/kitchen has a working fireplace at one end, surrounded on all sides by bookcases (*Happy All the Time* in Finnish was on a lower shelf). Big comfortable Morris-style chairs are cozying up to the fire. The kitchen, unlike those in many New York apartments, is not left over from "Let's Pretend." This one is bedecked with spice jars, quiche pans, Portuguese earthenware, china teapots, wire whisks, and scores of cookbooks, all adjacent to an airy, sunny room partially filled with Rosa's block collection and a large, inviting dining room table. Here Colwin, unlike the stereotype of the silent author who writes but doesn't talk, holds court. And she has a lot to say — on every subject.

Colwin's latest book, *Home Cooking,* evolved from an article she wrote for *Gourmet.* She realizes that for many cooks the attempt to try something new is frightening. "Someone gave me a sourdough starter and I'd like to write a little about that because I was really intimidated. I made jam last year for the first time; that was intimidating but it was really easy to do. There are many things that are very delicious and very simple." Colwin says she is "surrounded by people who work and are in a constant snit about what to feed their kids. . . . What happens is that these Yuppie parents go out and eat all these extraordinary things . . . and their kids are eating these really disgusting things. I think it's terrible. . . . I'm actually sort of hysterical on this subject without being nutty." She notices that "there are a lot of people I know whose children only eat peanut butter and jelly or hotdogs and I have always wondered about this. . . . I realize that people have expectations about how children should be, what childhood is like, what children will eat, and it is sort of like the whole idea of gender. People say it's impossible to have a gender-free childhood because no matter what you do . . . people's cultural stereotypes and people's expectations are so deeply rooted" that it is hard to effectively change patterns of behavior or response. If girls "play with a truck or boys touch a doll, their mothers . . . have nervous breakdowns thinking [about] how they are going to grow up to be 'fairies,' and these things are so rigidly in the hearts and minds of people that there is no way that children can escape."

Colwin says that her "particular bugbear in life is the fixed idea" and that "they are all over the place. They are in cooking too, and they are very hard to break. It's the same thing with childrearing and . . . with literary criticism." It's even difficult to tell people that "you don't have to have sugar to make bread" as you did "when yeast was unstable and they had to make sure it wasn't dead," because then "they'd say, 'How about a little molasses?' "

Laurie Colwin thinks of herself "as a kind of blank slate. I don't watch television. I never go to the movies, I didn't finish college, so I didn't imbibe these cultural stereotypes. I am kind of a native and I really do think I come to something without a lot of fixed ideas." No one, however, would accuse her of leaving a subject without "a lot of fixed ideas."

On the subject of books she said that "American literature is not my tradition at all. I really think my roots are [in] British literature. I grew up reading a totally different group of writers. Someone I do admire was questioned about who his mentor was and he said 'John Gardner.' I thought, John Gardner is this guy's mentor? . . . Why not Chekhov? I think what happens is that . . . younger American writers grow up reading other American writers and this was not my experience. . . . I remember when I applied to college. One application said, 'What book did you enjoy reading?' I said *Vanity Fair* because American teenagers in the sixties, and certainly now more than ever, were just incapable of reading Victorian novels. I did take a Victorian novel class with Carolyn Heilbrun [at Columbia University, who] is the best teacher I've ever had. She's so smart; she just opened Victorian literature for me. I read *Middlemarch* over and over, I read *Persuasion* fifty times, I read *Vanity Fair* a thousand times. I read Evelyn Waugh, who I consider my mentor. I read Angus Wilson, a tremendously underrated writer, in my opinion. I read Bridget Brophy and Iris Murdoch — who is excessively underrated. She is a fabulous writer! Her bad books are good! *A Severed Head* is brilliant [and] she is not given her due, especially in this country, [where] nobody thinks of her as a literary person, but she is really fabulous." Colwin says that recently she "was thinking about Nabokov, who was probably the smartest writer of the twentieth century." His writing style is complex but "it has to be that way. . . . It is a literary portrait of his mind. I'm not sure that is the case with Henry James" or "if the complexity of [James's] style . . . reflected a true complexity of intellect or if he just had a very complicated style."

Colwin remembered when the critic Janet Malcolm wrote an essay about Edith Wharton, and it "was perfectly clear from this article that [Malcolm] felt that Edith Wharton wasn't a very good writer." Colwin considers Malcolm to be "very smart," and since she herself "had never read Edith Wharton in my whole life . . . I decided it was time to read" her. "I thought [Wharton] was terrible. I thought she was morally confused, intellectually nowhere and I thought she had no idea about what she really felt about the characters. . . . This was the worst kind of writing in which the narrator and the author were not in agreement about how they felt, the narrator revealed things about the author that the author was probably not aware of, and I thought, 'Why does this woman have this stellar reputation?' I wouldn't publish her if I found her, or if an agent sent her in a manuscript box. She is," says Colwin, "a dope," unlike Emily Dickinson, who "is not a dope; it's a pleasure to read her."

Since Colwin teaches occasionally at New York University, I asked her if she planned to complete her degree. She said that she "cannot think of one single reason to get the degree. I just can't imagine it. I hated school and one of the reasons I'm keen on my daughter's school is that she loves school. . . . They build with blocks till they are eight. There is no blockbuilding corner for boys and no housekeeping corner for girls. Everybody does everything. They all cook, they all do woodwork, they all sew, they all use saws. Nobody says, 'This is what a little girl is supposed to be,' and 'This is what a little boy is supposed to be.' They say, 'The experience of childhood is to learn. Here are the tools. There are very few of them; see what you can do with them; they are yours.'" Most of the schools program children to think "little girls should do housekeeping chores and little boys should be doing woodwork. You can do a lot to dispel these things but then you look around and everywhere you go, little boys have short hair and are very 'butch' and little girls have ruffles. It's parents, it's the culture, and it takes a lot to make sure you don't end up with one of those nasty stereotypic children." Colwin is particularly outraged at the widespread use of I.Q. tests by New York private schools that service the children of certain social and economic groups. "Parents," she says, "especially of New York kids, should rise up as one body and tear down these . . . schools. To put children under that kind of pressure is immoral. . . . It's an outrage. It says vile things about ambition, success, elitism . . . and nice people allow it." She is also a passionate foe of television, which in her opinion "is the great bane of the late twentieth century. It's made people moronic, it's robbed people of their ability to think. It's done tremendous damage, and every single household that has a small child should take it and throw it out the window."

Laurie Colwin continues to be best known for *Happy All the Time,* which she says is a "book about people who are in a cheerfully anxious state. These people are anxious!!! One of the things that bothers me about the way I am viewed is that people say, 'Oh, the books have happy endings.' There is not *one* single happy ending in any book written by me. They are all unresolved endings. In the end of *Family Happiness* you don't know if this woman is going to stay with her husband or go off with her lover — and I don't care. My mission was to describe a certain kind of struggle."

For all her outspokenness, Laurie Colwin is a person who believes that "a life without religious feeling is not worth it" and who has "many feelings about God with no particular vessel to put them in." (In spite of an "assimilated" upbringing, she feels "strongly Jewish" and has "a great affection for the Catholic Church.") People, she says, "have longings which can only be called religious, and they have to be answered in some way." Religious people are "lucky" because "the rest of us spend the rest of our lives trying to figure it out." Clearly, most people spend no time at all trying to "figure out" their feelings about nutrition, religion, society, politics, childrearing, education, or entertainment. It is equally, and resoundingly, and definitely clear that Laurie Colwin does.

M.P.

BOOKS BY LAURIE COLWIN

NOVELS

Shine on, Bright and Dangerous Object. New York: Viking, 1975; Ballantine, 1979.
Happy All the Time. New York: Knopf, 1978; Penguin, 1985.
Family Happiness. New York: Knopf, 1982; Harper & Row, 1990.
Goodbye Without Leaving. New York: Poseidon, 1990; Harper, 1991.

SHORT STORIES

Passion and Affect. New York: Viking, 1974; Penguin, 1984. [Published in England as *Dangerous French Mistress and Other Stories*. London: Chatto & Windus, 1975.]
The Lone Pilgrim. New York: Knopf, 1981; Washington Square Press, 1982; Perennial, 1990.
Another Marvelous Thing. New York: Knopf, 1986; Penguin, 1987.

NONFICTION

Home Cooking: A Writer in the Kitchen. New York: Knopf, 1988; Bantam, 1990.

Joyce Carol Thomas

BETWEEN DOWNTOWN Berkeley and the University of California are steeply sloping, tree-lined hills. Joyce Carol Thomas lives on such a hill in a Spanish-style house that she calls her city-country home — city out the front door, country out the back. From her study on the second floor, productively cluttered with computers, books, and manuscripts in progress, she can look west over the San Pablo and San Francisco bays or south over an avocado tree in the garden that figures in her latest novel, *Journey*. We sat on the couch in her living room, framed by a huge blossoming lemon tree just outside the picture window behind us.

Joyce Carol Thomas has written poetry (four volumes), plays (five, all produced in San Francisco), and young adult fiction (four novels) — all celebrations of black culture. Characterized by lyrical language and compelling narratives, her fiction takes place, as Maya Angelou has written, "on a real-life stage." Her first novel,

Marked by Fire, which won the National Book Award in 1982, was recently made into a musical named after its main character, "Abyssinia." (It played to rave reviews in Washington and is now on its way to Broadway.) Thomas's fiction is classified as "young adult" fiction not because pain is avoided (it's not) but because the central characters are aged twelve to twenty. "Sometimes people think there can be no conflict in young adult fiction," Thomas pointed out, "but without conflict there's no story."

Thomas realized that she was fundamentally and essentially a writer in a sudden revelation in the early seventies while working on her doctorate in education at Berkeley: "I was in my stat class and I looked down one day at all the numbers on my paper, and around the border were poems I had written, and I said, 'I'm a writer.' I never went back." Now she realizes she had in fact been preparing to be a writer all her life, from her early childhood in Ponca City, Oklahoma, where "in church I fell in love with the rhythms of those who testified," through her young adulthood in Tracy, California, where "I loved hearing the Spanish workers talk and sing. I always loved languages. I loved words and the sounds of words, but I had no idea I wanted to be a writer."

Thomas was born and lived until the age of ten in Ponca City, the setting for *Marked by Fire,* which takes Abyssinia from her dramatic birth in a cotton field through a traumatic early rape and a deeply spiritual relationship with her godmother from whom Abyssinia inherits the role of town healer at age nineteen. Ponca City is presented in the novel as a cohesive, supportive community whose inhabitants reach out to one another. I mentioned that I was intrigued by the ending of *Marked by Fire,* when Abyssinia, despite her excellent high school grades and the clear option of college, decides to stay in Ponca City and learn the medicinal arts of herbs from her godmother. "I think that's important," said Thomas. "Many times going and staying away is not always the best answer. I just finished another play called *Nightingale* about three sisters, and one goes to the big city, the measure of success. She writes these letters about how dreadful the city is, about how people keep warm by burning oil in garbage cans, about how she misses the beauty of flowers and gardens. Often people say 'Go out into the world and make your way,' but if you look at where they are, they're no happier. In fact they're often isolated and cut off. So I kind of wonder about what we call success in living."

Thomas acknowledged that many of the events in *Marked by Fire* happened to her or her friends. "I know I romanticized it [Ponca City] because when I went back it looked a lot different. I remember going up this tall hill when I was a kid and rolling down and getting stung by a bumblebee. What I thought was a hill was just a bump. The memory is accurate, but it's the memory of a child; the sights and sounds and smells and tastes were much more sharp. Poetic license allows imagination to pick up colors in the vivid way we look at things when we're much younger."

Since all of Thomas's fiction and much of her poetry are about family life, we talked about her own family. "My mother lost a few children before she had one that lived, and she always wanted a girl. When she married, she had a girl doll and my father threw it away. She had thirteen pregnancies and nine of us lived, and I was fifth of the nine, so I was the ninth try before she had a girl. She had me and then my sister and then three more boys." Her mother never explained why she wanted a girl so badly, but "my brothers were gifted in the way males can be gifted. They took apart a whole car, an old car we had. They didn't know how to put it together; maybe my mother wanted someone to put something together."

Leona Haynes, Thomas's mother, kept many things together. She cared for nine children and cleaned houses for a living; she also "crocheted and embroidered" pineapple pincushions and other objects with elaborate designs and patterns. We agreed that the kind of patience her mother displayed was a mixed blessing, the particular heritage of women of her generation. "I don't have her patience. Sometimes I wish I had and other times I'm glad I don't because some of the things she put up with she probably shouldn't have. It's very difficult to unravel what she did and what she put up with from the person."

When Thomas was ten years old, she moved with her parents and siblings to "this tiny California town called Tracy, the first town in the San Joaquin Valley, and we lived in the country of the town, so you can't get any more rural than that." I asked her whether one of the patterns running through her novels — an inversion of some ordinary notions of inside space and outside space — is related to her experience of spending so much time working and playing outdoors when growing up. In the fiction, outside space is usually associated with pleasure and freedom and beginnings (the central characters of both *Marked by Fire* and *The Golden Pasture* are born outside), whereas inside space is often unsafe, subject to invasion from hostile persons or forces like fire. Thomas responded, "Outside space is important to me. The backyard to this house goes on forever. When I'm outside, it's as though I were in the country. Houses were places people could invade. One time in Tracy, the health people came to inspect our house. I remember feeling so violated — our house was always clean!" There was no clear reason for the visit by three or four white men. "I didn't say anything, but I was so outraged. I was about eleven; one of them looked at me as though he understood my anger."

It was also hard to find privacy in a house with eight siblings. Even though she now has a double bed to herself, "I curl up under the covers in this ball. It comes from sleeping four in a twin-sized bed. Part of it may be protecting myself in the fetal position; the other part is claiming this little space on the bed."

I observed that adults in her novels usually give their children a lot of space in the sense of freedom and responsibility. Thomas remembered that as a child she "was probably given enough space, but also I went inside myself. I think about the time I put my father's hat in the refrigerator. I was supposed to clean the kitchen. My father worked at the Studebaker place, and he never went to work without his hat. When he couldn't find it, he decided to make a cup of coffee to calm his nerves. Opening the refrigerator, he howled for my mother, 'Come and see what this gal's done.' There between the butter and the milk sat my father's hat. I had really tidied the kitchen."

While she was growing up, Thomas ignored the racism around her as "a way of surviving, of paying attention to your own needs without spending an inordinate amount of time reacting to what's going on." When she used the phrase "innocent racism," I asked her if there was or could be such a thing. She said that she wasn't sure, but gave me an example: "I'm doing a mini-autobiography for Gale Research and they want pictures from important stages in [my] life. So I got out this picture and article [about a spelling bee that she won at age thirteen], and the funny thing is, the runner-up got all the headlines. There was some innocent racism going on. She was white and I was black. Although I won, she got the headlines and the bold print. It was so fascinating to know that I was living under that and unaware of it. It was riveting to look at this picture in 1988. It was as though I didn't win." As in the Ralph Ellison novel, she was the "invisible girl."

When Thomas came to San Francisco shortly after high school to live with her aunt (partly to get away from "an early marriage that wasn't working for me"), she worked for the phone company during the day and took courses at night at *both* the City College of San Francisco and the University of San Francisco. "I didn't have sense enough then to know I shouldn't be doing all that." For the last two years of her B.A. she attended San Jose full-time; she also attended Stanford University full-time for her master's degree, while simultaneously caring for her four children. She has taught both French and Spanish, and has done teaching and individual testing in the reading program at San Jose State. She resigned her last permanent academic job in 1982 to write, "doing the thing that's going to count and not always playing it safe."

Thomas likes teaching, however ("writing is so lonely"), and occasionally teaches a creative writing course. She will publish a story by one of her students at the University of California at Santa Cruz, "an absolutely wonderful writer, a very shy Korean American, a serious young man who writes all the time. When Langston Hughes published his anthology, he published a young student named Alice Walker, so I'm following a tradition."

We talked about living as a writer in the San Francisco area, about the sense of some writers here that they are disadvantaged by being so far from the large publishers in New York City. Thomas feels that the disadvantage can be balanced by having (as she does) a New York agent. "Writers in New York socialize a lot. I imagine that, living there, it would be difficult to be left alone. If you have to do ten drafts, that's hard." We both groaned about the phone bills on calls between the two coasts, although Thomas has the good sense to call before 8:00 A.M., when the rates are lower. "Some writers may feel they get more attention there, but I find that if you holler loud enough, they pay attention to you."

Living in San Francisco has given Thomas the opportunity to see her plays through production. She met Nora Vaughn, the head of a black repertory theater, a woman now almost seventy, after Vaughn heard her reading "Church Poem" (a long poem that describes the weekend ritual of churchgoing in a black family) on the radio. "Vaughn said, 'I have to find the person who did that. It's what I look for in playwrights . . . that kind of respect for and celebration of black life.' This was a period when people were producing [a type of] play which I've never liked because not every black person walks the street talking under people's clothes." Thomas's profound admiration for Vaughn was cemented when she worked with her for a "short stint at the theater at a time when their productions were in a storefront that was always packed at every performance." Through persistent political action, blacks now have their own theater, built after Vaughn staged a sit-in at City Hall.

Thomas also admires the black woman who plays the part of Mother Barker, godmother and teacher of Abyssinia, in the musical version of *Marked by Fire*. "They call her Mother Vera, which is a better name because it means 'truth'. When she sings, people in the audience jump up. She read the book and really understands who this woman is. In the playbill she dedicated her performance to the spirit of her grandmother. It's wonderful to have the interpretation match what I wrote." Thomas recalled that "a male reviewer of one of my plays [which are primarily about women] said, 'The women dominate.' One of my woman writer friends said, 'They think everything has to be about them.' It's a burden on women to be in a world dominated by men, but it's a burden on men to be dominators and I don't think they realize it. If the female voice or the female vision speaks, they don't listen to it. They don't listen to the voice within themselves, and they don't listen when women speak."

We talked about our belief that many men don't achieve full

"personhood," that condition of knowing your own feelings and those of others and giving private relationships as much attention as worldly success and status. Thomas had recently come across the statistic showing that married women have a shorter life expectancy than single women: "Men require a lot from women, and taking care of yourself as a person is a full-time job. If you're taking care of yourself and another grown person, something is taken from you. Men who are married live longer than men who are single. I'm not anti-men, but I think that they ought to become persons, and then they don't have to lean so heavily on the female that she loses part of her life."

In *The Golden Pasture,* the story of a relationship between grandson and grandfather, Thomas created a male universe almost without women. "My son, then fourteen, [had] asked me why I never wrote about boys. Also, I wanted to write about the participation of blacks in the West, the black cowboy. Nobody's done that that I know of, and I wanted to reach for what hadn't been done." As a child she attended black rodeos like those in the book. We agreed that the book's grandfather, who is a terrific cook and super-sensitive to his grandson's emotions, is a genuine "person."

When asked what kind of daily schedule she follows, Thomas replied, "I work best in the morning, so I get up early. Sometimes the writing wakes me up in the middle of the night, and if I heed the call good things happen. When I was working on *Journey* a character woke me up in the middle of the night just after I had sent the last draft off to my editor. I got up and went into the study. The character changed her name from Margarite to Memory and when I'd done that, she told me other things to do, details that I didn't have access to until she spoke to me. So I went through the whole manuscript and stayed there and then called my editor and said, 'Do you know that final draft of *Journey* I sent you?' And she said, 'Yes, it's wonderful.' I said, 'That's not it. There's another draft.' When she saw it, she said, 'It's incredible.' "

In the course of our chat a young black woman named Bridget, a student at the University of California at Berkeley, came to xerox materials for Thomas's current project, a collection of short stories she is editing for Harper and Row called *A Gathering of Flowers*. "I wanted it to be multicultural — white authors, black, Asian, Latino. I wanted everybody represented, but I also wanted the best stories, so I decided to ask award-winning authors from these different groups to write original stories that might be of interest to young adult readers. They all responded — Maxine Kingston, Lois Lowry."

During the interview the front door of Thomas's house opened and closed at least half a dozen times as young people came in and out. We stopped talking only once, when she got up to give instructions to Bridget. She has a fierce ability to listen and to concentrate; perhaps that is how she remembers the songs of the cotton field and the rhythms of the black preachers. She has an openness that I, as a stranger, had no reason to expect. Perhaps that is why no bitterness impedes her poetic exaltation of black culture. The poetry, plays, and fiction of Joyce Carol Thomas look squarely at the black experience in America and burn through pain and humiliation to triumph and love. I am reminded of her poem "Aretha": "She has the gaze / Of the gods / In her voice / Her song is / The wind / Set free."

K.U.H.

BOOKS BY JOYCE CAROL THOMAS

NOVELS

Marked by Fire. New York: Avon, 1982.
Bright Shadow. New York: Avon, 1983.
Water Girl. New York: Avon, 1986.
The Golden Pasture. New York: Scholastic Inc., 1986.
Journey. New York: Scholastic Inc., 1988.

SHORT STORIES

[Ed.] *A Gathering of Flowers: Stories About Being Young in America*. New York: Harper & Row, 1990.

POETRY

Bittersweet. Fire Sign Press, 1973.
Crystal Breezes. Fire Sign Press, 1974.
Blessing. Jocato, 1975.
Inside the Rainbow. Palo Alto: Zikawuna Press, 1981.

PLAYS

A Song in the Sky. Produced 1976.
Look! What a Wonder! Produced 1976.
Magnolia. Produced 1977.
Ambrosia. Produced 1978.

Shirley Ann Grau

SHIRLEY ANN GRAU, who won the Pulitzer Prize in 1965 for *The Keepers of the House* comes from "a loosely structured family of eccentrics if there ever was one" who were "splendid [but] forgot they had children for long periods of time. Everybody was so interested in whatever they were doing they had very little time to organize others. When they remembered us, they *were* very concerned about it. Everybody was expected to go their own way [but] we were not expected to *do* anything at all. So you either did, or didn't. In either case, [it was] your problem. They'd say, 'That's very nice, dear.' It was sort of monumental indifference [but] I don't remember anything traumatic. Nothing seems to have happened."

Grau, who graduated from Sophie Newcomb College of Tulane University, lives now, as she has from early adulthood, in New Orleans, where she raised four children (with James Feibleman, a writer and professor of philosophy at Tulane, now deceased) who "have all come out different." They are "an amazing variety" who range from "extremely conservative to extremely liberal." Two are married, and one of the unmarried children "will marry, at the first twinge of arthritis. When he gets up and there is a twinge, he will marry the next 'girl.' " She said with some serious-ness that "it's very nice to begin to see them go away," that children are "wearying . . . one grows tired." The fact that they get married and leave home "is one of the few good arrangements in nature's plan." In any case, she said philosophically, children follow "their own genetic imperative," you can't "really influence too much" since "there are billions of possible [genetic] combina-tions. Some throw up physical flaws, [or] mental or moral flaws; they are now checking the genetic material of murderers. . . . It works or not. . . . When you think of the number of genetic pos-sibilities and possible combinations, it makes a lot of sense" that her children "are just about as varied a lot as you can have."

Grau reminisced fondly about living in the French Quarter during the early 1950s in an apartment where "one wall was black and there was one kind of purply wall" in the days "when it was a small town . . . not the Quarter you see now" and "you could have a very comfortable apartment behind a big courtyard and hear nothing except the cats climbing the roofs at night." Now it is "a very different place" with "such an obvious dark side, a drug-laden and prostitution-laden side. It bothers me when you see a young girl with eyes running, nose running, standing on a street corner, obviously waiting for a 'buy.' When you see young boys and their pimps . . . working the streets, it's obvious and depressing." There is "such a contrast between the lovely arch-itecture and the incredible sordidness of the people walking around the streets. . . . Too bad."

Nine Women (1985), Grau's latest work, is a collection of complex and unusually disturbing stories about women ma-rooned in the often muddy waters of emotional crisis. The collec-tion is her first published work since *Evidence of Love* in 1977 and is markedly different in tone and subject from earlier novels like *The Hard Blue Sky, The House on Coliseum Street, The*

Condor Passes, and *The Wind Shifting West*. The lead story in *Nine Women*, called "The Beginning," which she says is "a basically simple, ordinary story [about] a hooker and her child," a "variance on a fairy tale," will be incorporated into a novel she is writing now.

Grau seemed reluctant to discuss her work in any detail. She said, "If I look at people abstractly at all, which I don't, it's a never-ending parade of eccentricities and amusement . . . a grab bag of possibilities, [and people] are remarkably good at passing blame." What is important in her work "is whatever the reader sees, not what the writer thinks he [*sic*] puts in it. Whatever you see in a story is there." That is the "wonderful thing about words, their overtones, and the meanings they drag along with them." The finished product is "sort of an enormous Rorschach blob that everyone reads differently. Words are symbols, and all the associations they carry can't be controlled. They can only *approximately* be controlled and the rest, who knows?" But the stories do seem to have in common a sense of the often ungathered threads of a middle-aged woman's life, which one somehow expects to be more neatly braided or arranged. There is a haunting quality here which has to do with the unfinished scenario of experience, the unresolved complications of fluctuating memory, and the familiar insight that the character (or the reader) does not understand the reality of her own experience as well as she might have expected.

Grau's women seem caught in that amorphous middle place between the initiation of events and their resolution. In "Hunter," for instance, the heroine, Nancy Martenson, for whom "time came and went in a pattern of overhead fluorescent tubes," and who finds herself the sole survivor of an airplane crash in which her husband and daughters have perished, spends the insurance money on cross-country flights, awaiting her own death in the statistically inevitable plane crash. In "Letting Go," Mary Margaret, the daughter of ardent but uncharitable and unloving Catholics whose lives are demarcated by empty rites and rituals, is "running with fear from something she didn't know, something that might not have been there, something that might even have loved her." "Housekeeping" has a similar message: nothing is satisfied or in place, and one waits for the ghost-like past to be jettisoned in favor of the present. "Widow's Walk" is an open-ended story of a woman, Myra Rowland, who is alone, without answers, entrenched in the boring patterns of the advantaged country-club life she shared with her now-dead husband. What underscores this story is the sense many women have, in retrospect, of having been too young and unknowing for the youthful, demanding years of marriage and childbearing, and too aware but disillusioned for the later, less stressful, more disgruntled years. It is the familiar story of many women, who experience themselves as out of time and place but who understand the mechanisms of daily experience, and for whom the frustration and emotional ennui remain daily irritants.

Grau, whose first published work was a collection of short stories called *The Black Prince and Other Stories* (1955), said that, in her opinion, "very few courses on the short story are taught in colleges but collections of short stories are selling like mad." There is "a big difference between what teachers choose to teach and readers choose to read, and there is not much correlation." She "puzzles over the effect that teaching has on reading habits" in later years. "You wonder how many literate people go back and reread *Hamlet,* [which they] were assigned in college," since most "students leave school actively disliking the printed word and it takes eight years to get over four years of college."

We talked at some length about a book on mother-daughter relationships that I was working on, and she told me about "a meeting [in New Orleans] a couple of years ago [that featured] mother-daughter pairs" and to which she took her own daughter, who is a lawyer. Her opinion is "that some people are just so hooked into eternal self-analysis . . . they think about themselves incredibly, and they are *all alike!* You'd think if you wasted that much time on yourself, you'd come up with something different!" This conference convinced her that "this [kind of] introspection is encouraged by analysts and magazine articles" and "what bothers me is not that [some people] are so self-concerned, but that they are so basically dull-as-soap and so very, very boring." One daughter said her mother "had had ten or twelve children" and made them "kneel down every morning to say the rosary, with no wiggling. If they wiggled, they had to start all over again, which strikes *me* as barbaric and cruel. I'm not sure that, deep down in the daughter's mind . . . she didn't think it was barbaric too, but she didn't tell this story as a complaint. She said, 'I was raised very strictly.' This was an example of strictness. A few things like that just curl your hair. After all, the woman was thirty-five."

This conversation seemed particularly revealing because the encoded message suggests that few conflicts are ever totally resolved and the painful experience continues to reverberate in seemingly innocuous but powerful moments, much like those depicted in *Nine Women*. None of the conflicts described there is resolved, and that is perhaps related to their author's statements that "there are so many irritations in the world that I try to limit squabbles" and that "I tend to avoid anything labeled 'feminist' [because] it tends to be awfully strident." These seem to be the words of a writer who has a particularly pragmatic, practical, and unsentimental view of the world: that people's lives are "the most amusing jumble of things," and that there is, in spite of her best fictional efforts, very little explanation for, comprehension about, or resolution of, that "jumble of things" to be found. For every writer, however, there is the recognition and the description of that "jumble," and at that, Shirley Ann Grau has been doing an exemplary job for more than thirty years.

M.P.

BOOKS BY SHIRLEY ANN GRAU

NOVELS

The Hard Blue Sky. New York: Knopf, 1958.
The House on Coliseum Street. New York: Knopf, 1961; Avon, 1986.
The Keepers of the House. New York: Knopf, 1964; Avon, 1985.
The Condor Passes. New York: Knopf, 1971; Fawcett, 1973.
The Wind Shifting West. New York: Knopf, 1973.
Evidence of Love. New York: Knopf, 1977.

SHORT STORIES

The Black Prince and Other Stories. New York: Knopf, 1955.
Nine Women. New York: Knopf, 1985; Avon, 1987.

Kate Braverman

KATE BRAVERMAN, author of two novels and five books of poetry, lives in the Beverly Hills section of Los Angeles for safety and a good school for her seven-year-old daughter Gabrielle. Her heart and work, however, are closer to the Berkeley of the sixties or the Venice Beach section of Los Angeles or the barrio in East Los Angeles. Braverman is taut with energy and intellect, a brilliant woman who writes from a profound, fully articulated aesthetic that encompasses the political, the linguistic, and the personal. During our interview in her large study/bedroom, she was expressive not just with words but with dramatic gestures and frequent leaps for books and manuscripts, to read me a paragraph from her latest short story, or some lines from a poem, or a notice of her poetry readings.

She summarized her life succinctly. "I was born in Philadelphia; I grew up in Los Angeles. I was one of the flower children in the sixties. I graduated from high school in Berkeley and went to college in Berkeley — there is some part of me that will be forever Berkeley." She was active in all the protest movements and returned to Los Angeles in 1971 to become involved in the Venice Poetry Workshop. "I believe that I made a certain commitment in the sixties to be a certain kind of person, have a certain kind of sensibility and vision that would be permanent. There are aesthetic principles and moral principles that were implanted in me during this process . . . that come out in my work" which is "organic, and those aesthetic politics are part of the fiber of my being."

Palm Latitudes, a long poetic novel of the thoughts and experiences of three Hispanic women living on Flores Street in East Los Angeles, earned rave reviews from almost every critic in the country. Michiko Kakutani of the *New York Times* credited Braverman with "a magical, incantory voice and the ability to loft ordinary lives into the heightened world of myth." Braverman says that "the main thing I tried to do in *Palm Latitudes*" is "to tropicalize and feminize the language." Despite all the women writing today, "when we talk about literature, we're only talking about how men have written about the world." The women in *Palm Latitudes* are deeply intuitive and sensual. When she first started writing she "wanted to write like a man" but "over the years I've come to think more and more that you can write like a woman." In the novel she went with "my feminine sense of this region — a region I love." She perceives Los Angeles as "southern and hot and tropical and dense and overgrown" and believes that it has "a texture and scent and gods and reasons and a destiny that is different from the ordinary United States." She pointed out that "angular, cold church steeples and the sounds of little New England villages are very different from the sounds of a Palm Tree Plaza."

Some of the less positive reviews of *Palm Latitudes* came from a few feminists and from one Los Angeles paper. A Latin filmmaker reviewed it and said, " 'This woman doesn't understand life in the barrio and this is what it is really like' and proceeded to deliver a lecture. He said I called the Latin men insensitive and yet he behaved very much like an insensitive Latin male." Braverman, who speaks fluent Spanish, said that she "lived life in the barrio" but doesn't believe that her biography "should be anyone's business. Especially as a woman, it's so important to just deal with the work and not let them take away your legitimacy."

The novel was also attacked by some feminists because it clearly associated intuition and sensuality with women. "That's not done; that's considered essentialist, and it's the anti-essentialists that are powerful right now in the feminist movement." Braverman admitted that the novel "does say that women are different, but they own the language. I set out to use English in a way that I felt it had never been used before." She added that "Los Angeles, Our Lady, Queen of the Angels, is a female city." Braverman said she once believed that the idea of woman was a social construct, but her personal experience, especially "the experience of having a child, was quite edifying." Now she believes that by "being one woman, truly and wholly, you will be all women — tend one garden and you will birth worlds."

We talked about differences between critics' treatments of men and of women. Braverman said that "men want the same thing from their writers that they want from their wives, a certain type of predictability. For example, women are not allowed to write about hard drugs." As evidence that men writers are granted more freedom, she recalled that Larry Thornton, who had never left Indiana, wrote a book about Argentina and said, " 'As a writer, I need no passport for the realm of the imagination.' But there are different standards that apply to women. People have to know the biographical details, and those details are dealt with as being the character. The character and the author, there's this bleed between them. When one of my male students writes a book with spiritual audacity, it's called an 'epic urban tale,' whereas the same book written by a woman is another neurotic housewife having a long identity crisis."

Braverman agrees with many other writers I interviewed that "the novel doesn't belong to men any more; the novel belongs to women." She also noticed about ten or fifteen years ago that "all the interesting poetry was being written by women because their lives have changed. Women are having children without being married; they are having children and working. They have to live their politics." She also believes that "the novel doesn't belong to Anglo people that much any more." The novel "mutates or evolves and is not what it was in the fifties. The historical imperative now belongs to people with different accents and different rhythms, and it's this infusion that makes the novel continue to be dynamic." The novel was once about the "neurotic thoughts of an urban Anglo man," but "that story is over." Today, with the vast numbers of homeless people in cities, "the thing to do is go out with food to hand people." People are just not interested in "trivial neurotic things, the problems of whether you are going to get a divorce or stay with a company." She used "the Indian mythology of Mexico" in *Palm Latitudes* because "that is to me a vibrant and immediate and meaningful culture."

Braverman believes that emphasis on memory is "a quality about feminine sensibility." Her own interest in memory is related to the fact that "so much of the world I inhabit is not an empirically verifiable world. Creation myths, memory — the things that give us integrity and inform our lives are not really what we put in the bank or what we drive." Most Western literature, she says, "believes in empirically verifiable, logical progressions, whereas her own fiction, which she terms 'anthropological' in its vision, "believes in cycles, in wild leaps to magical positions."

Braverman is an associate professor of creative writing at California State at Los Angeles. She loves teaching and "I just live in Los Angeles as if I were on a small campus. I teach my classes, walk in the hills." She seldom goes out socially because "just being in a room with myself is almost more stimulation than I can bear." The job requirement she dislikes is driving on the freeway every day. In her ideal environment, "as stripped down as possible, I would just walk by the same manageable clump of trees, to my same manageable, small office every day." It is important for her to have a job "congruent with my sensibility" because, with a child to raise, no other kind would allow her to write. "I'm doing more than I can do right now."

Braverman's students call her regime for writing "Braverman's

Boot Camp. I tell them, 'You have to give away your TV; you have to read out loud two hours a day minimum, Neruda or the Bible aloud. You have to walk in the hills alone and always carry a notebook.' " Although for many years "I was able to rely on inspiration," she now believes strongly that "the creative life is a set of disciplines. I keep myself removed from the culture; I don't go to movies or read newspapers." Except for time spent with her daughter, "I am ruthless with my time." Braverman has been following this regime for seven years and describes the experience as "the sound of one hand clapping."

Braverman objects to the distinction between fiction and poetry as artificial, even a form of prejudice. "I've got a unified, hemispheric, aesthetic theory of literature. There are certain forms of literature that the in-vogue sensibility doesn't want to deal with. It's like racism and sexism. When we say 'it's like poetry,' we are saying we don't really have to look at it, it's not important or really that serious. It's an artificial category designed to hurt a certain kind of fiction that maybe is not going to sell." In fact, she asserted, all good writing is built "one good line at a time. You build a novel the same way you do a pyramid. One word, one stone at a time, underneath a full moon when the fingers bleed."

In her own work she moves easily back and forth between poetry and fiction. "Whenever I get lost in a novel I just throw a poem in. What it does is flare up, and it's so illuminated that I'm able to see where to go. I write between these illuminations." Braverman wrote her first poem shortly after graduating from Berkeley as an anthropology major. "I was writing stories the way I thought stories were written." They were about "lawyers' wives and other things with no connection whatsoever to me. I was working very hard but had not found the dialect in which I was fluent."

Then one day she had "a spiritual experience. The walls fell down and I wrote my first poem, only one page long. The lines just stopped because if you are writing anything that matters, your body tells you where to stop. Writing a poem is physical." A few years after that spiritual experience, Braverman returned to

Los Angeles and started giving highly theatrical poetry readings in coffee houses, often with music, "trying to shake, rattle, and roll here on the streets and alleys of Los Angeles." She believes that "if I had gone to New York or London I'd be putting [spires on] Gothic churches and writing the colors of the Danube and the Thames; I'd be gray and metallic and more conventionally acceptable." That UCLA always imports poets from the East Coast for readings confirms her belief that Los Angeles "practices regional self-loathing."

Braverman says that, whereas a principal influence on the novel in the fifties was film, for her generation it was music. If you think of the American novel "in terms of the bleed into cinematic sorts of structural premises that went on at one point in its evolution, you see the energy of the cinema going in and how writers dealt with it. The influence for a writer my age is the rock music of the sixties." This music has given her "a sense of cadence and rhythm" and a feeling "that I am not writing but composing and what I do with words are riffs and improvisations." For her fortieth birthday in February, "I've got this wonderful punk band that is going to play some dates with me. They back me up and we have live arrangements with the drums on the poems."

When I told Braverman that her poems have raw energy and searing images that remind me of Plath, she said, "I think that the two great poets in English this century are T. S. Eliot and Plath." When her students read Plath aloud, she sees "pleasure come over their faces, because most people in those classes have never said a line of poetry before." She admires Plath for "her sense of persona, her technical dazzle" and also loves "the Spanish poets Neruda, Garcia Lorca, Octavio Paz." She talked about the "magical realism" of Garcia Marquez and other Latin writers, and said, "They do it with a capital M; I try to do magical realism with a capital R because that to me is American, that realistic sense, multidimensional characters." Among American novelists "I like Joan Didion a lot and I used to like all the boys, Bellow, Philip Roth — never Mailer or Updike." She has taught Salinger's *Franny and Zooey* to her feminist writing class with exciting results. Franny "starves herself and has many of the mannerisms found in women — she puts herself down — putting a feminist interpretation on it is so interesting."

Braverman has recently been writing short stories, and before I left she read to me parts of two, "Desert Blues" and "Falling in October." They are linked stories about an emotionally fragile writer named Diana Barrington, very different from her other writings, set in the midst of a plague in a post-nuclear southern California. I found her reading powerful and disturbing, and she said, "I'm in a state of terror. No one has seen these. I'm afraid to send them to my editor." Six months after the interview, the story "Falling in October" was published in the *Los Angeles Times Magazine* together with stories by Harriet Doerr and Amy Tan and two male California writers.

Braverman also wrote a poem called "Falling in October" ("I fell into this riff about falling in October") which was beautifully printed in a limited edition. Before I left she gave me a signed copy inscribed "En la dia de trembler," in honor of an earthquake that had shaken Los Angeles early that morning. The poem is a love poem that ends, "Days later I am still shaking. / You say abandon yourself / To the possibilities / And I remove my skin." Kate Braverman is a serious writer with the courage to explore and the craft to exploit all the possibilities of literary art.

K.U.H.

BOOKS BY KATE BRAVERMAN

NOVELS

Lithium for Medea. New York: Harper & Row, 1979; Penguin, 1989.

Palm Latitudes. New York: Linden Press/Simon & Schuster, 1988; Penguin, 1989.

SHORT STORIES

Squandering the Blue: Stories. New York: Fawcett, 1990.

POETRY

Milk Run. Momentum Press, 1977.
Lullaby for Sinners. New York: Harper & Row, 1979.
Hurricane Warnings. Illuminati, 1987.
Season of Women. Illuminati, 1990.
Postcard from August. Illuminati, 1990.

Louise Erdrich

MY INTERVIEW with Louise Erdrich took place while she was trying to hold onto her "wonderful, healthy" *active* eight-month-old baby (ten and a half pounds at birth!) in Cornish, New Hampshire, and I was trying, in New Jersey, to hold onto my $1.99 rubber dart-gun gadget from Radio Shack that allows you to both tape and talk to someone on the telephone.

The baby, Aza Mirion, is the third child of Erdrich and Michael Dorris, author of the much acclaimed nonfiction book on fetal alcohol syndrome *The Broken Cord* (1989), and of *A Yellow Raft in Blue Water* (1987). They also have three children who were adopted by Dorris before their marriage, one of whom suffers from fetal alcohol syndrome.

Erdrich is the author of *Love Medicine* (covering the years 1934–1984), *The Beet Queen* (1934–1980), and *Tracks* (1912–1924), three parts of a four-part backward spiral into the lives and lusts of the Kashpaws, Lamartines, and Morriseys, characters and families who grew mainly from the richness of her mixed Chippewa and German heritage. No one who has read Erdrich will forget Eli Kashpaw, a loner who "couldn't rub two words together and get a spark," or "stark and bony" Pauline Puyat of *Tracks*. She tells the story of Fleur Pillager, "wild as a filthy wolf," who "messed with evil." Fleur is a hysterical martyr who wears potato sacking for underwear, her shoes on the wrong feet, and betrays the Chippewa as part of her own misguided penance and self-destruction. With Erdrich's unique genius for creating a mythical space called Argus, she has given the reader a mysterious, lusty, comical world full of elders, shamans, and mystics who are both foreign and, at the same time, familiar to the more culturally homogenized reader.

"I think," she said, "that if you believe in any sort of race memory, I am getting a triple whammy from my background — in regard to place and home and space." First of all, "the connection that is Chippewa is a connection to a place and to a background, and to the comfort of knowing, somehow, that you are connected here before *and before* the first settler. Add to that the (I think) overblown German Romanticism about place" inherited from her father's family. "Add into that that the German part of my family is most probably converted Jews" and the Jewish "search for place, and you have this 'awful' mix. A person can only end up writing — in order to resolve it. You can even throw in the French part of the background — the wanderers, the voyagers, which my people also come from. There is just no way to get away from all this, and the only way to resolve it, without going totally crazy looking for a home, is to write about it." The "Germans have a word for it — *unziemliches Verlangen,* unseemly longing" — and it's the incorrect kind of longing that you have. I always put [those people longing for home] into this box and that's the label that I give it, the unseemly longing that [Germans] have. It's really unfortunate. Someone said, 'I don't know how the average person feels the pain of death and the pain of longing and the joy — these great extremes — without art.' I feel that I am very fortunate to have some place to put [these longings] because otherwise they would become very destructive."

Erdrich said that she was "born and brought up in the flattest, most open, exposed part of the United States. The Red River valley of North Dakota hasn't a tree in it in certain places. I *love* imagining and thinking back to those spaces, although I write [now] in a very enclosed place" of "trees and coziness. That's what the landscape is about out here." But there "*is* a certain freedom in and peace that comes from home, the feeling of having a homeland."

I wanted to know whether the open spaces associated both with some Native American nations, and with American fiction generally, remained true for the women in her fiction, or whether Erdrich's fictional spaces, like the spaces of so many of the writers in this collection, were closed. Adelaide (in *Beet Queen*), who flies off with Omar, Aeronaut Extraordinaire, leaves her children behind at the ironically designated amusement park. Adelaide, and June Kashpaw, who, in a drunken stupor, freezes to death in an endless expanse of snow, were two of the characters I had in mind. These seemed to be two examples of women in open, undefined space which becomes, in effect, closed, limiting, and entrapping. Erdrich agreed that "it has a lot to do with where I grew up. I set myself back in that pure, empty landscape whenever I am working on something . . . [because] there's nothing like it. . . . It's the place where everything comes from." These characters, she continued, "*were* out in that open space, but their destination was home. June headed out into that open space, she was going across it, but she was heading home. She was heading into that wonderful and difficult mixture of family and place that mysteriously works on a person, that is home."

She added that Dot, the non-Native American character in *Beet Queen* who "is flying up in the cropduster's plane, up in pure space (which is the atmosphere), also makes a decision to come back, to come home, and to be at her home with her mother. The one person who doesn't make that decision is Adelaide, who gets into the plane and flies off into nothingness. And it is a nothingness of madness for her, as a character." She leaves her children mired in their own vulnerability and helplessness, in sharp contrast to the air images which are associated with her as the missing mother. "You see her later," said Erdrich, "unable to reconcile her longings — with her life — unable to ever get over the fact that she has abandoned her children for this space and for this freedom."

The freedom of open space "is there but it's nothing that someone stays in. People aren't 'lighting out for the territory.' The women in my books are lighting out for home." She added that "going home for most people is like trying to recapture childhood. It's an impossible task; you're not a child, and unless your parents have, by some grace of God, grown up with you, it's almost impossible to go back and stay and live. In extraordinary families there are people who can do this, but it's not done very much any more." The treks and journeys in her work, I suggested, are both a desire to leave and a longing to return. "I think it's both," said Erdrich. "And I don't think there's any judgment in that." She said that she "loves going back [home] and that it's a combination of true complexity [because I have] a very large extended family and there's a drama per minute. But it's also very comforting. . . . I have parents who really have become friends over the years."

I asked her if she ever had thought of moving back, of going home. "I think about it a lot, and I think it's quite impossible. I am probably an Easterner who mistakenly grew up in the Midwest. I never felt very accepted or at home in my hometown. There are terrific people there but I found growing up there difficult because the emphasis is on conventionality. You have to conform, because otherwise there is a lot of psychic pain that you have to go through. My parents happen to be truly intelligent, and my father is a little eccentric in his intelligence. And it is only after years and years and years that he was able to find a niche where he can be the person he is and be loved and accepted in the town. That is terribly important, and as a child growing up I was subjected to all sorts of pressures to 'be nice,' to conform, to be [a certain] sort of person. . . . I found it extremely difficult. I have thought often about going back but I don't think I would. I don't think I *want* to in the end. I love being out here [in New Hampshire], really being ignored."

We talked at length about silences, about whether her fictional women had made a tacit decision to be silent, as have many of the fictional women created by the writers in this collection. I asked her whether this was linked instead to the experience of the Native American woman. "It's very true that if I were writing about a traditional Native American woman you would say, 'This is a woman that has been silenced because she's not allowed to speak in her native language.' " She mentioned Lulu Lamartine, who appears in all three novels (producing eight sons along the way by eight different men) as "someone who has an interesting background. This doesn't appear in the fiction, but she is sent to a boarding school, and in government boarding schools during the time she would have been going to school, children would have been punished for speaking native languages. So she has a very lyrical and very unconventional way of speaking." Lamartine speaks "the way I would like to speak but can only do in fiction. But she is someone who was never allowed to speak and is punished for speaking the language of her childhood, so she grows up taking on English and, because of her peculiarities" her language very much reflects that. "You find this with a lot of native women of a certain generation, having their own way with the language, using it in an interesting way — and she does that." Like many people of various cultures who were denied language and the subsequent ability to name things, she is disempowered. Erdrich said that Lulu Lamartine was "punished for [language], punished for being your most fluent and absorbing and interesting self, because self and language are so much the same." There is an inalienable bond between "what you express and who you are" and the denial of Lulu's native language had to "have been an act that destroyed the self. We really have very few people who talk a lot about what that was like. You read some people who have reflected a lot more thoroughly on what language deprivation does to a person. Although I am *not* making any comparisons here — I think of Primo Levi's reflection in *The Drowned and the Saved* on what it was like to be thrust into a concentration camp setting and not to have the language of survival, not to have German" — it is "a truly profound reflection on the entire idea of being silent. I am *not* making a connection between being a child in a boarding school and being in this other horrific holocaust." It is fair to say, however, that in both instances you lose the ability to be connected, to link with those forces that you perceive as protective.

Erdrich's three novels are also defined by her use of nonchronological time, and by the reappearance at various ages of the same characters. I asked her if these techniques, associated with Modernism, were related to the amorphous quality of what she has called "the insistent tug of memory." "It probably does have to do with that — the unreliability of memory at any given moment. The memory is so unfixed, so fluid, you never know what's going to surface. I have a hold on a certain number of characters, it seems, so when a story surfaces it is usual that one of the people is in the story. I can't really go to the source and say, 'Here's what I want' and 'I want it in a nice package.' There is no way to control what happens, or when, or when somebody comes up with a story." I related incidents told to me by Rosellen Brown and Francine Prose, about taking down, almost like stenographers, stories that were dictated by the characters. She said "there are moments like that, but it rarely happens. . . . I truly think that you can't go and stock your material, you have to leave the door open, and whatever *chooses* you, chooses *you*. You can't go and wrestle it to the ground. I've never been able to do that. There are times when I'm desperate to talk about something or write about something in particular, but it's never been my real choice." I asked her which characters keep coming back most often. "Right now, it's Dot and Marie [in *Beet Queen*] but at any given time it's someone else. Who knows why?"

Louise Erdrich told me that she "grew up with all the accepted truths [of Catholicism] but," she added, "I don't have a central metaphor for my life. I only have chaos. I now read that there is some kind of order even in chaos, and that's comforting." What seems more comforting for her readers is that she continues to reach back into the not so deeply submerged fullness of her multilayered racial memory to produce fiction that is full of sexual and spiritual power, death, derangement, the miraculous and the mundane. Since it was praised so often by the other writers in this collection, who are of various ethnic, religious, and racial backgrounds, it is clear that from that chaos has come something universal and of inestimable value.

M.P.

BOOKS BY LOUISE ERDRICH

NOVELS

Love Medicine. New York: Henry Holt, 1984; Bantam, 1985.
The Beet Queen. New York: Henry Holt, 1986; Bantam, 1987; Caedmon, 1990.
Selected from Love Medicine. New York: Literary Volunteers of New York City Staff, 1988.
Tracks. New York: Henry Holt, 1988; Harper/Perennial, 1989.
[With Michael Dorris]. *The Crown of Columbus*. New York: HarperCollins, 1991.

POETRY

Jacklight: Poems. New York: Henry Holt, 1984; Abacus, 1990.
Baptism of Desire: Poems. New York: HarperCollins, 1991.

TEXTBOOK

Imagination. Westerville, Ohio: Charles Merrill, 1981.

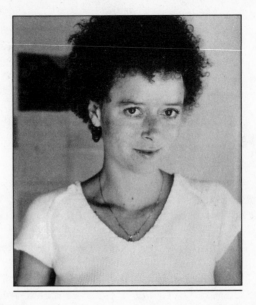

Anne Lamott

ANNE LAMOTT lives on the ground floor of a large house built on the side of a wooded canyon in Mill Valley, California, a small town just across the Golden Gate Bridge from San Francisco. The top of the house is level with the road, and hundreds of stone steps descend to her apartment. Lamott herself is small, spunky, funny, completely candid and (at the time of our interview) pregnant. At thirty-five, she is the author of four well reviewed novels, most recently *All New People*, set in Tiburon in the sixties, when that now-elegant suburb was a small railroad town. (The *New York Times Book Review* called *All New People* "a comedy in the best, classical sense [that] faces the dark and still manages to give forth the sound of laughter.")

All of Lamott's books are set in the small rural towns of Marin County, where she grew up; her characters are usually warm, funny, generous, and often economically marginal. When I asked whether her characters were distinctively Californian, she said, "I try to write about what we're all like on the inside, what it is to be human, what it is to be female," but she added that the communities in her novels are "very distinctly Californian. They're not New York or Upstate New York. They're not even Cambridge. They are not funky little artist colonies on the East Coast. They are really distinctly West Coast." Lamott said that one meaning of California is "the last place you can go; it's as far away as you can go."

Lamott thinks of herself as a "Northern California writer. Southern California to me is about 98 percent of the people trying desperately to get what 2 percent have. Everybody is sort of on the make. Northern California to me isn't about that; it's about people who have sacrificed some degree of sophistication and possibly being at the top in their profession because it's so beautiful here and really so peaceful." She says people in Northern California are "hooked in kind of desperately to the natural world. We walk, we hike and we bicycle ride. They don't bicycle ride in L.A."

Lamott was born in San Francisco and has lived in Northern California all her life. Except for a "phase in high school and early college where I thought I wanted to be a professor of philosophy," she "always knew I was going to be a writer." Her father, Kenneth Lamott, was a professional nonfiction writer. "I knew it could be done and I just loved the attention. I remember when teachers would come up to me and be really impressed by something that I had written and it was such a rush. I just wanted to do it again and again and again."

At Goucher College she wrote a column for the newspaper. "It was during the McGovern/Nixon campaign, and I was writing a lot of really impassioned, bleeding-heart liberal treatises. Some of them were really funny and some of them were very mockish but very passionate. That's when I knew that that was what I was going to end up doing. I grew up around books, around it being the center of everything, books and the literary world."

After two years she dropped out of Goucher and became a Kelly girl. "I was writing a lot, doing the all night coffee house routine [at] the Haven on Polk Street [in San Francisco]. I would write all night; I'd be tortured; I smoked and drank a lot so I looked the right part. I knew I was funny, but I didn't really have anything to say." She finally got a permanent job on Billie Jean King's magazine *Women's Sports,* where she wrote "little pieces. I was doing stuff like headlines, joke stuff, but then I was also going home and being the tortured writer. I'd go home and open up a jug of red wine. I wasn't even twenty-one yet; I remember because it was always hard to get the amount of alcohol I wanted, but I'd smoke all night and drink and be a famous writer in my mind. I wrote and wrote. My dad's thing always was, if you are going to write, you sit down every single day or five days a week, whatever you are going to commit to, and you write, and you practice it like you practice piano scales, and you are bound to get better. I was luckily able to get that going and that's really what saved me — that I put in the time every single day, no matter what."

In 1974 Billie Jean King fired her editor "over a political issue" and "the whole editorial department quit." Unemployment compensation gave Lamott means and time to write. She described the pain/joy of committed writing. "I love the actual composing of stories. It's just that magical thing that happens when you sit down [at the typewriter]. You saw something on the bus, you overheard a snippet of dialogue on the bus and you start trying to recreate it, and pretty soon you are putting all the details in, and it's triggered your imagination and these old, old, thirty-year-old memories." As you are weaving in the memories, "all of a sudden you are trying to imagine who the little girl really was on the bus. You remember who you were and then pretty soon you are just jamming and time is passing and you are just like a musician jamming. It's such a ball, even though it's torture sometimes."

Lamott wrote a lot of vignettes after leaving the magazine but didn't really have anything to say until her father became ill when she was twenty-three. "He said, 'I'm going to write down my version. Why don't you write down your version of this?' " Her version evolved into her first novel, which deals with a family's idiosyncratic responses to their father's surgery for brain cancer. "Probably half of *Hard Laughter* was written before he got sick but it was just about the town, the family, it was about the stuff with the best woman friend, Kathleen, who was several people rolled into one. All of a sudden there was some structure and there was some order, and there was a point A where the book begins and a point B where the book ends. I became a writer."

Lamott was in her mid-twenties when *Hard Laughter* was published. "My dad died in 1979. Then I wrote *Rosie*. Then I just moved so many places. . . . I lived in Petaluma for about a year; I lived in Tiburon for a while." *Rosie* is about a spunky little girl who tries to prevent her mother from falling into alcoholism. The book turns upon an incident in which Rosie is sexually molested by her best friend's father. When I mentioned that many women's novels are now dealing with child molestation, Lamott said that she met many women around 1979 who were molested as children. "I started looking into it [and found that] it was totally in the closet, child abuse. It had not come out yet; it had not had the 'TV disease-of-the-week' treatment yet." She talked to a child protection agency which told her that "four to five [out of ten] women were molested by someone in the family by the time they were eighteen."

To understand the character of Rosie, she also talked to a lot of seven- and eight-year-old girls. She found that they hated alcohol, partly because they associated it with doctors, but "the other thing they experienced with alcohol is that their parents left . . . either just left the house or left in that way you leave when you are loaded and you become a different person, quite possibly a bad person or a neglectful person. I was such an alcoholic that I knew I could write about it." Lamott says that she is Elizabeth in *Rosie*, "Ray is me, too, so is James, so is Rosie. If you put everyone together you would probably have me."

Lamott is very open about her own addicted past and very generous in helping addicts, both publicly and privately. She believes that her problems are related to the suppression of emotions in her home and her alienation as a child. "I was a class clown, but everything always hurt. My feelings always hurt, my insides always hurt." *All New People* is about this kind of pain. "The main character's name is Nanny and the family isn't my real family, but the girl is definitely me. It's just about that excruciating shyness and that excruciating sense of alienation. That you are somehow inherently flawed and that all the other girls are okay, and that they look okay and they seem okay and their families are okay, and you can see that your family isn't okay, that your family is in fact a mess and it's a big secret. It's that thing about comparing your insides to other people's outsides. Other people's outsides look good, they look like a TV sitcom family, and you know how hard it is on your family. There is never quite enough money, whatever the internal traumas and conflicts are. It turned out nobody is okay. It turned out that the people who were really popular, the eighth grade girls, were totally un-okay, they hated themselves, they are [now] shy and sick and using and drinking."

Lamott says that all of her books are about being lost and being found. The character who "finds" others is usually a woman, and Lamott said that *All New People* talks about "that profound relief about finding your best friend when you are a woman. It's one of the most profound feelings of relief that you can ever have. Then you are okay and you are found." About the most nurturing of her heroines, Louise in *Joe Jones*, Lamott said, "She would just breast-feed you back to life if she could. Part of it is beauty and part of it is co-dependence. Part of it is that beautiful huge heart; it's like the hugest gift God can give you, and the other part of it is the sickness. . . . Women became that way [because they were] told that they were going to be abandoned if they weren't that way, if they didn't fix people. Louise is the higher power in *Joe Jones*. Louise is the only person who really believes in God and she is also the higher power of that family. A lot of us were the higher power for our families, mostly the girls. We took on fixing people and we took on using our blood as crazy glue and would lose blood to fix other people and became givers, just huge givers. And part of it was about having very low self-esteem. It wasn't [all] about this radiant large heart that God had given us."

Lamott believes that the only way out of this dilemma for

women is "to get into recovery for it. I think it is a disease that kills people, co-dependence. I think you probably have to go to a twelve-step program to do it. You certainly need therapy to do it. It kills people because it's about sucking down your own feelings. As soon as you are sucking down your own feelings, then you get into all those stress-related disorders, some of which lead to death. My dad died of a stress-related disorder, brain cancer. His last book was called *Anti-Stress: How to Stop Killing Yourself.* He was very New England, very stiff-upper-lipped; we were just not allowed to be emotional in my family. If you were having emotions, it was, 'Okay, honey, you're having emotions, why don't you go to your room.' We went to our room without food, that's how we were punished." Lamott has learned little by little that "you do get to have feelings, you don't have to be polite. A lot of us were raised that the most important thing was politeness." Lamott says that her own recovery has been made possible by "a lot of therapy and Al-Anon."

Although she believes that women have a harder time professionally than men, "men have paid through the nose for this [privilege] and it's why they die so early. I think they have shut down in so many ways, [but] they do get to concentrate in a way that women don't get to because women haven't shut down in those same ways. Men are just so good at being workaholic. It's . . . their drug of choice." She thinks that women, because they "don't use work as a drug," have more "aware time" in the course of a day than men. "A woman who goes through the express line is going to have an entirely different experience than a man who goes through the express line, because if the person ahead of him or her is very sad or upset, the woman is going to get involved. The woman is going to listen and to help. The woman is going to carry things out to the car and find something to say that may be some kind of bandaid for the person. The woman's heart is going to be engaged. The man is going to be wanting to look away, and not wanting to make eye contact," or if he's a writer, "studying it for possible details." In the life of a woman writer, "all these things are marbled into whatever hours there are for writing; they are just marbled with 'I hope Natalie's okay (Natalie's a best friend), I should call her, I should make myself work.' It's probably not going to come up for the man in that same way. I think it is probably easier to concentrate if you are a man."

Lamott believes that these differences between men and women explain "why women's novels are dominating the country. People are getting hip, going through a lot of changes. There is a big movement going on in this country to get aware, a huge twelve-step movement moving in huge droves that's about starting to tell the truth, the emotional truth, and it's about all the old rules having been broken. It's about things not being anywhere as neat and tidy and orderly as men would have them be."

Lamott's business card, by way of protest against the category of "woman writer," says "Anne Lamott, girl writer." She says that women writers are not taken as seriously as men who write. "Someone like Susan Sontag eventually has to be made kind of a joke [because she is] that brilliant and that accessible and that outspoken. People think of her as sort of a self-parody. If she were a man, if she were John Kenneth Galbraith, she would just be revered totally. Men writers aren't thought of as 'men writers'; they are thought of as great writers. It would be fine if the men writers would be called 'men writers.' It just never comes up — 'Updike [or] Bellow, he's a really great man writer.' " But we frequently hear, " 'Margaret Atwood is a really incredible woman writer.' I say what a crock of shit."

I asked Lamott what writers she read when growing up and what writers she reads now. She said that she "started out with Pippi Longstocking; I think a lot of us who did that ended up being trouble-making women. Of course I read those *Little Women, Little Men* books and loved Nancy Drew." In high school, "I was really taken by Vonnegut, [and] like everybody, I loved Salinger." She has always loved Virginia Woolf and Jane Austen and George Eliot. "More than any other book, I think I love *Middlemarch* the best of all books."

Among contemporary writers "I really love the South and Central Americans. I belong to this reading group — in fact, it meets tonight — along with about six other writers. Alice Adams is in it, Deirdre English from *Mother Jones,* and four men. What we read is usually the most important thing I'm reading, and we've been reading recently J.M. Coetzee from South Africa and Nadine Gordimer. I really love Gordimer. I'm friends with and I love Ethan Canin and . . . I love Alice Adams's books. I love Evan Connell's books; I think he's a genius. I love Don Carpenter. Alice Munro really knocks me out."

Her "secret" is an addiction to Stephen King. "I'm really ashamed of myself, but I'm always so happy when there is a new Stephen King book out. It's the best way I can check out — there is nothing left I'm using, [but] if I have a Stephen King book I'm completely covered. It means I can come home, it doesn't matter what's happened in my life. That's the best thing about a book."

Lamott says that she always feels behind because she can't afford to buy books until they come out in paper or come to the library. She supports herself completely through her writing and has done so "for a long time. I think of myself as continually poor, but I guess I'm not. I do this food review which pays about two-thirds of my bills every month. It's like hit or miss, rain or shine, feast or famine. You get an advance and then you go out and get the facial and go to Jiffy Lube instead of getting someone to put some oil in your car. You do that for about three weeks and life goes back to normal and there is no money again for a while. I've done a bunch of short pieces, nonfiction. Those have paid." She has not worked at a nine-to-five job for a long time — "I think I'm completely unemployable."

Lamott turned down a large advance for *Joe Jones* because she felt betrayed by the East Coast publisher of *Rosie.* "The promise had been that if *Rosie* got the reviews we were hoping for, there would be all this advertising. It got wonderful reviews and there was not one cent ever spent on advertising. Then my editor went somewhere else and he made me a wonderful offer on the new book and I thought, 'I hate that whole East Coast, I hate what happened to me on *Rosie.*' I took an advance that was about one-third from North Point because I was just so desperate to be at a small press, somebody that was out here. If I have a problem I call Berkeley." North Point now publishes all of her books. "They put ads out everywhere for *Joe;* they really pushed *Rosie;* they put it in the front of their catalogue. They pushed it with Farrar, Straus [the distributor], and that means they will push it with a bookstore. I have nothing but raves for North Point."

Before leaving I asked Lamott if she was excited about having a baby. She answered emphatically, "Yes, I'm really happy to have a baby. I've always wanted babies. I hoped I would have a husband, too, of course. I'd always been with men who didn't or couldn't make a commitment to me or men that were married. Now I'm so single; I'm really profoundly single. A friend of mine, Don Carpenter the novelist, said (this is when I was being friendly with the father still), 'Support is not going to come from that man, it's going to come from your tribe; the tribe is going to be there for you.' I am real active in church, I'm real active in the community, I have a lot of really tight friends and that's my tribe. I've got all these people around — women, my little brother, a bunch of people."

Pregnancy has made her feel unprotected. "I realize why people have had husbands, men around. It might be the hormones, but I have felt so vulnerable, just incredibly vulnerable. I felt a lot of times like a really ugly, skinny, twelve-year-old kid that is going to have a baby. When you're pregnant you should have a football player around to run interference." However, she says that at the moment, "I'm really not afraid. I'm glad I'm religious. I think it's going to make it easier." When I said that it takes courage to be a single parent, she retorted, "I think it takes guts to be a *parent.* It's a good profession to be a single mother in. I'll just rock the baby with one foot."

In August 1989 Lamott gave birth to a baby boy named Sam. I have run into them both twice since then, once in a restaurant, and once in a bookstore at a signing of *All New People.* At the signing Sam was getting even more attention than the book, and I thought how aptly its title reflects the integration of Lamott's life as mother, friend, woman, and writer.

K.U.H.

BOOKS BY ANNE LAMOTT

NOVELS

Hard Laughter. New York: Viking, 1980; North Point Press, 1987.
Rosie. New York: Viking, 1983; North Point Press, 1989.
Joe Jones. San Francisco: North Point Press, 1985; Ballantine, 1987.
All New People. San Francisco: North Point Press, 1989.

Josephine Humphreys

JOSEPHINE HUMPHREYS, who says she is "a social recluse," was educated at Duke and at Yale, and lives quietly in Charleston, South Carolina. She arrived in New York on one of those snowy weekends when the winter-weary inhabitants are energized by some event of fleeting celebrity or instant social significance to leave their insulated apartments for the sleety streets. This time it was the Andy Warhol exhibit, then playing to full houses of art groupies and other enthusiasts of popular culture, and the lines at the Museum of Modern Art were long, long, long. (The day before, Humphreys was on her way to Brooklyn in what turned out to be an unlicensed cab. The cops were very nice and "no one got arrested.") The interview was quickly moved to a luncheonette down the block, where the English muffins were half raw, the coffee was cold, and the waiters were screaming at each other in Greek, Spanish, and Korean. Fortunately, you don't need good food, peace and quiet, or southern ambiance if you have Josephine Humphreys to talk with.

Dreams of Sleep, which won the 1985 Ernest Hemingway Award from PEN for a first work of fiction, was followed in 1987 by *Rich in Love,* which Pat Conroy said "is an even better book than [her] first novel." Alan Cheuse added that it "might have been composed by one of the elder states[women] of the South. Kate Chopin. Ellen Glasgow. Flannery O'Connor. Eudora Welty. And Josephine Humphreys. That's my list."

There is no question that Josephine Humphreys is one of the best writers in the South, but what this interviewer finds most exceptional in her work are the unusual and varied versions of mothers and daughters. Alice Reese, the native South Carolinian in *Dreams* who is trapped in her own inertia, lives with her two daughters and her obstetrician husband in the nongentrified part of Charleston, and is learning about "the loneliness of marriage" and about "how effortlessly and smoothly things go from ripe to rotten; it is nothing but a waiting game." Iris Moon, her seventeen-year-old babysitter, one of those people put on the earth to nurture it, is the daughter of an emotionally impoverished mother and a deserting father who sweeps through town periodically like a modern marauder to abuse his former wife and their daughter. As Alice's husband (who is having an affair with his impatient nurse, Claire) remarks, "they all seem sad . . . the nurses, the women driving Volvos through the streets, with sunglasses on their heads and sadness in their faces. What can you do when the women are like that?"

Rich in Love is the story of seventeen-year-old Lucille Odom, whose mother walks out of the house and out of her twenty-seven-year marriage, and whose erratic sister Rae comes home from her job in Washington — pregnant and disenchanted. In this novel as well, there are various "missing" or maladjusted mother figures who need taking care of, and wise, precocious, and durable daughters who take on that job. "Lucille makes her own little world. Her world is her brain. She is very removed from things around her but not the same way that Alice is in *Dreams of Sleep.* It's more of an adolescent construction really. And it's very similar to what I did as a teenager — operate in the real world but everything important is completely hidden from everybody else."

I asked Humphreys why she wrote about mothers and daughters, as so many women do, and whether she had consciously chosen to do so. There are issues "I think about, but not consciously. . . . When I write there is detachment that prevents me from analyzing what I'm doing. . . . I can't sit down and say, 'I am going to write about mothers and daughters.' It's too much of a conscious interpretation." She said that she "was trained as a conscious interpreter . . . and I couldn't write until I dismantled that whole apparatus of critical approach." Now "I try not to ever ask myself, 'What am I *doing* here, what does this mean?' . . . and ironically, a lot more comes out — the real stuff that I want to say." Humphreys said that no "sustained narrative in my two books reflects real events" although "my own childhood and family are real important in the making of the stories." The events "are so transformed, but I know that underneath every word and three removes away is something actual. I think," she said, "that I write about mothers because in real life I find it very difficult to understand my relationship with my mother and I don't really deal with it. I've removed myself from it and I feel more comfortable writing about it in a fictional mode than I would if I were to tell the true story. I think one of the reasons it comes up as a subject for fiction is that it is a difficult and complex thing to deal with in real life so we come at it sideways and in disguise and on more neutral ground." That way "you don't have to tangle with it in your heart."

Humphreys is now the mother of two boys, but as a child her "whole world was girlhood. I didn't even know any boys. . . . I didn't have a whole view but it was interesting in that I had a very specific and intense view of girlhood. If I'd had daughters I might not be able to write the same things [because] in writing *Rich in Love,* I found myself drifting back to thinking about girls, thinking about the relationship of a girl and a mother." Her own mother, she said, "ended up living a truly isolated life with [an] amazing brain that consumed books, [but she did] everything she could do to still stay at home and be removed." So this subject matter is "not something I would have chosen, I didn't really want to do it, but that's what came."

We talked about the ways in which women have become the safekeepers of the memories in which families are invested. Her mother, who went to Vassar but left school to get married, was "the custodian of all the information and the genealogy," but as a teenager Humphreys "didn't want to hear any of the family mythology. I thought it was very limiting and restrictive. . . . I have a feeling that in the South it's worse. In my part of the South there's such a big emphasis on the past and the need to continue and to not break with traditions. This need to preserve the past and the mythology comes from fear, and I don't want it. I don't want that fear for myself, and I don't want it for my children, so I rejected it, and in that process was able to understand it and become more comfortable with it. I get along well with my mother" and "it's very comforting and reassuring to me that we were able to come to an understanding after those bad years." Humphreys spoke for many daughters when she said that "I was never sure what she wanted me to be; I could never figure it out. I could never figure out what was the *right* thing to do, so I actually began my adult life doing the same thing she had. I was in graduate school and had done everything exactly right and had fellowships, good grades, and I quit, got married, continued to teach but neither one made me happy. Writing was a way to do both; I can do something I think is important but I'm still in the family situation that she wanted."

Her parents, she added, "told me from age four that I was good at [writing]. How did they know? I think they made it up, I think they liked the idea, and I believed them. It was something I could do, and wanted to do, and that they wanted for me." One of the positive aspects of living in this "girl world" was that Humphreys was "never aware of any limitations on me because of my gender. . . . My parents never indicated that there was any reason that I couldn't do anything that I wanted to do. I thought it was possible to have the traditional southern life and to be a lawyer, be a doctor, be a writer." It was only later, at Yale, for instance (where the one women graduate students' dorm was full and it was too far and too dangerous to walk from her apartment to the campus), and in publishing, that she became aware of the limitations on women.

Humphreys says that in her writing, imagination is as important as memory. "I think a lot of my narrative, my ideas . . . come
[as much] from my reading as they do from my experience. Reading for me was always the most important thing. As a child I *read*
more than I *did,* and so in many ways my memories are not only
of real events but of books and of stories and of ideas." When she
was writing *Rich in Love,* Humphreys said, her mother "said to
me one afternoon, and she had said this before, 'You live in your
own little world.' So the next morning that line went into my
novel, but it is said by an older sister. Rae tells Lucille, 'You live in
your own little world,' and Lucille says, 'She was right, half right;
it was my own but it wasn't little,' and that is really for me the
little seed."

It's natural to think of privacy and silence, issues that are
pervasive in her novels, when Humphreys says that "one of the
things that we were never allowed to do was to write a letter to
the newspaper. We read everything and discussed it at home" but
if "somebody said, 'I think I'll write a letter to the newspaper,' my
parents would turn white in the face. Being public in any way,
going on the stage, taking a part in a play, was a terrible danger —
something you were not supposed to do." When it looked as if
her novels would be published, her father said, " 'I don't want my
friends to see me in your book,' and I said, 'Well, you're not *in* it.
Of course you're not in it. . . . He said, 'Well, there's a father in
the book, isn't there?' I figured that I knew what I was doing and
I was careful to not actually use them in any substantive way —
except in the deepest way that nobody else would notice." After
Dreams of Sleep was published, her younger son said, " 'Did you
make us into girls' — because there are two daughters in that
book and there are two sons in real life who have the same age
difference. I said 'no' but the truth was 'yes.' But it was true and
it was not true. The two little girls are not my sons but I know
what it is like to have two children, so it was a comfortable way
to get into the story for me. If I had put three daughters [in the
novel] people would have thought it was me and my two sisters.
The number becomes an immediate signal towards which truth
you are dealing with. . . . I settled on two but in a way he was
right."

Humphreys says that "I am different from most women I know and run into every day, and the main difference is that I am totally incompetent in the household and I am extraordinarily messy. Clutter piles up around me, and I've been like that since I was twelve years old, and it's pathological." It's the "kind of messiness that disgusts other people, and I've never understood it. People tell me it's just laziness and I am refusing to impose order. . . . Sometimes I think that there is clutter in my head, that the clutter around me sort of reflects the clutter in my head. What's in my head is not a mess, but it's a vast amount of stuff. It's not ordered or clean, it's very confusing, but it's interesting and I like it that way and I certainly like to have a house that way. I like it to be full of surprise and disorder."

The only thing she likes "better than writing is children, and that has been a big surprise to me. I never knew as a girl that I would be interested in children. . . . I never held a baby till I had my own. . . . I expected I would be a sort of distant mother, but I'm not. I would rather have a baby than a book, but I did find myself at one point making the decision whether to have another baby or a book. . . . I wanted the time to write . . . but I'm still fascinated and in love with children — not just my own, but all of them. It's one of the nicest surprises in my life that I enjoy this so much and I didn't think I would."

Unpublished or fledgling novelists would do well to remember that Josephine Humphreys started writing when she was thirty-three and then "took a long time . . . five years of total privacy." Until *Dreams of Sleep* was published she "didn't know a single writer except Reynolds Price who had been my teacher," and she "hadn't seen or talked to him in fifteen years." She "kept writing with one goal in mind, which was to finish, to do the work." Her many delighted readers are grateful for that.

M.P.

BOOKS BY JOSEPHINE HUMPHREYS

NOVELS

Dreams of Sleep. New York: Viking, 1984; Penguin, 1985.
Rich in Love. New York: Viking, 1987; Penguin, 1988.
The Fireman's Fair. New York: Viking, 1991.

Harriet Doerr

HARRIET DOERR lives in Pasadena, California, the city just outside Los Angeles where she was born in 1910. Pasadena is not a product of Southern California's recent expansion, but a place of quiet streets lined with huge trees where the homes and the families go back a long way by California standards, to early in the nineteenth century. As we stood on the porch of her hillside house, looking down over terraces of lemon trees to her rose garden or up to the San Gabriel mountains in the middle distance, she said, "People say it's silly to live alone in such a large place, but I love it and will do it as long as I can." She led me through rooms filled with sun and antiques and comfortable sofas into an old-fashioned kitchen, where we chatted while preparing tea. I immediately felt the vitality and intellectual acumen of this woman who became a writer in her mid-sixties after channeling her energy into traditional female roles for most of her life.

In 1984 Doerr published *Stones for Ibarra,* a subtle and moving novel about the cultural tensions between a California couple who go to rural Mexico to manage a copper mine in 1960 and the native Mexicans who reside there in Ibarra, a "declining village of one thousand souls." (The CBS dramatization of the novel on the *Hallmark Hall of Fame* with Glenn Close and Keith Carradine did not do justice to Doerr's stark, unsentimental prose.)

When I asked her whether she thought of herself as a writer during her years as homemaker, she said that "when the children were little I was in a housewives' writing group [that] wrote character sketches; we were all amateurs. The sketch presented a person on page one and some sort of problem on page four, and on page eight it was solved. It didn't occur to me that I might write a book."

Doerr believes that she would not have become a professional writer without the encouragement of teachers she met upon returning to college three years after her husband's death. It was 1975 and she was sixty-five years old; her children challenged her to complete her degree. She admits to a moment of complete panic before her first class at Scripps College in Claremont: "I got to the class a little after nine and the door was closed, and I almost went home. I thought, 'You are a ridiculous old person. Why are you standing here entering this young people's Spanish class?' Then I remembered Bob Gibson, the legendary pitcher of the St. Louis Cards, who said, 'I don't believe in standing around on the mound waiting for the catcher's signals and trying to scare the batter; my philosophy is, just hum it in there, baby, and let's see who's best, them or me.' I think it's the most beautiful thing; it's like Shakespeare, all one-syllable words, poetic. So I went in and the teacher said 'Buenos dias, Senora,' and I said, 'Buenos dias' and sat down. The minute he spoke Spanish, I said, 'I'm home.' "

Since she owed Stanford University only one five-unit history course to complete her major there, "I made up as much as I could by going to Scripps; I took Spanish and music and creative writing and had a wonderful time." She recalls with particular pleasure her creative writing teacher, Clive Miller, who gave her "a wonderful lift" by writing things like "Can't wait till you try longer pieces, Harriet" on her papers.

She liked being around young people, quickly discovering that she had to be "interested and shock-proof. I don't have grandchildren, so I didn't have exposure to young generations. It's marvelous to know what they're thinking and doing and why they're doing it." When I commented that young people can learn a lot from older students, she at first expressed doubts, then reflected, "If you live a long time you have a long view, you look back a long way. I had a goal in mind and a deadline, so I didn't fool around. Now I feel the same way about the book I'm writing. You cannot just waste time. Otherwise you'll die to regret it."

Doerr planned to move near Stanford for just a few months to complete her degree; once there, however, she had such a good time that she stayed for five years. "One year I had a Stegner Award; then I went back as a nonmatriculated graduate student for another two years." She feels a particular debt to John L'Heureux, professor of English and director of creative writing at Stanford. She first met L'Heureux when "I handed him a few stories I'd written for Scripps to get into his class. We went to the Union and sat under an oak tree and had cottage cheese with peaches in it and had this interesting conversation. He had been a Jesuit priest. I said to John that I don't understand [the concept of] grace, so he explained it to me, but I still have a few problems with it. You don't know when you have it, so what's the use of having it? It's a particular moment that's enclosed; you are walking with grace."

Doerr said that she belongs to no organized religion, perhaps partly because her religious training was lacking in passion. "I was brought up going to Sunday School, but no one seemed to care; I retired from devotional exercises. It isn't that I believe in nothing; the trouble is that I believe in everything, [but] not formal documented beliefs. You see things everyday when you go outside which make you think somewhere there's order that's bringing these things about. I believe in that order, but I don't know what to call it."

It was not simply L'Heureux, however, but the other members of the creative writing class who encouraged her to publish her work. "John and that class handed me a future, a whole different conviction of what I could do. It made the future absolutely full, because you had a purpose. No matter how long I live there will never be a dull moment." Visiting writers also played a role in her vision; Eudora Welty and E.L. Doctorow each took a workshop with her class and did a public reading. She thinks Welty is "marvelous, a wonderful person" and recalled that Doctorow said he "sits at his typewriter every day from 9:00 A.M. to 12:00 or 1:00. One day he sat for forty-five minutes and no thought came, so he typed 'the wall,' because that's what he was looking at, then 'the room,' then 'the house,' then '1902,' then he wrote *Ragtime*. All he had to do was get to the date of the house, then came Houdini, J.P. Morgan, and Stanford White. Sometimes a little thing can pull you into a big thing."

Doerr's experience at Stanford in the seventies represented a return after an interval of over forty years. She had met her future husband in Pasadena when she was sixteen and he was eighteen and about to enter Stanford as an engineering major. After a year at Smith College, she transferred to Stanford; then she left college to marry at age twenty. They returned to Pasadena, where he had a job in a steel company, just after the stock-market crash of 1929. He "was laid off from time to time," but she believes that Southern California did not suffer from the Depression as much as many places in the United States. "You were lucky to have a job and keep your car going, but you didn't see starving people or bread lines. My son was born less than a year after I was married; my daughter, four years later."

With the exception of fifteen years in Mexico (the total from several different sojourns) and a brief stay in Philadelphia during World War II, Doerr has lived her entire life in California. Two memories stand out from her stay in Pennsylvania, both experiences that only a Californian would have. Despite her husband's engineering background, "we almost killed ourselves the first night with fumes from the coal furnace. It was an old house and we weren't used to furnaces." The other memory is of the garden that bloomed behind the house after the thaw. "Tulips and freesias and lilies of the valley sprang up; I loved the forsythia and lilac." Doerr had never seen forsythia or lilacs growing before. "They don't do well in California because it isn't cold enough. I tried planting forsythia here, even putting ice around the roots, but you can't spend your life trying to make a plant believe it's winter."

Her family was back in Pasadena in time to witness the rounding up and incarceration of the Japanese in 1942. "My husband and I both signed a petition the week that this horrible thing took place; he was at Lockheed at the time and was immediately put on the FBI list. We were near the railroad [station] getting gas and across the tracks were all the Japanese with their suitcases. I said to the children, 'Look and remember, this is the most terrible thing our country's ever done.' She wishes now that "I'd gone and said how sorry I was to all of them. Or I could have lain down on the tracks and been hauled off to jail."

In 1950–51, she and her husband and daughter lived in Mexico City, where her husband worked in a family business. They returned to Mexico in 1960, this time to a small town. Although *Stones for Ibarra* is not strictly autobiographical, Doerr says, "If I hadn't lived in a village, I wouldn't have been able to write the book. I had to have some idea of the people who have roots there, whose fathers and grandfathers and great-grandfathers have lived there, what their philosophy of living is." Although she did exaggerate certain features of the town — "making the mountains higher," for example — she tried to remain faithful to the character of the Mexican people. "I'm not sure anyone can say they know another whole people — really know — because there are so many and such deep differences, but you know enough to understand, and they can find out about you, and mutual respect forms."

Sara and Richard, the American couple in the novel, have few memories of their past lives in California; the reader does not even know whether they have children. Doerr said that the omission was deliberate: "I just gave them a point of entry. I wanted to keep it in one place; if they'd had children in another place it would have been diluted. I wanted it to be a section of lives."

She originally submitted the work to publishers as a collection of linked stories. "It came back with mystified remarks; then Cork Smith at Viking took it and said, 'With a little feather dusting this could be a novel'; so I worked on it for about three months, making it chronological, adding bridges. When putting it together I realized how much death there was in it, violent deaths and murders and suicides. When I was writing separate stories, it just seemed like Mexico. Richard's death was slow and calm, but in Mexico death is all around you in the things people tell you; you're very aware of it, especially in a little town. When you ask how many children, they say, 'nine, three dead' or 'six, two dead' as if they are still a part of the family — even if they're stillborn. When a child dies in the country, you see a little procession on the shoulder of the road with one man carrying the coffin walking to the cemetery. Once I saw a child's coffin on top of a bus. When I asked, 'Is that the custom?' the person explained, 'Where else? You can't put it under the seat.' You see pigs and chickens and fodder for cows on top of the bus. So much of what they do is reasonable and honest and clear-sighted."

In *Stones for Ibarra* the tensions between the agnostic, classical music-loving, restrained American couple and the volatile, sometimes violent but generous Mexican Catholics are gradually transformed into mutual affection and respect. Although Sara, the main character, has few memories in the beginning, she builds up memories of incidents and people who touch her life. The title of the novel comes from the Mexican, or Indian, practice of placing stones to mark the place where an accident has occurred; they are a form of honor and remembrance. At the end of the novel Sara partly sees, partly imagines, a pile of stones outside her gate. She thinks of what she was told; when people pass and remember, they bring stones.

Doerr planned to leave for a visit to a quiet spot in Mexico two days after our interview. The novel she is writing now will take place in "a town called El Molino, the mill. I adopted the lake, the houses, the church. On the mesa above the town I have installed Americans. The Americans in this book are completely different, as are the Mexicans they live with. My imagination and thoughts are in the '50s and '60s, when I was exposed to another people; the difference charmed and startled me. I still operate on that marvelous relationship of surprise on both sides." Doerr observed that "now there are complex changes in the economy and political situation, demonstrations in the main plaza of Mexico City, right under the presidential palace. This would have been unthinkable twenty years ago."

Doerr asked me, "Do you think that I should write about Pasadena instead? I can't think of one thing to say." She is critical of the materialism of many Americans and observed sadly that when Mexicans come here, "the vision [of education] they have for the children there somehow evaporates. The desire to be North American blots out better goals, like enormous respect of children for parents. They want cars and television sets. I don't think our culture is so superior."

I asked Doerr about her favorite writers. "Katherine Anne Porter is marvelous; Eudora Welty is marvelous. I love the Latin Americans, Garcia Marquez and Juan Rulfo for the sense of Mexico, honesty about Mexican people, heart-breaking short stories with no sentimentality." I remarked that *Stones for Ibarra* is totally free of sentimentality, no small achievement given the tragedy and poverty that surround many of the characters. Doerr responded, "Sometimes I think I'm on a tightrope; you have to be terribly careful."

She is currently writing an essay for an anthology called *The Writer on Her Work*. Her essay, entitled "Houses," is "focused on three different houses" in which she has lived — the one she was born in, a California adobe house built in 1816, and another in Mexico. She asserted that the three houses are a way of looking at segments of her life, but she cannot analyze her motives for writing. "At the end I say, 'I don't know why I love these houses; I don't know why I write.'" She testified that she needs complete solitude to write. "I don't think I could have written with a family all around me. If anyone lived in the house I'd jump up and say, 'Do you want some tea? Come and talk.' The place I'm going to in Mexico I went to last summer, a posada in Cuernavaca, flowers in the rooms but no television. I was the only guest. Between meals there is nothing to do but read and write."

When I asked Doerr why women have excelled at the writing of fiction, she said the answer may have to do with leisure and imagination. "Men as a group were thought of as the providers; women had more leisure to wander about and think about things. Men weren't allowed to be dreamy." She added that this is of course an absurd generalization "because of all those male writers like Faulkner; they must have dreamt all the time. Leisure has a lot to do with imagination and allowing your mind to form a picture. Even driving on a freeway by [myself], I hear a phrase in my mind; out of that might come an idea. In Mexico I try to listen. I always ask people in the posada about their families."

Before I left, Doerr showed me her new word processor, an Apple PC, which she is in the process of mastering. I thought of all the people half her age who are frightened by the new technology, and recalled that she had remarked earlier in our interview, "Reading and understanding are the only important things, don't you think? Even though in your whole lifetime you only get that much. But you can try for it."

Harriet Doerr's prose style describes events and persons with a precise objectivity that arouses strong emotion in the reader. It might be a metaphor for the person herself, a remarkable woman of strength, graciousness, and an intellect that roves over all it touches.

K.U.H.

BOOKS BY HARRIET DOERR

NOVELS

Stones for Ibarra. New York: Viking, 1984; Penguin, 1985.

SHORT STORIES

Under an Aztec Sun. Covelo, Calif.: Yolla Bolly Press, 1990.

Elizabeth Winthrop

ELIZABETH WINTHROP lives on Riverside Drive, that quintessential New York space, tree-laden and pigeon-marked, full of joggers, dog walkers, playground parents, Walkman wearers, and retired professors from Barnard, Columbia, and City College out for a stroll. The park across from her windows is posted with the usual New York signs — "No Parking," "No Littering," "No Radios," "No Ball Playing" — to which nobody who calls him or herself a New Yorker pays any attention — but, in addition to the city-produced list of restrictions, it has temporary neighborhood fliers flapping from the fences that read: "Call police if you see a man abducting squirrels and pigeons — his car (tan station wagon) is registered to ———, Brooklyn."

This combination of the absurd and the extraordinary, which *is* New York, is now the home of the elegant Washington-reared author of a three-generation novel about mothers and daughters,

In My Mother's House, who is the first novelist in "a family where there are writers all the way back" — uncle, aunt, grandmother, and a poetry-writing great-grandmother. But Winthrop, who is the only daughter among six children of the late Washington columnist Stewart Alsop (to whom, "unconsciously, I was proving myself for a long time"), uses her middle name because, although "I liked my father and was close to him and proud of what he did, when I came to write . . . I chose not to use the name Alsop." She shares the problems of writers with famous or prominent parents but she now has "a far bigger reputation as Elizabeth Winthrop in the bookstores than any Alsop does any more." "That's the name I created," she says, and "I have made it on my own."

Winthrop works in a spacious, book-filled room with fourteen-foot ceilings, at a light oak desk, full of cubby holes and niches, but she is feeling a bit "closed in" by the omnipresent computer and the printer, which sit like reproachful sentinels, one component on each side. Winthrop's desk faces the wall, not the Hudson, but, like many women who are writers and mothers of school-age children, she knows that she doesn't need the often-welcome distraction of the tankers and luxury liners sailing by. She already has a doorman who is psychologically incapable of receiving a package without calling on the intercom to announce its arrival, and two teenagers who, like everyone else's children, are unable to walk through the door of an apartment without the news that they've "flunked the math test," made the soccer team, or need money for (this is a fill-in-the-blank item) school supplies, rock concerts, sneakers, or class trips. During the working day she keeps the answering machine on low so she is not tempted to pick up the phone if someone interesting is on the other end. Each morning she swims for an hour at a local gym to provide a space between wife/mother and writer, and she keeps her knitting out on the dining room table (which is big enough to seat America at Thanksgiving) so she can pick it up when she would rather be eating a danish.

For many readers, her apartment itself would be distracting enough, full, as it is, of mahogany sleigh beds from her grandmother's basement, forest green and white skirted tables, giant jade plants on the painted windowsills, and pictures of Washington superstars like John F. Kennedy hung in nonprominent places on the hallway walls. It is a nourishing, friendly place, one of those rambling, old-world apartments that look little like an interior designer product and very much like a place where educated, well-read, and accessible people who like books, children, nature, and art actually live. This is even more endearing, since Winthrop, who is friendly, understated, and aristocratic all at the same time, had as grandmother someone who was the niece of Teddy Roosevelt and the first cousin of Eleanor Roosevelt and Alice Roosevelt Longworth.

Winthrop is the product of Sacred Heart Schools. Her father was an Episcopalian and her mother "an English Catholic, an Evelyn Waugh Catholic . . . more Catholic than the Catholics." Her father said to her mother, "You can educate the girls; I get the boys," and "Mummy lost because she got one girl. . . . I got all the Catholicism." From Sacred Heart, "where we weren't allowed to talk between classes," she was sent to Miss Porter's School for Young Ladies in Farmington [Connecticut], "where I thought I'd died and gone to heaven because we were allowed to talk. . . . A couple of years went by and I realized that wasn't real life either!" She moved from that safe and homogeneous environment to Sarah Lawrence, "which was special to me," and in "1966 was a wild place to go," full of ethnics, Jews, hyphenated-Americans, "and people who tried to kill themselves at freshman mixers. I hit life." And there "was Sarah Lawrence's whole attitude toward education which worked for me: 'You do it, you fix it, we're depending on you, the student, to do the work.' And there were a lot of people who just couldn't handle it. But for me," she said, "it was great. I could walk in freshman year and say, 'I want to be a writer. I want to write every single year and I want to write a lot.'"

One of Winthrop's mentors was Grace Paley, "who I adored. She was great fun," although they "come from *totally* different backgrounds and points of view." Winthrop says she was at Sarah Lawrence during "the great upheaval, 1968 and 1969," and Paley "was always marching and often in prison. So you would get to the door of the classroom and they'd say, 'Send your stories to Cell Number 42 at the Women's Prison.' " "I love her as a person," but other teachers, her "wonderful don," Joe Pappaleo, and Jane Cooper, the poet, who first suggested that she write for children, had more effect on her work. During senior seminar, for instance, "six students and six teachers came together as equals" and everybody read from their work. "I remember that E.L. Doctorow was reading from *Ragtime* and we had the audacity to say, 'Well, I don't like that paragraph too much.' Ah, to be young," Winthrop said with a hearty laugh; "It was a very heady experience."

The title of Winthrop's novel, *In My Mother's House,* "which I've written three times," was suggested by a friend's comment: "There is 'in my father's house are many mansions.' Why not 'in my mother's house?' " It is an interwoven story of multiple sets of mothers and daughters who are all trapped in a long-buried memory. Lydia Franklin, the grandmother, an unmothered girl, is sexually molested for many years by her much-loved Uncle James, who "before he went over the line . . . was wonderful." He is, she said, "not an out-and-out villain" because "in every villain there is a hero, and in every hero there is a villain." In early adulthood Lydia suffers an almost inevitable nervous breakdown, brought on by "the terrible consequences of silence," by the entrenched training of women to be both compliant and quiet, by guilt, the power of secrets, and by the absence of a sympathetic and effective advocate. The ramifications of her loneliness and deep-seated feelings of loss and helplessness are not only pervasive in her own life but effectively distort the upbringing of her daughter, Charlotte, whom she attempts to make into a steel-willed and assertive woman. "I will give you," says Lydia, "a tough shell, a way to protect yourself."

Since Lydia's mother died in childbirth, she has had no experience of having been mothered, and consequently she has no facility for mothering. Her overwhelming need to protect her daughter, Charlotte, serves both to strengthen and to alienate the daughter, who marries an alcoholic, a man both loving and violent. The childhood trauma intervenes in the life of her grand-daughter, Molly, an artist, whose deep-seated fears about sexual abuse are also a legacy from Lydia.

The issue of sexual molestation is central in this novel, as it is, for instance, in Joyce Carol Oates's *You Must Remember This.* Winthrop believes that "all women's boundaries are crossed at one time or another" and "they are crossed continually." She told me about an informal but extraordinary discussion with a group of "ladies in their sixties and seventies . . . my mother's genera-tion . . . who have known me for years at this club and that club," for whom sexual abuse, rape, and the social issues that dominate the nightly news and the front pages happen in another world to other, very different people, "and when they read the book they were horrified." But Winthrop said, "Let's have a bit of truth here" and was not surprised when a seventy-year-old matriarch recounted for the first time that "she had been raped by her doctor at the age of eighteen . . . locked in his office, and she had never told *anyone.* ALL of them had a story. . . . Some had seen men expose themselves to them at the Paris Opera! One had an older brother who had pushed her into a closet. . . . It was an amazing session." She has "had very honest women call up and say, 'How did you know? My uncle did this to me.' " Winthrop agreed that what seems to be a kind of prescience is "terrifying," but, she repeated, "all women's boundaries are crossed," and she quietly tells the callers, "I hear you."

She read to me from "a terribly disturbing letter" whose corre-spondent said that Winthrop "has churned me all up. . . . How could she have known so much. . . . I wish I could read without being haunted." But her point is that this correspondent, and other readers, are "walking around in this book" because of their own encoded memories. The many stories she has absorbed are wound together here with the unknown, tacit memories of many strangers.

Winthrop looks at this particular novel as "a kind of sym-phony. In Part One there are only a couple of instruments play-ing. . . . It is a very tight opening." It was written at the Virginia Center for the Creative Arts "and there is something incredible about working there, or at any [writer's] colony. . . . All of this 'mothering stuff' is gone, and you are dignified as a writer. Not only are all your meals cooked, and your beds made, but you aren't even disturbed at lunch time for fear that you might be creating some astounding thought. Now that is *so* different from children" barging through the door. "I produced more than I had ever produced . . . twelve or thirteen pages a day, which was unheard of for me; I normally hit around five." But, she said, then "the symphony had to open up. The whole orchestra had to play in that middle section." But in Part Three, "the same spaces . . . close down."

We talked for a long time about the usually confining, imprisoning spaces of women and about how Charles Franklin, Lydia's father "closed his wife's bedroom [after she died] so that the maids had to turn up the gaslights in order to clean the staircases, and everything about [that house] became very entrapping and dark." Part One is filled with imagistic but ordinary spaces — closets and fenced gardens. Charlotte's section is more open; it takes place largely in the farmhouse to which Lydia escapes from "that musty, dark brownstone on 38th Street, that horrible place where Uncle James could find her." But that farmhouse is also the scene of Charlotte's painful afternoons on the "painting porch" with an autocratic, controlling mother who dictates solutions and overreacts to childhood weakness in her need to be "the good mother." Section Three, where Molly confronts her matriarchal past, is again rife with limited spaces — the painting porch, a shoebox filled with Lydia's diaries (containing the story of her sexual molestation by Uncle James), the kitchen (which is the space of a surrogate mother, Agnes, the housekeeper), a closet, and a car which becomes a movable prison. "The house is a very specific house that I loved, and the jacket photo is based on my grandmother's sun porch" in Avon, Connecticut. "My grandmother actually did paint there."

Winthrop is now working on a book "which in my head is called *The Handmaiden to the Patriarch*," based on her observations of women in their forties "whose mothers both died ten or twelve years ago," and the ways in which "even feminists can become handmaidens to incredibly powerful, incredibly important, egotistical, patriarchal men. Every feminine bone in their bodies disappears when they get around these men. . . . They bring them their Postum at 3:00 in the afternoon, they make sure the lights are low. . . . These are women I greatly admire in business and they are great feminists, but when they get around these men they turn to Jell-O." When "you are working on something," she said, "you get some key word in your head [like patriarchy] and you see everything about it." It's the "Lady Di syndrome."

Elizabeth Winthrop is not an overnight sensation; she is the practiced, skillful author of thirty-four books for children, and she won the Dorothy Canfield Fisher Award for *The Castle in the Attic*. She brings both to young people's fiction and to this novel a special sense of interior and exterior spaces, of the psychic battle and the public pose, and, most specifically, a gentle compassion for those lives haunted, over generations and without respite, by unfriendly and unyielding ghosts.

M.P.

BOOKS BY ELIZABETH WINTHROP

NOVELS

In My Mother's House. New York: Doubleday, 1988; NAL, 1989.

CHILDREN'S BOOKS

Bunk Beds. New York: Harper & Row, 1972.
Walking Away. New York: Harper & Row, 1973; Dell, 1977.
A Little Demonstration of Affection. New York: Harper & Row, 1975; Dell, 1977.
That's Mine. New York: Holiday House, 1976.
Potbellied Possums. New York: Holiday House, 1977.
Knock, Knock, Who's There? New York: Holiday House, 1978; Dell, 1980.
Are You Sad, Mama? New York: Harper & Row, 1979.
Journey to the Bright Kingdom. New York: Holiday House, 1979.

Marathon Miranda. New York: Holiday House, 1979; Bantam, 1981; Puffin, 1990.

I Think He Likes Me. New York: Harper & Row, 1980.

Miranda in the Middle. New York: Holiday House, 1980; Bantam, 1982; Puffin, 1990.

Sloppy Kisses. New York: Macmillan, 1980; Viking/Penguin, 1983.

Katherine's Doll. New York: Dutton, 1983; Dutton, 1991.

A Child Is Born: The Christmas Story. New York: Holiday House, 1983.

Being Brave Is Best. Beverly, Mass.: Parker Brothers, 1984.

Tough Eddie. New York: Dutton, 1984; NAL, 1989.

Belinda's Hurricane. New York: Dutton, 1984; Puffin, 1989.

Grover Sleeps Over. New York: Golden Books, 1984.

[Adapted by]. *He Is Risen: The Easter Story.* New York: Holiday House, 1985.

The Castle in the Attic. New York: Holiday House, 1985; Bantam, 1986.

Lizzie and Harold. New York: Lothrop, Lee and Shepard, 1985.

Shoes. New York: Harper Junior, 1986; Trophy, 1988; Gollancz, 1990.

Story of the Nativity. New York: Simon & Schuster, 1986.

Maggie and the Monster. New York: Holiday House, 1987; Holiday House Paperback, 1988.

Bear and Mrs. Duck. New York: Holiday House, 1988; Simon & Schuster, 1990.

The Best Friends Club: A Lizzie and Harold Story. New York: Lothrop, Lee and Shepard, 1989.

Sledding. New York: Harper & Row, 1989.

Luke's Bully. New York: Penguin, 1990.

Vasilissa the Beautiful. New York: HarperCollins, 1991.

A Very Noisy Girl. New York: Holiday House, 1991.

Bear's Christmas Surprise. New York: Holiday House, 1991.

Janet Lewis

JANET LEWIS has written five novels, five books of poetry, five libretti, and many beautifully crafted short stories. Living in Northern California, where her work is widely read, I wanted to interview her but felt that perhaps at age eighty-nine (now ninety) she was entitled to peace and quiet. However, when friends reported to me that they had met her at a large wedding in Los Angeles, I sent her a letter the next day. She called me immediately and we set a date.

At age ninety Janet Lewis reads avidly, goes to the opera, and still writes — most recently, poetry and libretti. She lives with two friends, including the composer Alva Henderson, in Los Altos, a tiny city of foothills that adjoins the more populous Palo Alto. Her house is old-fashioned in the best sense — the rooms are cozy and lived in. She made me a cup of tea and we sat in her living room and talked about books, the writers she knew in the twenties, the two women's movements, and her current reading ("There are things I'm reading late; I'm catching up.").

We also talked about the way the world has changed since her childhood in Michigan and her early married life in northern California, where she has lived for over fifty years. The towns around Stanford, now home to wealthy venture capitalists and executives from high technology industries, were agricultural when she and her husband, the poet Yvor Winters, arrived in 1927. She said that now these towns "even speak a different language — money language, automobile language. Metaphors come from things like that. We get in sync; we get in gear."

The story of how Lewis came to California is interwoven with the stories of her marriage and her love of poetry. When she entered the University of Chicago as a junior in 1918, Winters sent her an invitation to join the Poetry Club. Before they could meet, however, he developed tuberculosis and left to "cure" at a sanatorium in Santa Fe. Lewis said that "the people in the club who were fond of him shared his letters. We sent him poems and he sent back comments. It was extraordinary." After World War I, when Lewis herself developed tuberculosis, Winters helped her get a tutoring job at the same sanatorium, which was "a wonderful place to be, although that may sound a little odd." Winters was teaching in a remote mining town in New Mexico. "He'd come up on weekends to Santa Fe and we got acquainted in person, and at the end of the year we were engaged." After another bout with TB which kept her in the sanatorium for several years, Lewis and Winters, now married, came to California because "he thought it would be a good climate for a TB patient," and Stanford offered him the chance to do graduate work in English.

Lewis, whose brother was a painter, started writing "as soon as I could hold a pencil." Her father was a scholar and teacher at the Lewis Institute, and Lewis said that "by the time I was ten years old I had soaked up the Greek myths." She described her education as "Tennysonian" in its pattern — "the classical English Lit" with Shakespeare and "a lot of French, which I'm sure was influential." She said of influences on her writing, "The ones in early life are so obvious that you overlook them." She believes that both her father and her husband were strong influences on her style.

Lewis was also active in and influenced by the *Gyroscope* group of writers who founded a literary journal in 1929. The spare, classical prose style of Lewis's fiction as well as her deep concern with moral righteousness reflects the tenets of this group, their adherence to classical style and themes, their rejection of Modernism. Lewis explained that her husband started the group his second year at Stanford, when his status changed from student to teacher. "He wanted to get a group of young writers together, such as we had at the University of Chicago, because they are very good for each other, lead each other on and criticize each other." The group was important to Lewis and the other writers who belonged because "then, perhaps, you don't get so idiosyncratic."

Among other writers who belonged, "Howard Baker was a fine poet and a novelist, too. . . . Henry Ramsey started as a poet. My husband was in touch with people like [Allen] Tate and Hart Crane and they sent contributions." She and Winters got to know a lot of writers by letter, "especially Tate, Katherine Anne Porter, Caroline Gordon." Lewis saw a lot of Porter when she came to Stanford to teach for a quarter; she said Porter was "absolutely charming" but a "difficult girl to deal with." One day when they were visiting, Porter told her, "I've had one publisher and four husbands" and Lewis responded, "I've had one husband and four publishers."

I asked Lewis how, as a poet and French major, she came to the writing of historical novels. She said that she became interested in the history of the Ojibway nation and the Johnston family when she was growing up on the Michigan side of the St. Mary's River. (Her father, also a writer, had another cabin on the Canadian side.) "I'd been doing short stories about small things in my life, and my neighbors. I was going to do a small story about Miss Molly Johnston, whom I had known as a girl growing up, and suddenly decided that I had to do her ancestors, and suddenly I was doing *The Invasion*." When I noted that this epic novel must have required vast research, Lewis said, "My father did a lot of scouting for me. He was back on the ground and could talk to the Johnston descendants. Chase Osburn, who had been governor and was fascinated by Michigan history, lent me a book that was out of print. Lots of people helped me." She said that she taught herself history "in the area in which I was working in fiction, so that there are certain what you might call 'illuminated spots' where I know my way around, and then there are acres and acres of unexplored territory."

Lewis typed parts of *The Invasion* with her baby literally on her lap. "I got a contract suddenly and there was a time thing on it. I believed seriously that if I didn't get it in on time, they wouldn't take it. I was scared to death." *The Invasion* earned rave reviews for the "cool translucent beauty of the writing" and was called by J.V. Cunningham in 1932 "the best example we have of the regional novel." (Lewis has also written two books of poetry about Native Americans: *The Indians in the Woods,* about the experiences of the Ojibway, and *The Ancient Ones,* about the Navajo and Hopi villages of the Southwest.)

After writing a domestic novel, *Against a Darkening Sky,* Lewis decided she worked best from historical plots and began her famous historical trilogy of novels which includes *The Wife of Martin Guerre.* "My husband had this book called *Famous Cases of Circumstantial Evidence* and so I decided to look through it. . . . I found the one about *The Wife,* which interested me because nobody knew why she did what she did. . . . I made some notes and then plunged madly into it." Lewis published *The Wife of Martin Guerre* in 1941 and *The Trial of Soren Qvist* in 1947, and completed the trilogy with *The Ghost of Monsieur Scarron,* in 1958. In the early sixties the critic Fred Inglis argued in *Studies in Modern Fiction* for the superiority of Lewis's "honest and courageous" exploration of moral issues to "Hemingway's adolescent nihilism."

We discussed the fact that historian Natalie Davis served as consultant to the movie version of *Martin Guerre.* Lewis said that her book had been bought for a movie by "the Stanley Mann who did *The Mouse That Roared.* . . . Eventually I sent a message and he called me and said that he had written the most beautiful screenplay of his career and that somebody had taken over and rewritten it and ruined it and then got cold feet and didn't produce it." Even though a different version served as the basis of the film, Lewis's book was made into an opera with William Bergsma. "It was because of that opera that I met Henderson, because when it was presented in San Francisco, he was a singer."

Lewis, whose granddaughter is studying music at Yale, said, "I love music, but that doesn't mean I know anything about it. I think a good many poems fall in the category of songs; they are at least singable." Lewis glowed when talking about her libretti. "It's great fun. You work with somebody; it's not as lonely as writing." She wrote an opera based on *The Invasion* called "The Legend of Neengay" for a Cleveland composer and was amazed when its performance was attended by descendants of the Johnston family. (Neengay, the daughter of the chieftain of the Ojibway, married John Johnston, an Irish fur trader, in 1791.) Lewis told me that "one of the descendants of the Johnston family started a newsletter which he calls *The Waubogenes,* which is a terrible pun. He has rounded up I don't know how many descendants of the original couple, and they got in touch with each other. They turned up at the opera *en masse* and brought relics and family trees." They plan a reunion in 1992, the two hundredth anniversary of the interracial marriage that produced eight children. Lewis said that "after you write about these people, you think that you've made them, invented them. It was startling to discover that they were real and started talking back — as it were — through their descendants."

Our discussion of history reminded me that Lewis had grown up during the first women's movement, and I asked her how it felt to be a writing woman at that time. She said, "We were part of the generation. It seemed quite natural to me that women should write. One of my friends at the university was Elizabeth [Madox] Roberts and I knew of so many women who were very active — judges, for instance, or the head of United Charities in Chicago." Lewis said that she had a friend in the sanatorium "who was going to be a pediatrician when she got home." Although this young woman did become a doctor, Lewis acknowledged that "I was aware from her stories that sometimes she was the only woman in the class. There were lots of fields still to be taken over, but the atmosphere that women were moving in was so natural that I didn't think about it as a revolution. It's what we were doing."

Lewis believes that "after the second world war, the scene changed. Before the war, through the twenties, the important figures were people like Edith Wharton, Elizabeth Roberts, Esther Forbes, Ellen Glasgow, probably lots more, and suddenly, after the second war, [the novels] are all war stories and the big novels are all by men. Women have been coming in, but they sort of come in on the edge, like Joan Didion and this wonderful woman in Africa, Nadine Gordimer." I asked Lewis if she thought that after the war there was discrimination against women writers. "I don't think it was because they were women writers. I think that people who hadn't been in the war were passionately interested in it."

Lewis herself, who has two children (a son and a daughter, both teachers) and several grandchildren, said, "I see no point of pushing motherhood out of the picture just for the sake of a career." Before her marriage Lewis worked for a time at the American consulate in Paris and also taught in her father's school. She taught at Stanford after her children had grown up. She believes that women who wanted to write did — "If you want to write, you write" — and also that "the funny thing about history and women is that there have been startling and tremendous women all along, regardless of what the culture thought." At the same time she grants that "there is a lot yet to win, most certainly" and expressed her admiration for Eve Merriam's book *Growing Up Female in America.*

Believing that women "have always been storytellers," Lewis said, "I write as a woman." In her stunning collection *Goodbye, Son* most of the stories are about family life. One of the longest stories, "People Don't Want Us," is about the close emotional bond between a woman and her Japanese housekeeper, who is about to be relocated because of the war. Lewis said, "I think that the bond between women and servants is a very close thing. Wonderful housekeepers have held a house together." She recalled one of her favorite Edith Wharton stories, "The Bunner Sisters," about "an older sister who tried to arrange the life of her younger sister, sacrificing something herself. The moral is you cannot arrange someone else's life for them. But there was the concern and the deep feeling."

Lewis has been reading Nadine Gordimer "in small bits" because "she's depressing and I feel depressed because I have not written any books about the social terrorism of the age." She believes that Gordimer is "doing a great social thing," but "I don't live in her world and therefore I can't write it." She also reads French writers and has been "reading with a French group." She has just finished reading James's "The Aspern Papers" because "I saw the opera, beautifully put together and very strong. After 50 percent of it was crafted on a Henry James story, but the James story was very slight and not one of his best." Of all the writers I interviewed, Lewis was perhaps the most interested in the conversion of literature into opera and film. Of the various renditions of James into visual media, she commented that "*The Golden Bowl,* which you would have thought would be most difficult, . . . turned out beautifully."

Lewis spoke with admiration of Eudora Welty and Harriet Doerr, who "wrote a beautiful book. She makes me feel very lazy." Lewis acknowledged that she has *never* really been idle. At age eighty-seven she participated in the Aspen Writers' Conference: "I enjoyed that very much. I still write to some of the people who were there." In December 1988 she published a book of poems entitled *Late Offering.* Although she is not working with a group now, she talks often with "a number of friends who are writers." One of her latest poems is dedicated to a retired editor of the *Southern Review* whom she'd known from Michigan when "he was reading Latin with my father."

"Really," Lewis mused, "why does one write poems? I don't know." Yet to the reader who knows this remarkable woman, the answer seems clear. Her poems, which celebrate natural beauty, enduring loyalty, and commitment to family and friends, are an expression of her deepest self.

K.U.H.

BOOKS BY JANET LEWIS

NOVELS

The Invasion: A Narrative of Events Concerning the Johnston Family of St. Mary's. New York: Harcourt Brace, 1932; Athens, Ohio: Swallow/Ohio Univ. Press, 1964.

The Wife of Martin Guerre. San Francisco: Colt Press, 1941; Swallow/Ohio Univ. Press, 1967.

Against a Darkening Sky. New York: Doubleday Doran, 1943; Swallow/Ohio Univ. Press, 1985.

The Trial of Soren Qvist. New York: Doubleday, 1947; Swallow/Ohio Univ. Press, 1959.

The Ghost of Monsieur Scarron. New York: Doubleday, 1959; Swallow/Ohio Univ. Press, 1982.

SHORT STORIES

Goodbye, Son and Other Stories. New York: Doubleday, 1946, Swallow/Ohio Univ. Press, 1986.

POETRY

The Indians in the Woods. Monroe Wheeler, 1922; Matrix Press, 1980.

The Wheel in Midsummer. Lone Gull, 1927.

The Earth-Bound, 1924–1944. Aurora, N.Y.: Wells College Press, 1946.

Poems, 1924–44. Denver: Swallow Press, 1950.

The Ancient Ones: Poems. Portola Valley, Calif.: No Dead Lines Press, 1979.

Poems Old and New, 1918–1978. Swallow/Ohio Univ. Press, 1981.

Late Offering. Florence, Kentucky: Barth, 1990.

CHILDREN'S BOOKS

The Friendly Adventure of Ollie Ostrich. New York: Doubleday, 1927.

Keiko's Bubble. New York: Doubleday, 1961.

LIBRETTI

[with Alva Henderson] *The Last of the Mohicans,* 1977.
Birthday of the Infanta. Los Angeles: Symposium Press, 1981.
The Swans: An Opera Libretto in Three Acts. Santa Barbara, Calif.: John Daniel, 1986.
The Legend: The Story of Neengay. Santa Barbara, Calif.: John Daniel, 1987.
The Wife: A Libretto for an Opera in Three Acts. Santa Barbara, Calif.: John Daniel, 1988.

Irini Spanidou

THE FLOOR vibrates in Irini Spanidou's fifth-floor apartment "between the Korean greengrocer and Bartley's Bar" in New York's Greenwich Village when she is trying to write, because "the guys who live downstairs work in a disco and play their music very loud." They have, she said, "very fancy equipment. . . . I am able to write with this and [with] people having quarrels. The only kind of noise that bothers me is television, for some reason. It's a harsher noise with continued interruption; it's too much to tune out." But as for the ambulance sirens, the raucous university students, the street merchants selling everything from tacos to T-shirts, and the cacophony of New York life, "what happens is that when I concentrate, I stop listening."

A shortened version of this interview appeared in *Belles Lettres* 4, no. 4 (Summer 1989): 11.

Readers of *God's Snake*, Spanidou's partially autobiographical first novel about a pre-teenage protagonist caught between the dictatorial and repressive cruelty of her authoritarian father (a Greek army major and a man of two verbs — "to obey" and "to command") and the indifference and fragility of her beautiful but emotionally crippled mother, can be thankful for her powers of concentration.

Spanidou has not blocked out much of human experience beyond the noise, however, because *God's Snake*, as Doris Lessing has noted, has "the harsh simplicity of a Greek myth . . . a very old story, as much as it is a new one." It follows the classic pattern of a monomyth — a journey, an initiation into experience, withdrawal for meditation, a search for self, the trials of experience, and a confrontation with death. But it is a mythic story that is unusual in its use of a young girl as a wandering hero. Spanidou says that she "made [the hero] a girl because, to some extent, the book is autobiographical so I saw no reason to change the sex of the [character]. About one-third is true and the rest is made up. It didn't even occur to me to make the protagonist a boy because . . . I wanted to write about myself; I wanted to be truthful. In the book I am working on now, it was a more conscious, deliberate choice. I wanted to create a protagonist who would be a woman and who would be seen as a heroine *in the real sense*. Because most women characters, in the books that I was reading when I was growing up, were passive. Many books have been written about them. But those novels are usually [about] their suffering, because many things were done to them. If they are adventurous, at the end, there's always a man and that is the fulfillment. I wanted to create a character who would be a woman but who would be active in life, that actually wanted to pursue things other than matrimony and to be excited about them. I remember that as a child, I used to identify in fairy tales with the prince because I could never fantasize about being in a castle — waiting — I could never fantasize about that! And the only way to have adventures would be to pretend that you were the prince or the knight, or whatever it was in fairy tales."

We agreed that the knight (or hero) has space, open space, and that when women write fiction, across international borders, what seems to be emerging as a vision of space is invariably imprisoning. *God's Snake* ends with a scene in which Anna is in an open space, tossed by her father into the openness of the sea. Spanidou says that "my intention [in that scene] was defiance. At the end of [*God's Snake*] I was already seeing a second book." That scene "is a vision of what my direction would be. When I was starting out, I was trying to work with memory. [And it represents] freedom. Water, as we know, is often used symbolically, and," said Spanidou, "I have often had dreams about water and about sailing. At a time in my life when I was very unhappy, [when] things were very difficult for me, I would have this recurring dream: I was in a boat, a sailboat, and I wanted to sail. (I wasn't sailing it myself; there was a captain.) But instead of water, there was mud and the [boat] did not go. . . . I was caught, trapped, the boat would not move. Finally, when things in my life started to get better, I had this dream [again]. It was the same boat, but I was in water, real water, and I was sailing. . . . So symbols of water, to me — sailing, swimming — mean freedom, feeling alive." There is a sense, she said, of "possibilities, cleansing, feeling buoyant."

God's Snake is also a novel about evil and entrapment. Each chapter is an interweaving of the destructive and regenerative qualities of people and animals, and each chapter is dominated, in ascending evolutionary order, by a snake, a crow, a calf, a deer, or a dog. The animals replicate or suggest the savage potential of the child molesters and the child beaters, the sad and sensitive orphans and the lonely women and tuberculars who populate this novel. If these are not people who believe devoutly in evil, as I suggested to Spanidou, they are characters who "accept its existence, that evil is connected to God, not separated from Him. You can't get one without the other. They don't worship it, they understand its existence. That," she said, "is in the ancient Greek culture . . . treachery and jealousy. The Gods were not pure by any means; they were not virtuous entirely. They had virtues but those were counteracted by a lot of weaknesses. There was an acceptance of the complexity of both nature *and* human nature.

So you have beautiful sunlight *and* earthquakes. It is an unquestioned acceptance of that [complexity]." If this is a Greek angle of vision, Spanidou says that it is "not in the blood. But your mind is trained, if you're brought up reading in certain formulas, but I was not conscious of it while I was doing it." Anna's mother, in particular, is a woman who has been overpowered by so many people for so long that she seems encapsulated in the evil forces that encircle her. Like the other women in this novel, the mother is a human version of an orphaned and victimized animal.

Anna's grandmother — melancholic, enigmatic — is a woman thwarted by destiny from her dreams. And her unmarried and married aunts, who hunger for love and buy felt hats because, as they tell Anna, they are "durable," all live lives in opposition and of submission, and, like the animals, and the soldiers who are Anna's father's subordinates, they learn to obey.

Since this novel was published during an avalanche of books that examine the often deleterious influence of mothers, aunts, and grandmothers on daughters, I asked Spanidou how this mother had influenced Anna. Spanidou replied that a less fragile mother would certainly "have made a difference later in the way the girl develops," but that this particular girl is missing more than a strong mother. All the things that would make her strong — a sense of place, solidarity and permanence among them, are denied her. But Anna is not caught in the web of her mother's inadequacy. "Somehow the child is not influenced by that, because she tends to identify with the father. She sees in the women characters — defeat. . . . It's not exciting. She wants to go out and do it herself." The father, demonic and degrading though he may be, says Spanidou, "also encourages her, though he has a negative effect. . . . He makes her feel bad about being a woman. In order [to persevere] she has to deny the fact that she is a girl. . . . She doesn't think of herself as a girl who is going to go out in the world but almost as a kind of neuter" and there is a decided androgynous quality about her. "She has to deny any identification with the mother in order to [get out]."

Anna's father, like her uncle and grandfather, gorge themselves with ideas of maleness that feed on anger, control, and mastery.

Her father, in particular, lives by the dictum that "you are a man or you are cannon fodder." To be a man, in his vision, is to dictate and control.

Spanidou added that the "lack of roots in her development psychologically [also] works in her favor. . . . You have to define yourself from inside because [since, as an army daughter, you are always moving] whatever you have attained in one place will be challenged in the next." Anna "does not belong anywhere." She is the product of separation and, by extension, of loss — of the nonexistent relationships associated with constant displacement, the nomadic loneliness of the army brat, the strained solitude of the outsider, the sadness of the unnurtured child.

Spanidou's next book, *Fear,* will be set in Salonika, Greece's second largest city. It covers one year of Anna's life, where, for the first time, "she is in a school with all girls and that is confining, all those girls in uniforms, and there is [her] house, and the going back and forth. So there is the sense of confinement, from authoritarian father to existing in a world of women. [And] because it is the city . . . with the [planned] streets, the tall buildings, [there is] the anonymity." In a smaller town, she said, "there is openness." The novel, "as I've worked on it, has been transformed almost entirely. It is the same girl and the same situation, but I'm focusing more on the relationship between Anna and the mother [who becomes] the central figure."

I asked Spanidou if she had made a conscious choice to link up with all those other Annas — Anna Karenina, Anna Livia Plurabelle, Doris Lessing's Anna Wulf, and so on. "No," she said, "but the name appealed to me because it is a sturdy name and yet beautiful, and it's not exactly common. . . . I didn't want a name that was too rare, too pretty, or symbolic of something — a flower, or Mary. I liked the simplicity of it. . . . I may have even checked on it at the time [because] I liked the A's, the repetition of the A — A-nn-A. I wonder why it has appealed to so many people on so many different levels. It sounds pure to me."

We talked about the recent change in Spanidou's life since she is currently teaching at Sarah Lawrence, from which she graduated after moving to the United States at the age of eighteen.

"Teaching at Sarah Lawrence is a very, very strange experience, [since it is now more than] twenty years later. For one thing, I had not really been conscious of kids that age so . . . suddenly going back, it made me feel older, and it was a shock, because the last time I was there I was *so much younger!* When I first went back the students were still unpacking their things and I could see the fear, the excitement, the sense that their lives are ahead of them, and I am sort of midway over mine. So at first it made me feel sad [with] lots of regrets for my youth and wishing I were starting over. But I would probably feel the same at any college if I were suddenly surrounded by nineteen- and twenty-year-olds." I suggested that she was seeing herself in the same place at twenty and at forty; she was seeing another version of herself. But Spanidou replied that "maybe this has something to do with our discussion of memory. I cannot see myself any more. That is the odd thing about it. . . . I felt I was myself. I could not really divorce myself . . . separate myself, and see myself as younger. I thought that would happen but it didn't happen at all. It was as though the person I was then was just dead, disappeared. . . . I could not really, truly, evoke myself."

Where did that person go, I asked, the person you were at twenty? "Maybe," said Spanidou, "she's been too well assimilated into who I am now." She added that at Sarah Lawrence, where, like Elizabeth Winthrop after her, she studied with Grace Paley, she was writing "New York stories." She does not think, as I suggested, that *God's Snake* might perhaps be a finer work because she had returned to her psychological and sociological roots, but that "going back was necessary, that her writing suffered in the intervening years, [that] she resisted writing the first novel and wanted to start with the second novel. I did not want to deal with the autobiographical material [and] I think it went against me."

I asked if every novelist has to use her childhood in an early book to "get it out of the way." "Most people have. . . . Sometimes it comes out indirectly. I shouldn't generalize because a lot of writers haven't done that but *so many have.* . . . It's a matter of catharsis . . . You have to get yourself out of the way of the writing. It's not a matter of using material or describing events; it's a matter of understanding the experience, a way of [not] being haunted by it — the pain, or the confusion that you might have grown up with. I think once you've done that, you can project other characters more fully. That's what I found. . . . A lot of material was beginning to intrude into the work; I wanted to put it in [but] it was coming in the back door just because I had not wanted to confront it. . . . It needed to get out; let's get it out of the way." What adds to the interweaving of memory and fiction for Spanidou is that some of the relatives in *God's Snake* "did not exist, so there is a lot of confusion about this. Even close friends, who know about my life, suddenly will ask me about a person from the book: 'What about so and so?' " and she has to once again deal with the line between identity, reality, and fiction.

Part of the considerable power of *God's Snake* is the way in which it forces the reader to reevaluate our own relationships with parents and authority figures and to estimate the degree of damage that is a natural component of childhood. Pain intervenes in the process of obtaining knowledge but, as Spanidou reminds us, it sometimes generates knowledge about power and evil, about fragmentation and continuity, and about the heaven and hell of childhood. *God's Snake* illuminates once more how we all, ultimately, must confront that power and that pain.

One senses that for Irini Spanidou this will be both an enervating and an exhilarating work of a lifetime, and that she will weave and reweave those twisted threads of a memory that is both mythic and poignant. But she remains, after the critical success of *God's Snake,* a slight, short-haired, unadorned woman remarkable for her steel-edged intelligence and her intense, encyclopedic ability to listen. This is a writer who understands deeply about pain, and she is correct when she says, "I say what I say in my work, and I believe that's sufficient."

M.P.

BOOKS BY IRINI SPANIDOU

NOVELS

God's Snake. New York: W.W. Norton, 1986; Penguin, 1987.
Fear. New York: Knopf, forthcoming.

Lynne Sharon Schwartz

"FOR TWENTY-FIVE years I have been unlearning what I learned in my first twenty-five years," said Lynne Sharon Schwartz, the author of *Leaving Brooklyn,* which "of all my books . . . uses memory the most." For "twenty-five years I was filled with everything that was Brooklyn — in the 1950s" — mores, folkways, and point of view. "But I thought, 'No, this is not going to be my life' and I've spent all this time undoing, unraveling. It hasn't been so much learning new things but unlearning, and this book was my apotheosis of that."

The novel uses "the image of peeling the skin, just peeling it off" the adolescent heroine, about whom Schwartz spoke as she recalled her own childhood. "I'm old enough now not to feel scorn. I don't condescend." But at some point, Schwartz decided, "It's just not going to be for me even if there are parts of it that I have to accept. I've done about 95 percent" of the cleansing. "I think that there's very little left. There are the Proustian things — little iconographic objects. When I see them, whole worlds come out. Certain signs . . . certain streets . . . the beaches."

"Brooklyn," she said, "was a beautiful city but you never saw it because the repression in Brooklyn was phenomenal." The ethos was "that if you didn't talk about something it would go away. If something happened in a person's life," and you wanted to ask, " 'What's happening with your life, your recent illness, your children, your health?' someone would say, 'Don't mention it! You don't want to bring up the things that would make people feel bad, that would make people suffer.' " The consequence was that "social intercourse or even friendship disappeared. There was so much niceness it was killing. It *was* nice. It was secure and smooth, but the things that were most important, most interesting, were left unsaid." Schwartz used to think "this was bad for a writer. But maybe this is *good* for a writer, because you come out of it with glee. Now my mission was to say *everything* and I've done that. . . . I feel very much that the person I am was there, as I am now, at six or seven . . . and all this stuff was layered on to me — defenses and veils and screens, which I use a lot, and to get back to myself I simply had to peel. So much of our growing up is breaking out, freeing ourselves, and for different people that comes at different times. . . . For me it was in my forties. I finally felt satisfied that I was my own person, whatever I am. This is now the person I have made. It is no longer the person I was programmed to be. And that's a big difference."

This difference is reflected in *Leaving Brooklyn,* which is "a new, experimental, even avant garde book not because it dealt with memory and memoir in a tricky way . . . but experimental or new because it places the woman in the center of her own experience. She is the heroine of her life and the grown-up narrator looking on at her sees this. For once, it's a woman not seen from a man's point of view. There are books written by women where the women characters are still seen objectively as in a man's world, from a man's context. In this book, the woman is subject, is center, and it's the world as seen by her. It's a recreated world, feminist in a sense. The men are the objects. The men are utilitarian" — the father, the eye doctor (who introduces the girl to sex), and it is the eye doctor who ends up in the trapped space so often associated with women.

Schwartz's writing, like that of her former Barnard classmate Rosellen Brown, is "very packed, very inclusive, everything but the kitchen sink is in there, everything is thrown in and described. . . . I feel a great literary kinship with Rosellen because of this." They are both writers who are dramatically unlike the minimalists who are in fashion now, "who don't have the density. I resent a lot of the minimalist stuff not only because it's so boring and horrible to read" but because "there is no space over them. . . . The trouble with minimalists is that they have anomie, ennui, and despair, which we all have (we older writers have much more cause for it), but they refuse to allow the richness of life, of the universe" to enter in. The minimalists "seem much more passive and victimized" than writers of the generation before them; "life just keeps hitting them over the head. Their characters are not powerful enough." But, she said, "the universe is alive, teeming with things . . . and they leave all that out of their work, and that is what I deplore. We may be doomed and mortal and all the rest of it, but nevertheless, that's only us. There is a lot outside of us, and they just won't put it in. They don't have a sense of the world going on without them. They think that when they have psychologically or physically described a character, that that is all there is to it. There is no sense of beyond, or transcendence, or largeness, or scope, and I don't like what they have done to literature because they have produced a generation of readers who are bound by their own skin. . . . From me to me. Where is it going to take you? . . . There is something else out there."

The younger writers, she said, "have grown up on literature written by writers in their twenties. To me it's inconceivable that anyone should publish in their twenties unless they are Keats. I think it should be outlawed. They simply don't know enough. Thirties is okay! . . . If they do write about war and larger issues, it is as they impinge on them. Matthew Arnold said that 'literature is a criticism of life,' which I still believe, but they don't want to do that. The younger writers prefer to retreat to technique and the intellect, a male thing really, when the emotional or the existential stance is too painful. You can always go to the brain; the difficulty you encounter intellectually can be solved or worked out. These books are a kind of escape from actually living, and the books that are about living are difficult. On the other hand, Louise Erdrich, whom I admire very much, writes books about actual people. Her books are not intellectual constructs . . . they are grounded in feeling; the good books always are. . . . Raymond Carver developed this trend (and did it quite well) of limiting your vision to what your characters see. You take an uneducated character who doesn't know that he's bumbling through life, so that's what you get. I actually don't think these characters are so narrow; they know more about their lives than their authors imply. Gogol's *Dead Souls* has characters bumbling through life as well, but you'd never know it because the writer brings so much vision to it. It's so rich." It's "too bad for the readers" that the fictional characters are often "trivialized" by the writers who create them, she added. "I feel as if I am part of a dying breed, and such people as Rosellen, Alice Adams, and Alison Lurie — we're all in there together trying to keep some tradition, some openness, some largeness in literature."

We talked at length about images of seeing and sight in *Leaving Brooklyn*, which opens with this line: "This is the story of an eye, and how it came into its own." Schwartz, who shares the wandering eye problem with her character, says that the "eye distorts the visual world, it breaks it up. The relationship of things shifts and changes because the center of vision is somewhere else. What was solid breaks into particles within the vision of that eye. That is what the artist has to do, since it is a book about the artist finding her vision. There is another thing this eye does, which is to see the things behind doors, and this I can really do. It's not magic. . . . my center is somewhere else because I don't use one of my eyes. So when I close one eye, the center shifts. I can see something that would ordinarily be behind a door. This is seeing into the hidden space . . . the unspoken, the silent space. For me, what was unseen and unsaid is what you need a special and subversive vision in order to see."

Balancing Acts, published in 1981, also has a young heroine who "at one point runs away into New York City and has this wonderful feeling on the suburban train that right now no one knows where she is! She could be off the world. Kids have the sense that wherever they are — someone, usually their mother — *knows* where they are. 'Phone home' and so on. I've always longed for that feeling. Even now I don't have it because, when you live with people, and in this kind of neighborhood [near Columbia University], people keep tabs on you: 'I'm here, I'm there', 'I'll be home late.' " The character "runs away to join the circus in Madison Square Garden, and she finds herself in free, grown-up space, and is totally bewildered. The book ends with a scene in the ladies' room where she's with this older woman and she's crying. And the older woman says, 'Enough already. Come out. Come out to the world.' "

Schwartz, who has often taught at writing workshops across the country, says that "writing has become a career track. It's like going to law school or medical school. 'I'll graduate, I'll go to writing school, I'll come out a writer.' It's like becoming a dentist. They come out and they think they're writers. I'm of the old school. Writers work, suffer, sit in cafes, talk to their friends — they live — and you become a writer alone. I'm very proud of this! I became a writer alone. When I get my academy award or whatever it is, I'm not going to get up there and thank anyone, although there have been people who were good to me all along, but *you make yourself a writer.* When you go to school, it becomes an academic thing and what should be a subversive and anarchic [activity] becomes institutionalized." What they should be saying at these schools, "rather than correcting technical flaws, is — do something with your spirit and your relationship to the universe."

For reasons associated only with scheduling and time, Lynne Sharon Schwartz was one of the last writers to be interviewed for this collection. But she talked about an issue that had been reflected earlier in the conversations of other novelists, one of importance to both aspiring and working writers. "Writing," she said, is "love, a mission, and a calling," and "how and where and why you write" are very crucial issues. "Getting away," as she had to, "from being 'a good girl' is important because it's impossible to be a 'good girl' and a writer at the same time. . . . When I was about thirty-two, it dawned on me that I had to make a choice: 'be good' or be a writer. And I decided to be a writer. Now, whenever I find myself being good, I have to stop and say, 'Don't do this.' " What this translates to is, "Leave the dishes unwashed and the demands on your time unanswered. Be ruthless and refuse to do what people ask of you." Or, as this very talented and intelligent writer would say, "Fight this almost irrepressible instinct to be 'a good girl' all the way!"

M.P.

BOOKS BY LYNNE SHARON SCHWARTZ

NOVELS

Rough Strife. New York: Harper & Row, 1980; Harper, 1985.
Balancing Acts. New York: Harper & Row, 1981; Viking Penguin, 1989.
Disturbances in the Field. New York: Harper & Row, 1983; Bantam, 1985.
Leaving Brooklyn. Boston: Houghton Mifflin, 1989; Penguin, 1990.

NONFICTION

We Are Talking about Homes: A Great University Against Its Neighbors. New York: Harper & Row, 1985.

SHORT STORIES

Acquainted with the Night and Other Stories. New York: Harper & Row, 1984, 1985.
The Melting Pot: and Other Subversive Stories. New York: Harper & Row, 1987; Penguin, 1989.

CHILDREN'S BOOKS

The Accounting. Great Barrington, Mass.: Penmaen Press, 1983.
The Four Questions. New York: Dial Books for Young Readers, 1989.

Mona Simpson

MONA SIMPSON, who wrote *Anywhere But Here* (1987), talked to me about her work in her apartment on the west side of Manhattan, which "looks like a flat in Berkeley or Palo Alto or Red Bluff or anywhere." On the white-painted radiator cover there's a stone mortar and pestle and two ripening red and green chili peppers, which Simpson says she uses for guacamole. Her novel is about Adele August, "a complex, ambitious woman in all the worst and most endearing aspects," and her twelve-year-old daughter, Ann Hatfield August. It opens with these lines:

> We fought. When my mother and I crossed state lines in the stolen car, I'd sit against the window and wouldn't talk. I wouldn't even look at her. The fights came when I thought she broke a promise. She said there'd be an Indian reservation. She said that we'd see buffalo in Texas. My mother said a lot of

things. We were driving from Bay City, Wisconsin, to California, so I could be a child star while I was still a child.

Later in the scene, Adele pushes Ann out of the car.

I got out. It was always a shock the first minute because nothing outside was bad. The fields were bright. It never happened on a bad day. The western sky went on forever, there were a few clouds. A warm breeze came up and tangled around my legs. . . . I lost time then; I don't know if it was minutes or if it was more. There was nothing to think because there was nothing to do. . . . I tried hard but I couldn't learn anything. The scenery went all strange, like a picture on a high billboard. The fields, the clouds, the sky; none of it helped because it had nothing to do with me.

Simpson said that she wrote "that scene, or the core of it, when I was twenty-three, before it was a novel and before I even thought about writing a novel. I didn't really know a plot then, I didn't know what this mother and child were running away from or struggling towards, but I just wrote this little patch about the impervious quality of physical landscape, even of beauty, how the great open monumental forms of the American West become drained for us without the infusion of love. So right from the beginning this novel was about deracination, about a kind of immigration. I hope the book holds not only the blankness of loss but the exhilaration of possibility in the new, the immigrant's greed, the American hope of self-transformation."

Anywhere But Here is suffused with images of loss, abandonment, and disconnection, part of which is expressed in "the power of Adele's delusion, in the face of bills, bounced checks, and a series of smaller, emptier apartments," which "competes with a growing sense of reality in Ann's sensibility." It is unusual because it is a story of a mother and a daughter on the road, "lighting out for the territory." Simpson says that "American literature gives us a long tradition of men going west, of trying to change their lives materially, of obliterating their origins. We have Willy Loman, Jay Gatsby, Thomas Sutpen. I wanted to write about a woman's way in this same attempt, with these driving desires. . . . Adele and Ann, on the road and settling precariously and provisionally in California, form a kind of couple, living far from their larger family and community." She added that "so many of the institutions that shaped the assumptions, the premises beneath the nineteenth-century novel, have irrevocably changed. Marriage as the conclusion of a novel would no longer make the kind of sense it made to Jane Austen's ordered world" but "it could be a beginning. Few institutions now [suggest] permanence. The church has changed. Physical mobility, particularly in America, has changed village and urban life, and we assume the possibility of choice in basic matters — where we will live, whether we will have a child we are pregnant with — unthought of in other fictional worlds. But families are still the basic element of any community life. Moral choices and virtues start, as they always did, at home. Even if that family is led by a single mother."

Since I had just completed a collection called *Mother Puzzles: Daughters and Mothers in Contemporary American Literature,* I was particularly struck by Simpson's statement that "writing about family life in the twentieth century may really mean writing about mothers and children. Fathers are present as absences in family life. Who really had a father? Even people who did have fathers didn't. I grew up in the fifties and sixties. Men were working."

Simpson's next novel, not surprisingly, will be called *The Lost Father.* "I was working for two years on another novel, called *A Regular Guy,* which I still feel close to and plan to finish. But this book, this story, took over, and for a long stretch it didn't feel like writing. I felt I was just taking down what came rushing out." (See interviews with Rosellen Brown and Francine Prose.) She said that "some of the people in *Anywhere But Here* reappear [but] it is a book much more saturated with men. It's about a search for a missing father. And about men and women trying to come to know each other." I asked if this father was dead or whether he had just disappeared. "They don't know," she said. "He is just gone, he has left, as a lot of fathers do. So his children are looking. As to who he is, his children don't have a fixed conviction. They have many ideas. Is he dead? Is he in prison? Is he prosperous somewhere? What does he look like? That's the thing about absence. The person could be anywhere."

Simpson, who attended the University of California, Berkeley, and went to graduate school at Columbia, was at one time a freelance journalist. "My roots as a writer come from two very different realms. I started as a poet, first and most deeply, but I also always loved journalism. . . . I interviewed circus performers, a carillon genius, doctors and nurses in the city's hospital for indigents, Buddhist bakers who start work at four in the morning at the Tassajara Bread Bakery, the man who dreamed up the Pacific Film Archive, my local *dim sum* chef, a woman leading an incest victims' group, performance artists, city attorneys, merchant marines. But I'm too slow, really, for daily newspapers, and also I'm not always interested in the 'news' of news. I once wanted to do a story on just a day in a food stamp and welfare application and distribution office. Nothing was new but there were a hundred old things that leapt out [and were as] startling as circus animals." The piece was never printed because she "couldn't find a good enough news peg."

Mona Simpson talked at length about the uses of revision. "I spend most of my writing life revising," she said. "I seem to work in layers. So a chapter or a story doesn't really find its shape and emphasis, its color, until the fifth or sixth draft, and I do many more [revisions] just to polish the stones. My generation learned many of our lessons from Raymond Carver. He revised twenty to thirty times, and his stories live on now as hard, perfect, compact monuments. He is truly our Chekhov. He made an entire diction out of spoken American English, a narrative diction, not only a diction for characters' dialogue. No one had ever done that before."

She spoke too of Proust and Flaubert, Austen, George Eliot, Chekhov, Tolstoy, and Conrad, describing them as her "great masters. . . . And the poets. I read Rilke and Emily Dickinson and poets like Herbert almost daily. Right now I am rereading the Old Testament, Van Gogh's letters to his brother, and *Absalom, Absalom!*, all books I have read many times before. [With] Proust and Tolstoy I look for a specific paragraph, find it, read it over ten times and then I keep going until I make myself stop a hundred pages later. I think you need a certain voice at a certain time, the way a pregnant woman craves food which contains a particular necessary mineral."

The most unusual aspect of this interview concerned the issue of work. Simpson said that she "learned how to work by having held jobs since I was fourteen, and not really working very hard at them. I've always had jobs. I worked as an ice cream scooper, a waitress, a stock clerk, a Christmas present wrapper, a neurophysiology lab assistant, a movie theater usher, an acupuncturist's assistant, an editor — everything. And in every office I ever worked in, I saw how lax the world was. We talked, we drank ice cream sodas, we broke up and reconciled with boyfriends on the phone, we taught each other makeup tips, balanced checkbooks, rubbed shoulders. Through all those jobs, writing was the thing I saved for — I waited for that sacred, peaceful time late at night when I could go on and on, just working. And now that I can write almost full time, I unplug the phone and close the door and just stick with it. I don't ever go out for lunch and I don't take vacations. I like to be awake [when] no one else is: either just before dawn in the morning or late, late at night. I always use the same pen, an old fountain pen I bought once in Boston, and I fill it up with blue or brown ink and write on yellow legal pads. Silence helps. Sometimes I sit at the desk at night with a candle."

Everyone, she says, "has their drug, whether it's liquor or dope or coffee. Mine is a certain kind of Swiss coffee that takes a half hour to brew. But I would try anything once for work. Anything."

M.P.

BOOKS BY MONA SIMPSON

NOVELS

Anywhere But Here. New York: Knopf, 1986; Vintage, 1987.
The Lost Father. Forthcoming.

Nancy Willard

NANCY WILLARD and I became friends several years ago in an unlikely place. We found ourselves, late on a Sunday night, precariously perched on adjoining mountains of luggage in the middle of a New York airport teeming with drunken students returning from spring break. We had been "bumped" off the early flight from Houston, where Willard, along with Stephen Donaldson and Brian Aldiss, had been a featured speaker at the "Conference on the Fantastic in the Arts," and we were both waiting for those people who were supposed to be waiting for us.

No more alien environment can be imagined for this soft-spoken poet and prize-winning writer of books for children and adults, who was trained as a medievalist at the University of Michigan, and lives, surrounded by plants and flowers, in a white house near Vassar, where she teaches. There, with her one-eyed cat Caspar asleep on the dining room table, we talked about fairy tales, her novel *Things Invisible to See* (set in Ann Arbor) and about "listening."

Willard's interest in these mythic and enduring stories is linked to her self-image, which is very much that of a listener, an oral historian, who grew up with a "difficult" live-in grandmother with "hardening of the arteries and memory problems, who seemed to be able to remember her early memories" if not the recent ones. "When I was growing up," she said, "we spent our summers in a small town in Michigan — barely on the map — and there was no newspaper in this village. (The nearest town was Oxford, and it had a weekly, so you can see how small we were.) My mother said, 'Why don't you start your own?' so we did. We had the world's simplest press — a Hectograph, which is a tray of jelly and a master pencil. You make a master copy, put it face down, the impression is in the jelly, and you run off copies. . . . There are no movable parts and nothing to break down. So I would go out every morning with a notebook and I would get news. But *nothing happened* here, you understand! I would knock on the door of a house and I would say, 'Has anything happened in this house?' Whatever anybody told me, I would write down, and when we had enough in the notebook, the paper came out. Occasionally a visitor would come and that was news!" But "it was a bit of a raw town. . . . People had terrible arguments at night. They drank and would carry on, the police would come out, but we couldn't put that in! *That* we had to leave out. But as a writer you're taking all that in." She thought, "I can't put it in the newspaper but I'll use it *someday*."

Willard said she "got used to hearing stories and I realized that it wasn't so much what *happened*, as *who was doing the telling*. . . . I heard a lot of people who were not well-educated people . . . many of them perhaps hadn't finished high school, and I learned a lot about listening to speech. I became interested in storytelling and the way people *tell* stories." Willard reminded me of an article by Paule Marshall called "A Poet in the Kitchen" that speaks to the issue of how and what women write. Marshall talks about "women's problems and their dilemmas as writers. It seems that men have it easy. They go off into the world and women are kept closer to home for a longer period of time, where all life seems to go on in the kitchen. [Marshall] says, 'Right, it does go on in the kitchen!' So women have a chance to hear everyday speech with all the nuances and the unsaid, the between-the-lines of everyday speech. They become great listeners and storytellers. Of course they know all life goes on in the kitchen." It gives them an advantage in understanding the encoded messages which for Willard's generation (and mine) were that you could be a nuclear physicist/president/the leader of the "free" world, as long as you lived in the white house up the street and made sure that everyone had a good breakfast and was wearing clean underwear. But Willard said, "The way it is encoded and how you get those messages is what is so interesting to a writer" because it is about the importance "of what isn't said. . . . Women have always been faced with encoded messages. Someone presents them with choices. But there is a more original way to look at this, a third solution. We don't have to make *those* choices that are presented to us. I remember reading an interview with Muriel Rukeyser in which people said you can have children, or you can write poetry, but you can't have both. *I believe it was the men saying it,* but women of this time were guilty of the same fallacy. She said, 'I want the whole thing,' but it took a leap of imagination" for her to say that.

Nancy Willard feels that in her own life, in a strange way, she "was probably at a great advantage. My parents wanted two children and they had a boy who died pretty close to birth. Then they had my sister and they wanted another boy. I came along. My sister and I were really brought up differently within one household because I was allowed to do things differently. I have a funny feeling that I had more freedom because they wanted the boy and I was the nearest thing to it. . . . I remember at the age of three being given a wonderful electric train, which I never asked for, but I loved it even though it was an odd thing to give a three-year-old girl, and my father [a chemist who later worked at Los Alamos] giving me a chemistry set. That didn't take; I wasn't good at math and that kind of science, but I loved being given it. It was like being given something magical. You could mix things and they would change color so maybe there was an advantage there." Later my father "had women graduate students getting Ph.D.s with him, so I had some model." But "the choices seemed clear — you could have a career . . . but it did seem hard [also] to have a family."

We talked too about Willard's involvement in literature for children and her love of fairy tales, "which have now been handed down to children but were originally for all ages. The fairy tales, I think, were told mostly by women to other women . . . children could listen if they wished." That is why they are so violent, sexual, and real but "the pace of them is emotionally right," said Willard. "So children are much less bothered by some of the violence in those stories than the adults are. I know this from having read *The Seven Ravens* to my son when he was six. Somewhere in the story is a girl who is on a quest for her brothers who have been changed into seven ravens. She is given a magic bone to use as a key to [the place] where her brothers are held captive. She loses the key and, by her leave, she cuts off her finger, puts it in the lock, and the door opens. Of course this is an ancient story and the point of it is that she has to sacrifice herself in some way," since she has become part of the problem. "When I read this to my son, he never batted an eye. Nothing was made of it . . . but I didn't sleep all night!" But, we agreed, "there is a rightness to some of the violence."

"I try an exercise with a class I teach on fairy tales," she explained. "Sometimes I give a scene in which no dialogue takes place and the scene is done in a few sentences. I ask the class to put it into dialogue. Hidden characters emerge; it's astonishing what happens when you take something that's told very abruptly, and suddenly you listen to it as speech. Someone had asked me to do a play, *East of the Sun, West of the Moon* (1989), a story I've always loved, and there's not that much dialogue in it. There were scenes . . . where [a woman] has long days in the palace by herself. How are we going to have a scene? Who is she going to talk to?" she thought. "Then I realized that in fairy tales everything is alive, everything speaks — the dishes, the tables, the chairs, and having to put it in dialogue really taught me about listening and what can talk, and the value of [that]. So I am very much interested in what is said between the lines."

For both of us, we agreed, the fairy tales "we seem to have gotten only showed the princesses, not the young women who went on quests. We all puzzle why this is so, why we didn't know these stories growing up. I liked *East of the Sun, West of the Moon* because it is, in fact, a story where the young woman rescues the prince." She talked about a collection edited by Michael Hearn that includes "The Girl Who Wanted to Be a Boy." In order "to go on her quest she dresses as a boy. (We taught this in fairy tale class here and my students were irate.) At the end she turns into a boy; that's her gift. The women [here] rose up. One of them re-wrote the story" and decidedly changed the ending. She was teaching this class with a Jungian, and "we asked the students to keep a journal of their impressions while they were reading this story. They included dreams — and we realized the strong con-nection between these ancient stories and what people dream." They become "more aware of their dreams, as I'm sure traditional storytellers always have been. Some of the stories seemed true to them on a level on which these stories have always been true. I guess that accounts for their resurgence in popularity. It's wonder-ful to see the popularity of Joseph Campbell's books, which have been around forever. Maybe things go in cycles and people are ready for some change. The culture is materialistic enough. And the next generation is saying there has to be some spirit out there informing all this."

Considering the recent popularity of the movie *Field of Dreams* and John Irving's book *A Prayer for Owen Meany*, "which starts with somebody getting hit in the head with a baseball," I asked Willard to talk about *Things Invisible to See*. It begins with the line "In Paradise, on the banks of the River of Time, the Lord of the Universe is playing ball with His archangels," and the ghosts of Christy Mathewson and Lou Gehrig appear. Willard said that "although people say that my book is about baseball, it is really *not* a baseball book. It's a book about life and death, and it's certainly not a book about fathers and sons. And the reason I have baseball in the book is because it involves a bet, a wager between life and death, and I was thinking about those medieval paintings in which death challenges the knight to a game of chess . . . (Ingmar Bergman does this wonderfully in the opening of *The Seventh Seal*), and you use the game as a way of winning a reprieve from death. [I] was talking about the Midwest, a small town, and who's going to know chess? So they have to find a game he knows, and the only game he knows is baseball."

For example, there's "an ancient Guatemalan book in which they go down to the underworld and there's a soccer game against death. . . . [The baseball players here] had to come back from the dead because it is, finally, life versus death, and life is going to win in this one. . . . I wanted to set up tremendous odds; I didn't just want the sons and the fathers, I wanted the women out there . . . [who] were playing for their sons' lives, so the stakes were *enormous*. Logistically it's complicated to set up, because you had to arrange things so there was an accident and the fathers couldn't play. The team of the dead come out and see . . . life, with all its sacrifice and love, [and they realize both] that it is *they* who have crossed over" and "what they wouldn't give to be back."

Willard mentioned that she had "grown up in a family with women who in fact saw things that other people didn't see. . . . My mother did sometimes know things that were going to happen before they did happen. We would all kid her about this; it was a very odd gift, and she was pretty accurate about it. My cousin could predict the sex of children before they were born. We didn't know how she did it and she didn't know how she did it either, but she was so accurate that we used to say she should open an office in Detroit! I think she missed on a set of twins once; . . . she didn't know there were two of them, but she got the sex right."

Willard said that her "father's sister . . . had a vision" of her own father's death on an operating room table. "She saw the whole thing when it happened." Her "mother's sister had the same sort of gift. It was she who had a ruptured appendix when she was fifteen and in fact crossed to the other world. She came back to tell us about it; it was a story that I often heard. She seemed to have left her body, and the vision that she had, I gather, is one that is very common — what she remembered is standing over the river and on the other side of the river were people in the family that were dead. . . . She described them and so you knew that they were relatives or ancestors who had died. She decided not to cross over and she came back in her body and lived many years. . . . My cousin said, 'Did she ever tell you the one where she woke up and saw a crowd of angels standing around the bed?' [So] I realize that what is real . . . for one person seems supernatural or very natural for someone else.

"I do remember when I was a child, stepping outside and seeing a large ship in the sky and not being too surprised, and thinking I wanted to share this with someone else. I went and got my mother, and by the time we got out there, the ship had gone on elsewhere. But she didn't in any way say, 'Oh, you didn't see anything at all.' It seemed perfectly plausible that something should be out there. And I didn't think it was so odd that it was there. I just thought it was nifty."

Nancy Willard is one of many writers who talked about their mothers and about their own role as mothers. Hers, she said, "seemed happy to have children who wanted to write but . . . did not seem restive" in her own role as traditional homemaker. "She would go out in a rowboat with a bunch of books and she would drop anchor and read to us. She would often read whatever *she* wanted to read and I suppose it was a way of getting her reading time in. But I think she genuinely enjoyed spending this time with us. I realized later just how amazing it was. . . . I hope I've carried over the same attitudes because I have enjoyed having my son, reading to him, sharing with him, spending a lot of time hanging around the playground. Because I don't drive a car, and I ride a bicycle, when I used to arrive on a playground on a bike, [the children would] think I was sort of a tall child and that I was on their side. I've talked to them as equals and I don't think I could do that if I hadn't had a child with me. Some of my writing did come out of listening, [and it helps] your own childhood memories come back to you."

As we walked from Willard's house to have lunch at the Vassar student center, I was struck by how appropriate it was for this writer to be on a campus that gives visitors a map of their trees — each one marked with its date of birth and donor. Many of the trees seemed to be guarding this special person whose house is filled with "spirits" enclosed in colored bottles (made by Willard) and a giant dollhouse (actually the prototype for *A Visit to William Blake's Inn: Poems for Innocent and Experienced Travelers*) that dominated the dining room and is often on loan to museums. She spoke about "shared space" and about sharing her work space with her son, now at college in the Midwest. But to see her 1936 Smith Corona typewriter (painted with pink stars), bought at a secondhand shop for $24, the sense of life and joy in every corner, and the flowers (even on the bathroom floor), is to know that Nancy Willard shares more than space with the rest of us. In a unique and extraordinary way, she enriches the space she is in, and that quality of perception, gentleness, and humanity informs every page of her thirty-three books. "I haven't a clue as to how my story will end," she has written. "But that's all right. When you set out on a journey and night covers the road, you don't conclude that the road has vanished. And how else could we discover the stars?"

You can almost see the moonbeams on her path.

M.P.

BOOKS BY NANCY WILLARD

NOVELS

Things Invisible to See. New York: Knopf, 1985.

POETRY

In His Country: Poems. Ann Arbor: Generation, 1966.
Skin of Grace. Columbia: Univ. of Missouri Press, 1967.
A New Herball: Poems. Baltimore: Ferinand-Roter Gallerias, 1968.
Nineteen Masks for a Naked Poet: Poems. Brownsville, Oreg.: Story Line, 1971; Harcourt Brace, 1984.

The Carpenter of the Sun: Poems. New York: Liveright, 1974.
Water Walker. New York: Knopf, 1989.
The Ballad of Biddy Early. New York: Knopf, 1989.
Selections 1991. A Nancy Willard Reader. Middlebury, Vt.: Middlebury College Press; Hanover: University Press of New England, 1991.

SHORT STORIES

Lively Anatomy of God. Austin, Tex.: Eakins, 1968.
Childhood of the Magician. New York: Liveright, 1973.
Angel in the Parlor. New York: Harcourt Brace, 1983.

NONFICTION

Testimony of the Invisible Man: William Carlos Williams, Francis Ponge, Rainer Maria Rilke, Pablo Neruda. Columbia: Univ. of Missouri Press, 1970.

CHILDREN'S BOOKS

Sailing to Cythera, and Other Anatole Stories. New York: Harcourt, 1974; Harcourt Junior, 1985.
The Merry History of a Christmas Pie: With a Delicious Description of a Christmas Soup. New York: Putnam, 1975.
All on a May Morning. New York: Putnam, 1975.
The Snow Rabbit. New York: Putnam, 1975.
Shoes without Leather. New York: Putnam, 1976.
The Well-Mannered Balloon. New York: Harcourt, 1976, 1991.
Strangers' Bread. New York: Harcourt, 1977.
Simple Pictures Are Best. New York: Harcourt, 1977; Harcourt Junior, 1978.
The Highest Hit. New York: Harcourt Junior, 1978; Scholastic, 1983.
Papa's Panda. New York: Harcourt Junior, 1979.
The Island of the Grass King: The Further Adventures of Anatole. New York: Harcourt, 1979.
The Marzipan Moon. New York: Harcourt Junior, 1981.

A Visit to William Blake's Inn: Poems for Innocent and Experienced Travelers. New York: Harcourt Brace, 1981; Harcourt Junior, 1982, 1988.

Uncle Terrible: More Adventures of Anatole. New York: Harcourt, 1982; Harcourt, 1985.

Household Tales of Moon and Water. New York: Harcourt Junior, 1982, 1987.

The Nightgown of the Sullen Moon. New York: Harcourt Brace, 1983; Harcourt Junior, 1987.

Night Story. Harcourt Junior, 1986.

The Mountains of Quilt. New York: Harcourt Junior, 1987.

[Et al.]. *The Voyage of the Ludgate Hill: A Journey with Robert Louis Stevenson.* New York: Harcourt, 1987.

Firebrat. New York: Knopf, 1988.

The High Rise Glorious Skittle Skat Roarious Sky Pie Angelfood Cake. Toronto: Lester & Orpen Dennys, 1990; Harcourt, 1990.

Pish Posh, said Hieronymus Bosch. San Diego, Calif.: Harcourt, 1991.

A Starlit Somersault Downhill. Boston: Little, Brown, forthcoming.

PLAYS

East of the Sun, West of the Moon. New York: Harcourt, 1989.

ILLUSTRATIONS

[By John Kater]. *The Letter of John to James.* New York: Harper & Row, 1981.

[By John Kater]. *Another Letter of John to James.* New York: Harper & Row, 1982.

[By Robert Pack]. *The Octopus Who Wanted to Juggle.* Baltimore, Md.: Galileo Press, 1990.

INDEX